Child Abuse and Neglect Worldwide

Volume 1
Understanding, Defining, and Measuring
Child Maltreatment

Volume 2
Global Responses

Volume 3
Interventions and Treatments

Child Abuse and Neglect Worldwide

Volume 1
Understanding, Defining, and Measuring Child Maltreatment

Jon R. Conte, Editor

PRAEGER

AN IMPRINT OF ABC-CLIO, LLC
Santa Barbara, California • Denver, Colorado • Oxford, England

Library of Congress Cataloging-in-Publication Data

Child abuse and neglect worldwide / Jon R. Conte, editor.
　　　volumes cm
　　Includes index.
　　ISBN 978-1-4408-0090-0 (hc. : alk. paper) — ISBN 978-1-4408-0091-7 (ebook)
1. Child abuse. 2. Child sexual abuse. I. Conte, Jon R.
　　HV6626.5.C4843 2014
　　362.76—dc23　　　　2013029939

ISBN:　978-1-4408-0090-0
EISBN: 978-1-4408-0091-7

18　17　16　15　14　　1　2　3　4　5

This book is also available on the World Wide Web as an eBook.
Visit www.abc-clio.com for details.

Praeger
An Imprint of ABC-CLIO, LLC

ABC-CLIO, LLC
130 Cremona Drive, P.O. Box 1911
Santa Barbara, California 93116-1911

This book is printed on acid-free paper ∞
Manufactured in the United States of America

For Meg, from whom and through whom all good things flow,

and

to professionals around the globe working every day to improve the lives of youth.

Contents

1

Introduction

Jon R. Conte

By any measure, including stories in the media, research published in scholarly journals, numbers of young people entering the helping professions to work with and for children, and even some governmental actions, the maltreatment of children has reached a level of attention globally that is unprecedented in human history. This is true even though, as is often pointed out, harm to children has been a recognized feature of human existence as far back as memory or historical record allows us to understand. Knowing what we know about human behavior and the tendency for those with more power and privilege to use and abuse those who have less, harm to children is likely to have always been an aspect of human life as societies have developed over the centuries.

Perhaps the first encouraging sign that things might change in this regard is the increasing attention child maltreatment is receiving almost everywhere in the world. Any traveler will note that stories in the local press about one or another aspect of child maltreatment are seen almost as frequently as local sports teams' scores. As an editor of a scholarly journal for almost 30 years, I have witnessed over the last decade an explosion of research studies from virtually every corner of the globe. Local, national, and international conferences on child maltreatment and other forms of trauma and trauma effects are common. Child maltreatment is a common theme in fiction, biographies, and movies.

Some of this content is based on accurate understanding of child maltreatment, some is sensationalized, and some presents inaccurate information to further the political agendas of those falsely stating a particular statistic, or for dramatic effect. While false information about child maltreatment or negative views of abused children and adults abused in childhood (e.g., that abused children become criminals, or that all sexually abused children become prostitutes) may have a negative impact on families suffering abuse and affect the public's views of the problem, there is nonetheless much to feel good about. Victims still come forward and disclose their abuse. Social systems such as child protection, criminal law, health care, and mental health care are developing ever more sophisticated and victim-centered policies and practices. The research foundation for our knowledge and practice in many aspects of child maltreatment is growing by leaps and bounds.

I am extremely proud to be associated with the authors who have prepared chapters for this text. Representing diverse regions, professions, and orientations, they provide a glimpse—indeed almost a report card—of the world's response to child maltreatment. They have been an exciting group of scholars to work with, and I have learned much through working with them.

The work of these authors is rich, complex, and thought-provoking. No introduction could do justice to the more detailed chapters that follow. As a reader of the volumes you are about to engage with, I would like to share a few thoughts that come to me, not as editor, but rather as a professional in the beginning of my fourth decade of work in our field.

DEFINITIONS

Several of the chapters will address what may well be one of the oldest issues in our field: How do we define child abuse? This has been a complex problem affecting research and social policy and goes centrally to the heart of how we define ourselves as professionals. With the expanding global perspective, we increasingly learn that child labor, child soldiers, children and young people used in pornography or for sexual trafficking, neglect of children as both parents go far from home to work, discipline in classrooms, children caring for younger siblings when both parents and other adult family members have died from HIV or in war, violent uprisings, natural disasters, etc., expand our ideas of what constitutes child maltreatment.

At a different level, at what age do we define an older child who has been sexual with a younger child as a "victim" or an "offender"? Is a 4-year-old child doing to a 3-year-old child the same thing done to him by a 15-year-old babysitter a victim or an offender? Certainly most societies would label the 15-year-old an offender. The label communicates both our understanding of the etiology of the offending behavior and what services are desired to correct the situation (punishment versus treatment). What about a society that allows an adult rapist to marry his child victim and thereby to no longer be considered as having committed a rape? What is the life of that now-married victim likely to be like? Not good would seem a reasonable prediction. The point here is not to judge a different culture but rather to point out that as a human race we lack clear agreement on what constitutes child maltreatment.

As noted in Chapter 9 of Volume 1, the UN Convention on the Rights of the Child (CRC) takes a rights perspective to define what children naturally should be able to expect from society. While this is not the same thing as defining forms of child maltreatment, it is a useful step along the way. Certainly there are other attempts to define the focus of our attention (e.g., "childhood adversities") that have advantages and disadvantages. Efforts to provide uniform culturally and historically relevant definitions of the various forms of child maltreatment will be useful in future research and policy making. Ongoing global discussions about what conditions, contexts, and experiences constitute child maltreatment can only improve policy and practice.

CHILD MALTREATMENT TOO NARROWLY DEFINED?

Important aspects of child maltreatment have been left out of these volumes and are planned for the follow-up compendium (e.g., child protective services, commercial sexual exploitation of children, understanding child sex offenders). The authors in this volume would no doubt tell you that the editor kept telling them to cut and cut, because they had so much more to say than space would allow.

There is no question that as a field of knowledge and professional practice child maltreatment is massive. Having said this, it is equally true that if the interested reader reads only within the topic of "child abuse," s/he will miss much relevant material from other fields, such as public health, trauma studies, and prevention science. Our field grew slowly at first with a group interested in physical abuse following efforts in the 1960s and Dr. Kempe's calling attention to battered children. Then in the late 1970s, sexual abuse emerged again, as it had early in the 1890s with Freud's first observations. The issue of child neglect, along with prevention of child maltreatment, lay somewhere off to the side of much of the intellectual and professional focus. While working in these fields made it possible to concentrate and learn a specific area of knowledge and practice, we now are coming to learn that overlap of forms of maltreatment is the norm.

Some children who view their mothers being abused are also abused. Male children who watch their mothers being abused grow up at times to become abusers. Combat warriors who develop PTSD often have histories of physical child abuse. Some adult rape victims have child sexual abuse histories. Sometimes children in natural disasters are sexually abused by rescue workers and some children react more severely to a natural disaster because they have histories of child maltreatment before the disaster. Just as we learned years ago that some fathers who commit incest abuse children outside of their homes and some rape adult women, we learn that some domestically violent fathers commit sexual offenses both inside and outside the home.

We need formulations of "victims" and "offenders" that recognize the overlap in the status of being a victim or an offender (i.e., some victims abuse others) and that victimization may lead to victimizing in some cases—and yet victimization may also lead to a lifetime of service to make the world a better place than the one the victim experienced. Many people have come to think that the term "trauma" represents a formulation that has this potential. Many highly stressful events or experiences (e.g., alcoholism in the family, severe neglect), however, may not rise to the level of a trauma yet have a profound impact on children.

It will be helpful to have thinkers work on this problem of how to define the parameters of our field and what adjacent fields we may draw on (e.g., child development or developmental psychopathology), and find ways to categorize the stimulus events we study (e.g., child abuse, neglect, war) as well as the responses (e.g., social, emotional, educational, health effects).

NOTIONS OF EVIDENCE-BASED PRACTICE

With the globalization of interest in child maltreatment and dissemination of knowledge globally, voice has increasingly been given to evidence-based practice. I am extremely proud of the chapters on evidence-based practice in this text. Each of the authors has communicated important research to the reader in clear ways, and has shown an expert knowledge of the real world of practice to which the evidence they cite will be applied.

What I am now going to say should not be taken as a detraction from my real belief in the importance of knowing the research and doing what the research indicates should be done. To not do what is known to be effective is not only ethically wrong; it also runs a high risk of hurting people who have already been hurt by adults, i.e., abused children. It would be akin to not giving a child antibiotics for a serious infection. Nonetheless, I think it is important to recognize that *belief in evidence* is a value and that evidence of what constitutes best practice is not necessarily applicable across cultures. Values express what is honored and important, and what is worthy. We should not privilege one value over other values. I personally hold values that culturally relevant practice, social justice, anti-oppression, and child safety are equally important. I believe that we must hold these values as dear as we hold evidence-based practice. In this regard, Angèle Fauchier and her colleagues in Volume 3, Chapter 9, make mention of the application of TFCBT in distinct cultures and with the use of less-trained therapists. These are incredibly important findings as they point the reader to understand that an evidence-based intervention may be applied in different cultures and in areas where there are insufficient numbers of highly trained mental health professionals. This line of research is important as it points to how values relating to evidence-based interventions, cultural relevance, and meeting unmet needs can be blended. Social justice would seem to call on many Western and Western-trained researchers to look for ways to extend or generalize their research to different cultures and locations around the globe.

THE WESTERNIZATION OF CHILD MALTREATMENT

As a number of the regional chapters that follow illustrate, there are exciting developments in many parts of the world. Laws vary, traditional ways of dealing with issues merge with new modern developments, and historical development over time impacts how societies respond to child maltreatment. The unique cultural and historical contexts summarized in the regional chapters point to potential risks as communities face developmental challenges, globalization, and pressures—conscious and unconscious—to form a single consumer culture.

Social networking, Internet dissemination of ideas (some good and tested, other untested and of questionable value), increasing travel to developed and developing countries, and the massive publication in print and media that gives privileged nations and professionals access to a global market are realities as this series goes to print. Certainly there are many positive aspects of this state of modern affairs. Rapid dissemination of knowledge; easy or at least easier access to ideas and techniques; and global sharing of innovations, concerns, and possibilities are all enabled by globalization and technology.

It is my impression that there may be a rush globally to view the Western model of medical evaluation, investigation, and prosecution of the abuser as the ultimate response to child maltreatment. It has long been recognized in the West that responses to child maltreatment involve medical, social service, mental health, and law enforcement professionals. It is not clear that evaluation, investigation, and prosecution are the only or even the best ways to protect children in diverse communities, rural and urban, with distinct historical and cultural development.

It is not clear to me how thoughtful the transfer of Western knowledge and practice is or can be. Many forces are beyond our control. To the extent that it is possible, however, I suggest that we must be careful in this state of rapid transfer.

First, not everything that is Western is good. I fear the Western model of multidisciplinary investigation with an emphasis on punishment of the abuser may not be the best solution for children and certainly not the best solution in all societies. Child safety first and then services to assist children in moving beyond abuse would seem a priority goal for our field, and it may well be that it can be accomplished in different contexts in ways other than we in the Western world have decided.

Certainly societies express social policy through their laws. The abuse of a child as a socially prohibited act would seem a good policy. Safety of that child and other children may often require separation and control of the person(s) responsible for the abuse. The ways that societies, through laws and social policies, make it possible for abusers to avoid responsibility (e.g., by attacking a child's credibility, marrying the raped child, attacking the professionals who received the child's disclosure) have to be carefully evaluated in light of child safety. One consequence of a system that focuses more on the offender and punishment is that child safety and healing are often second thoughts. Countries and professionals should be encouraged to support local and culturally appropriate, but child safety–oriented, responses to child maltreatment and not assume that a Western model is globally relevant.

Second, as societies become more aware of the issue, social actors other than child maltreatment professionals often shape social policy and social responses to child maltreatment. Media craves the new, the extreme, and the sensational, and not all press or media coverage always presents the most evidence-based, victim-sensitive, or realistic view of child maltreatment. Massive coverage of particular cases such as the Catholic cleric abuse cases in the United States and Ireland, as well as others in other countries, impacts how victims and their families, the public, and policy makers view child maltreatment. In such times of near hysteria, it is important for professionals to speak from a cultural and historical perspective as well as an evidence-based practice perspective to help the public understand what is unfolding in the press. In the long run, a rush to a Western solution may not be the most useful or appropriate response in some cultural contexts.

AUTHENTIC VOICES

Finally, as readers work their way through the following chapters, each one well written, based on data and experience, by experts with years of collective experience in child maltreatment, it is important never to forget that underneath these complex ideas, large bodies of research, and summaries of collective experiences there is, at the end of the day, a maltreated child and the adults who care for and influence that child's life. The authors you will meet in the coming chapters have presented the best practices available and put their knowledge, wisdom from experience, and expertise together to provide the reader with information. They also do not lose sight of the purpose of all of this, which is to help the maltreated child and his or her family.

Your test as a reader of the ideas put forth in the following chapters is easy: Will this idea make it easier for me to help maltreated children and the adults in their lives? I hope you will find the answer to be yes.

2

Defining and Measuring Child Maltreatment

Linda M. Williams and Edward G. Weeks

It is critical to clearly define child maltreatment and to know how to measure it if we wish to address the problem of child abuse and neglect locally and across the globe. This is true whether we wish to focus on legal, policy, and practice responses or on basic or applied research. In the twenty-first century, we find it increasingly important to understand the application of definitions of child maltreatment globally—across cultures and nations. This broader reach of our definitions has called for consideration of how to define child maltreatment in a manner that can be embraced more universally while permitting adaptations to reflect cultural and normative differences. This chapter is designed to help with our understanding of the importance of clear definitions and good measures to assess our response to child maltreatment.

INTRODUCTION

A critical first step to understanding child maltreatment is, of course, defining what we mean when we use the term "child maltreatment." How is child maltreatment (CM) defined? Once it is defined, we can begin to understand if CM means the same thing in every community and across the globe. Then we can study how definitions change over time, how the definitions are codified into laws and regulations that govern society, and how effective we have been in reducing the incidence of CM. The first part of this chapter offers definitions of child maltreatment that have achieved some consensus and discusses key issues addressed by the field in arriving at definitions that accommodate cross-cultural variations and potential changes in definitions over time.

ARRIVING AT A DEFINITION OF CHILD MALTREATMENT

Rosemary Chalk (2006) provides a good review of the evolution of definitions of CM in the United States and an insightful discussion of the many factors that have driven these definitions, including shifts in theories and paradigms used to understand CM (ecological, interactive, developmental), and different purposes for the definitions (surveillance, service, medical and clinical use, legal, and research). It has long been recognized that one of the difficulties with research and comparative work on CM is that often CM has not been operationally defined or that the operational definitions differ from one study or one venue to the next, thus resulting in findings (or even counts of CM) that are not comparable. In addition, we know that different approaches to measuring CM relate not only to the definitions used but also to the sources of the data.

Chalk (2006) has also discussed the ongoing issues that continue to challenge those who work on defining CM. For example, is child endangerment sufficient to constitute CM or must actual harm to the child be demonstrated? And, within the definitions, are severity and frequency of the behaviors taken into account, and how is any assessment of severity impacted by child victims developmental levels (e.g., a hit with a closed fist is likely to do less harm to an adolescent than to an infant)? Also, there has been consideration of perpetrator factors in formulating definitions of CM, including the perpetrator's relationship to the child (can any adult be seen as a perpetrator?), his or her intent to harm (must the harm be intended?) and his or her culpability (must the perpetrator be adjudicated guilty?) As one considers the definitions included in this chapter or those available in the literature for use in any setting, these enhancements or restrictions in definitions may, of course, be employed. So, for example, one could decide how broadly to define who can commit child abuse and if that person must be the child's parent or a caregiver or more broadly any member of the community, or even if the larger society could be included. The most recent focus, however, has been on separating these issues of harm, severity, and perpetrator from the basic definition of CM. While customarily the focus has been on behaviors by immediate caregivers, this narrow lens has shifted and the relationship of the perpetrator to the child is now more commonly less restricted in the definition of the CM (or it has varied with type of maltreatment). What is critical is that the definitions one uses are clearly operationalized.

In addition, definitions have variously, and with uneven success, attempted accommodation to cultural perspectives and practices. There are several arenas in which we confront difficulties in understanding how behaviors and the experiences of children across cultures fit definitions of CM. From comparative research and cross-cultural studies, we know that cultural norms concerning the treatment of children tend to vary somewhat from society to society. In addition, even within a given society, the norms may change over time. For example, in Laotian, Cambodian, and many other societies, leaving an infant in the day-long care of seven- or eight-year-old siblings is expected rather than considered to be neglect (Korbin & Spilsbury, 1999). In the United States today, however, both the infant and the seven- or eight-year-old caregiver child would be judged as neglected. Additional examples of these cross-cultural variations that challenge our definitions are discussed below in relation to specific types of abuse. As these issues are considered, adaptations of the basic definitions, particularly in regard to questions asked about behaviors that are indicators of CM, may be necessary.

Even beyond consideration of the definition of abuse or maltreatment per se, an important domain also having some cross-cultural variation is the definition of childhood. Who is a child? When does childhood end? We must define the terms "child" and "childhood" in order to have a useful definition of child maltreatment.

Generally, in international work to define and measure child maltreatment today, there is a movement toward addressing these issues by relying less on the local laws; by including maltreatment by persons other than the child's caregiver; and by applying the concept of "child well-being" to definitions of CM and including failure to meet children's needs or preventing them from reaching their full potential within society.

Defining Child Maltreatment

In 1999, a formal definition of child abuse was developed by a World Health Organization (WHO) consultation on child abuse prevention:

All forms of physical and/or emotional ill treatment, sexual abuse, neglect or negligent treatment or commercial or other exploitation, resulting in actual or potential harm to a child's health, survival, development or dignity in the context of a relationship of responsibility, trust or power. (WHO, 1999; Krug et al., 2002)

This definition suggests that abuse is anything that interferes with a child reaching his or her full potential. Abuse includes acts of commission (e.g., physical or sexual assaults) and acts of omission (e.g., neglect or failure to supply food). WHO stressed, however, the awareness of cultural factors and that baseline or cultural conditions or social factors beyond the control of families (poverty, lack of availability of proper nutrition or education, and social upheaval and war) must be considered in any identification and response.

Indeed, arriving at good working definitions of CM can be challenging and complex when considering applicability to our diverse international community. The WHO definition is in accord with part I, article 1, of the United Nations Convention on the Rights of the Child, which was developed in 1989 and has now been ratified by all but two member nations. This document reflects international consensus that children deserve special protections as a matter of human rights.

Because part of the task of defining child maltreatment includes defining who is a child, the definition of "child" based on the UN Convention on the Rights of the Child, part I, article 1, is helpful: "a child means every human being below the age of eighteen years unless under the law applicable to the child, majority is attained earlier." "Majority" refers to the age when a person is legally considered a full adult.

One organization that has played an important role in gaining a global perspective of child maltreatment is the International Society for the Prevention of Child Abuse and Neglect (ISPCAN). In 1992, ISPCAN issued its first report, *World Perspectives on Child Abuse: An International Resource Book.* A central part of the 1992 *World Perspectives* report included results from a survey sent to key informants identified by ISPCAN as being knowledgeable about CM issues within their respective countries (ISPCAN, 2008). ISPCAN reported:

> [T]here is an emerging global agreement regarding the major behaviors that constitute child abuse and neglect (e.g., sexual abuse, physical abuse, children living on the street and child prostitution). Although some differences continue to exist between the definitions embraced in developing versus developed countries, and local social conditions frame the relative emphasis that professionals may place on various behaviors, those working in diverse contexts are working with cases involving many of the same characteristics. Children who have experienced physical mistreatment, sexual abuse and

parental or societal neglect, can be found in many countries around the world, regardless of a country's economic conditions. (ISPCAN, 2008, p. 4)

For the 2008 ISPCAN *World Perspectives* report, participants from different countries were asked to indicate whether a series of parental or caretaker behaviors and social or institutional conditions were considered child abuse and/or neglect within their country. The most common behaviors considered to be child abuse and neglect in all or most regions of the globe were physical abuse by parents or caretakers, and sexual abuse defined as incest, sexual touching, or pornography (ISPCAN, 2008). According to this report, "these two behavioral categories were labeled as child abuse by all but three respondents (e.g., physical abuse by a parent was not listed as generally considered child abuse by respondents from Armenia, Iraq and China, nor was sexual abuse listed as a behavior commonly regarded as child abuse by respondents in Armenia and Malaysia)." Other behaviors were acknowledged by more than 80% of all respondents as abusive. These included failure to provide adequate food, clothing or shelter; abandonment by a parent or caretaker; child prostitution; children living on the street; physical beating of a child by any adult; forcing a child to beg; female or child infanticide; and abuse or neglect occurring within foster care or educational settings (ISPCAN, 2008).

In contrast to past years, in 2008 only three types of CM demonstrated significant regional differences in the definition of abuse or neglect. These included failure to secure medical care for a child based on specific religious beliefs, parental substance abuse, and physical discipline. In the case of physical discipline, this behavior was notably less likely to be listed by respondents from Africa and Asia than from elsewhere in the world (ISPCAN, 2008). Regarding parental substance abuse, respondents from the Americas and Asia were least likely to report such behavior as being commonly considered a form of child maltreatment. This variability may reflect the capacity of emerging systems in these regions to respond to any but the most serious forms of maltreatment or to very different cultural and religious contexts (ISPCAN, 2008). While not without limitations in the number of countries covered and the breadth of the samples interviewed, the *World Perspectives* report illuminates some broad consensus on defining CM.

Most definitions found in the literature include four major types of maltreatment: physical abuse, sexual abuse, neglect, and emotional abuse. It is important to note that although any of the forms of child maltreatment may be found separately, they often occur in combination.

DEFINITIONS

Physical Abuse

In the WHO documents (WHO & ISPCAN, 2006; Krug et al., 2002), physical abuse of a child is defined as the intentional use of physical force against a child that results in—or has a high likelihood of resulting in—harm to the child's health, survival, development, or dignity. This includes hitting, beating, kicking, shaking, biting, strangling, scalding, burning, poisoning, and suffocating. Much physical violence against children in the home is inflicted with the objective of punishing.

Key principles in the definition include that it is nonaccidental behavior with physical injury (ranging from minor bruises to severe fractures or death) that may result from acts such as (in addition to those mentioned above) punching, throwing, stabbing, choking, hitting (with a hand, stick, strap, or other object), or otherwise harming a child. Commonly, when a caregiver is involved, such injury resulting from nonaccidental behavior is considered abuse regardless of whether the caregiver intended to hurt the child. Physical abuse may also include any injury to a child that is not accidental or any action that could have seriously harmed the child, but luckily did not.

It is important to recognize that there are different physically abusive behaviors that are named or are identified in different communities or nations. Some of these behaviors are named to elicit responses in surveys and be sure that all abusive behaviors are included. While these behaviors all would fit within the definition provided by WHO and ISPCAN (2006), they provide further elaboration or additional key words to describe the behaviors that fit the definition of CM. For example, the United Kingdom specifies the following in its detailed definition of what constitutes physical abuse (additions to the definition discussed above are in italics): hitting, shaking, throwing, *poisoning,* burning or scalding, *drowning, suffocating,* or otherwise causing physical harm to a child. It also specifies that physical harm may also be caused when a parent or carer *fabricates the symptoms of, or deliberately induces, illness in a child* (DCSF, 2010).

A wide variety of additional behaviors are also listed in the measure developed by ICAST (Zolotor, 2010). Some of these behaviors may be more commonly practiced in one country than another. This list of physically abusive behaviors includes the following: threatened to hurt or kill a child; threatened child with knife or gun; pushed, grabbed, kicked, hit, beat, spanked with hand, spanked or hit on buttocks with object; hit elsewhere with object; beat up; severe physical discipline; choked or tried to choke, smother, or drown; shook child < 2 years of age; burned or scalded child; locked child in small place; pulled hair; pinched or twisted ear; knuckled or slapped back of head; forced child to hold heavy load or exercise as punishment; forced painful kneeling/standing; placed chili pepper in child's mouth; gave drugs or alcohol, including through mother's use of an illegal drug or other substance; and manufactured methamphetamine in the presence of a child.

In spite of an emerging agreement on definitions of physical child abuse and major behaviorally specific items that could be used to measure CM, across cultures there is room for ambiguity and disagreement. Definitions may challenge long-held traditions and beliefs. Indeed, cultural variations do exist as to what constitutes child maltreatment. "Spanked" is a behavior found on the list although in most countries physical discipline, such as spanking or paddling, is not considered abuse as long as it is reasonable and causes no *bodily injury* to the child, especially when delivered to the buttocks. In 2009, however, Sweden experienced its thirtieth anniversary of a national ban on corporal punishment. Since 1979, 24 countries have enacted legislation to ban corporal punishment within the home (Zolotor & Puzia, 2010). Still, in the United States, spanking and corporal punishment are considered a legal form of discipline despite any long-term psychological or other harm (Straus, 2001) that may result.

In addition, violence by the state generally has *not* been included in definitions of CM, although abuse and violence against children in jails or prisons, or through execution, could fall under the definition of physical abuse promulgated by the UN and WHO.

Sexual Abuse

Sexual abuse is defined as the involvement of a child in sexual activity that he or she does not fully comprehend, is unable to give informed consent to, or for which the child is not developmentally prepared, or else that violates the laws or social taboos of society (WHO & ISPCAN, 2006; Krug et al., 2002). Children can be sexually abused by adults or by other children who are—by virtue of their age or stage of development—in a position of responsibility, trust, or power over the victim. Sexual abuse commonly is seen to include activities such as fondling a child's genitals, penetration, incest, rape, sodomy, indecent exposure (exposing an adult's genitals to a child), and exploitation through prostitution or the production of pornographic materials.

Once again, we see further elaboration in the United Kingdom (DCSF, 2010), and the definition offers more specifics and includes forcing or enticing a child or young person to take part in sexual activities, not necessarily involving a high level of violence, whether or not the child is aware of what is happening. The activities may involve physical contact, including assault by penetration (for example, rape or oral sex) or nonpenetrative acts such as masturbation, kissing, rubbing, and touching outside of clothing. They may also include noncontact activities, such as involving children in looking at, or in the production of, sexual images; watching sexual activities; encouraging children to behave in sexually inappropriate ways; or grooming a child in preparation for abuse (including via the Internet).

Sexual abuse includes the employment, use, persuasion, inducement, enticement, or coercion of any child to engage in, or assist any other person to engage in, any sexually explicit conduct or simulation of such conduct for the purpose of producing a visual depiction of such conduct. It also includes rape, and in cases of caretaker or interfamilial relationships, statutory rape, molestation, prostitution, or other form of sexual exploitation of children, or incest with children.

Gilbert et al. (2009) defined child sexual abuse as any completed or attempted sexual act, sexual contact, or noncontact sexual interaction with a child by a caregiver. Some definitions in use today may specify that the interaction be for the sexual stimulation of the adult; this refinement of the definition requires more complicated assessment and may only be useful to help clarify how to apply the label of sexual abuse in situations in which there are differing cultural standards about contact and privacy. This could include norms about nudity in the home, sleeping arrangements, or accepted practices regarding what parts of the body are covered and what is displayed, as well as commonly allowed touching of children's breasts, buttocks, or genitalia.

A significant cultural issue that has made its way to the forefront of international debate on CM and sexual abuse is male circumcision and female genital mutilation (FGM). In western culture it has become a widespread practice to circumcise boys without their consent for cultural and religious reasons. Some argue that circumcision of boys is child abuse resulting in permanent disfigurement, while proponents state that the social and medical benefits outweigh the costs. FGM is a common practice in parts of Africa, Asia, and the Middle East (WHO, 2012). Estimates indicate that 140 million girls and women are living with the consequences of female genital mutilation and 3 million girls under the age of 15 are at risk for FGM annually (WHO, 2012). FGM procedures involve partial or total removal of the external female genitalia or other injury to the female genital organs for nonmedical reasons. Such procedures result in both immediate and long-term adverse medical consequences including infection and serious medical complications. Internationally, FGM is recognized as abuse and a violation of human rights for girls and women (WHO, 2012).

An additional example of disparities in the definitions of sexual abuse arises in regard to child marriage. Indeed, child marriage is now viewed as a violation of human rights and such violation has been proclaimed by many documents. (One of the first international instruments of the United Nations—the Universal Declaration of Human Rights [1948]—specified that "marriage shall be entered into only with the free and full consent of the intending spouses." This concept was also stated in the International Covenant on Civil and Political Rights in 1966 [article 23]; the 1962 Convention on Consent to Marriage, Minimum Age for Marriage and Registration of Marriages [article 1]; and the 1979 Convention on the Elimination of All Forms of Discrimination Against Women [CEDAW, article 16.1.b].) In many countries, and in some jurisdictions of the United States, marriage to children below the age of 18 is legal, and in some countries marriage can occur with children under the age of 15. Indeed, the Population Council research (Halberland et al., 2004) indicates that approximately one out of seven girls in the developing world (excluding China) is married before her fifteenth birthday. Child marriage facilitates the sexual contact of an adult with a child—the child bride—and thus can be viewed as persuasion, inducement, enticement, or coercion of a child to engage in sexually explicit conduct. Is such sexual contact child sexual abuse? Should we define child marriage as child maltreatment in countries where such behavior is legal? These questions represent some remaining difficulties in arriving at a more universal definition of child sexual abuse.

Neglect

WHO documents define neglect to include both isolated incidents, as well as a pattern of failure over time on the part of a parent or other family member to provide for the development and well-being of the child—where the parent is in a position to do so—in one or more of the following areas: health, education, emotional development, nutrition, and shelter and safe living conditions. The parents of neglected children are not necessarily poor. They may even be financially well off (WHO & ISPCAN, 2006; Krug et al., 2002).

In further elaboration, the following definition of neglect has been proffered (Straus & Kantor, 2005):

Neglect is *behavior by a caregiver* that constitutes a *failure to act in ways that are presumed by the culture* of a society to be *necessary to meet the developmental needs* of a child and which *are the responsibility of a caregiver to provide.* (p. 20)

Straus and Kantor (2005) include in the definition of neglect the phrase "presumed by the culture." They point out that, except possibly at the extremes when a child dies or is seriously injured by some form of neglect (which we almost all end up defining as neglect), it is important to recognize that neglect is a culturally constructed phenomenon. Neglect may include the following components: physical (e.g., failure to provide necessary food or adequate or safe shelter or clothing; lack of appropriate supervision, as in leaving a young child alone or with someone who is not able to care for him or her; driving while intoxicated with an unrestrained child in the car); medical (e.g., failure to provide necessary medical or mental health treatment); educational (e.g., failure to educate a child or attend to special education needs); and emotional (e.g., inattention to a child's emotional needs, failure to provide psychological care, or permitting the child to use alcohol or other drugs). Some countries (including many U.S. states) provide an exception to the definition of neglect for parents who choose not to seek medical care for their children due to religious beliefs that may prohibit medical intervention. Substance abuse may be an element of the definition of child neglect when use of a controlled substance or alcohol impairs the caregiver's ability to adequately care for the child.

In the United Kingdom, the definition of neglect includes the mention of *persistent* failure to meet a child's basic physical and/or psychological needs, likely to result in the serious impairment of the child's health or development. Neglect may occur during pregnancy as a result of maternal substance abuse. Once a child is born, the definition of neglect may include a parent or carer failing to provide adequate food, clothing, and shelter (exclusion from the home or abandonment is specifically mentioned); failing to protect a child from physical and emotional harm or danger; failing to ensure adequate supervision (including the use of inadequate caregivers); or failing to ensure access to appropriate medical care or treatment. It may also include neglect of, or unresponsiveness to, a child's basic emotional needs (DCSF, 2010).

Abandonment is defined in many of the United States as a form of neglect. In general, a child is considered to be abandoned when the parent's identity or whereabouts are unknown; when the child has been left alone in circumstances where the child suffers serious harm; or when the parent has failed to maintain contact with the child or provide reasonable support for a specified period of time.

Some behaviorally specific indicators that have been used in ICAST (Zolotor, 2009) include: the child went hungry or thirsty; the child had inadequate nutrition or liquids; the child had inadequate clothes; the child's medical needs were unmet; and the child was injured due to inadequate supervision.

The presence of these indicators or patterns, however, may not always mean that a child is neglected. Sometimes cultural values, the standards of care in the community (such as the aforementioned common behavior to leave young children in the care of seven- or eight-year olds), and poverty may be contributing factors. These may indicate that the family is in need of information or assistance. For example, in some countries it is acceptable, customary, and often legal to put children to work for long hours at very young ages. Elsewhere (in most countries), adulthood is associated with entering the fulltime workforce and occurs closer to the age of 18. Globally, we also see how violence in the form of war, civil unrest, or forced migration, for example, may mitigate parental responsibilities, leading to calls not to hold parents responsible but to broaden definitions to include societal and governmental culpability for CM.

Emotional/Psychological Abuse

According to WHO and ISPCAN, emotional and psychological abuse involves both isolated incidents and a pattern of failure over time to provide a developmentally appropriate and supportive environment. Acts in this category may have a high probability of damaging the child's physical or mental health, or his or her physical, mental, spiritual, moral, or social development. Abuse of this type includes the restriction of movement; patterns of belittling, blaming, threatening, frightening, discriminating against, or ridiculing; and other nonphysical forms of rejection or hostile treatment (WHO & ISPCAN, 2006; Krug et al., 2002).

Emotional abuse (or psychological abuse) is a pattern of behavior that impairs a child's emotional development or sense of self-worth. It may include constant criticism, threats, or rejection, as well as withholding love, support, or guidance. It includes making a child feel that he/she is not loved or that he/she is bad or has no value. Emotional abuse is frequently present whenever other forms of CM are identified. In western countries, emotional or psychological maltreatment is often considered when there is a lack of attachment between infant and parent, or when an infant shows a lack of responsiveness to his or her environment. It is also considered in cases where an infant has failure-to-thrive (a condition in which children show a marked retardation or cessation of growth), or when a parent is highly critical of and negative toward the infant/child. In the United Kingdom, what is stressed is persistent emotional maltreatment of a child such as to cause severe and persistent adverse effects on the child's emotional development. It may involve conveying to children that they are worthless or unloved, inadequate, or valued only insofar as they meet the needs of another person. It may include not giving children opportunities to express their views, deliberately silencing them or mocking or belittling what they say or how they communicate. It may feature age- or developmentally inappropriate expectations being imposed on children. These may include interactions that are beyond a child's developmental capability, as well as overprotection and limitation of exploration and learning, or preventing the child from participating in normal social interaction. It may involve seeing or hearing the ill treatment of another. It may involve serious bullying (including cyber bullying), causing children frequently to feel frightened or in danger, or the exploitation or corruption of children. Some level of emotional abuse is involved in all types of maltreatment of a child, though it may occur alone (DCSF, 2010).

Definitions of emotional abuse in the United States include psychological abuse, and also include more extreme emotional abuse such as tying and binding or close confinement of a child (Sedlak, Mettenburg, Brown, Basena, & Madden, 2010), which also have been included in the definition of physical abuse. Some indicators that have been used in ICAST include: screamed, cursed or shouted at the child; insulted the child; embarrassed or publically humiliated the child; expressed the wish that the child was dead; threatened to abandon the child or send the child away; threatened to invoke spirits to harm the child; refused to speak to the child; withheld food from the child; locked the child out of the home or locked the child in a dark or small space; and bullying of the child by another child at home.

Summary of Definitions

As we have seen, current definitions of child maltreatment focus on and reflect some consensus on several major (and sometimes overlapping) categories of child maltreatment, including physical abuse, sexual abuse, neglect, and psychological and emotional abuse.

As we consider these definitions, it is important to recognize that if we want to adequately measure CM, we must be conceptually clear in these definitions. The concepts must be "operationally" defined. Operationalization is the process of translating abstractions into concrete measurement processes (Greenstein, 2006). Operational definitions then lead the way to more sound methods for measurement. The definitions of child maltreatment, especially the ICAST behaviorally specific items, are (hopefully) a step toward translating more abstract concepts about child well-being into quantifiable behaviors.

MEASURING CHILD MALTREATMENT

For some time, we have been aware of how the absence of clear definitions of CM has hindered advancement of the field (National Research Council, 1993). Without clear definitions, we cannot understand the prevalence of CM (prevalence is the subject of another chapter), nor can we conduct meaningful research to understand the causes and consequences of CM and assess the impact of policies and practice designed for prevention or intervention.

Beyond the issue of operationalized definitions, we must confront the problem of detecting the often hidden behaviors that comprise CM. Clinicians, researchers, and policymakers customarily need to ask about specific behaviors to assess the incidence and prevalence of CM so that they can know how much of it (or how much of a specific type of CM) exists. Good measurement is important for nations as well as for local communities simply to get a reasonable understanding of the scope of the problem (How much child maltreatment occurs here?) and then to be able to examine and compare the occurrence (rates, meaning incidence and prevalence) from one location to another, as well as within the same location over a period of time.

In addition, we not only want to know how serious the problem is for children in our location, community, state, or nation, but also whether the social responses that we employ to prevent CM have lowered its occurrence, and for whom the rates have changed. So we might ask, "Is the rate of CM rising or falling? Have our programs or policies, or the changes that have occurred in our communities or in the political, social or cultural environment, been associated with any changes in child maltreatment?" This section of the chapter is designed to help with our understanding of good measures to assess our response to child maltreatment.

A key component of measuring CM relates to how we gather the data. Do we count the "official" reports of behaviors defined as CM? Or do we seek data directly from individual victims (either during childhood or retrospectively as adults reporting on their experiences from childhood)? Or do we seek data from other knowledgeable adults such as parents, or from reporters such as teachers, doctors, and others who interact with children in a given community?

In this section of the chapter, we look at measures of child maltreatment and approaches that have been used widely in official "counting" of CM, or are recommended for survey research by experts in the field. Any discussion of "counting" the amount of CM or detecting its presence in any community must take into account the fact that much CM goes unreported and undetected. Even with clear and agreed-upon definitions, the actual amount of child maltreatment is difficult to count in most venues. Frankly, it is impossible to have knowledge of all maltreatment that has been perpetrated against children. Most CM takes place behind closed doors and is not officially reported.

It is important to remember that measuring CM is dependent on the *definitions* of terms that each person holds at any stage of inquiry (the "what" of the definition); the *measurement approach* (the counting "process" and the impact of the tool on the resulting counts); and the steps (if any) one takes to determine the validity of the report of CM (the "how" of the counting process). These three dimensions have often been confounded, and create difficulties in understanding the key connections between how we *define* CM, how we *measure* it, and how we *count* it.

Official Reports and Measuring CM

Until recently, in many countries there was no formal mechanism for protection of children, no official identification and counting of CM. In the United States, on a state-by-state basis, laws have been enacted that designate people who are in certain roles as mandated reporters. Such designated "mandated reporters" must report any indication or suspicion of CM to the appropriate designated authorities (e.g., child protective services [CPS]). The threshold for reporting, and those defined as mandated reporters, vary from state to state, but may include anyone who has direct supervision of children, a caretaker, or any professional who works directly with children.

Alternatively, some CM is reported directly to law enforcement authorities such as the police, who assess whether a crime has occurred (as defined by the laws governing the place where the behavior occurred). As we know, in order for child maltreatment to move towards an officially reported "incident," the child or someone else must perceive and label the maltreatment as something that is reportable or wrong. At that point it may or may not be reported. Then, if reported, it must make it through the CPS.

In most societies, parents or other caregivers bear primary responsibility for socializing the child to the ways of the family and the community. These adults often are charged with keeping strict discipline. Children are physically dependent on others for many years and are weaker than their parents or caregivers. Clearly, children must be taught the ways of the community in which they live. However, because of the child's dependence and need for socialization to survive in the adult world, young children also may be most vulnerable to abuse. Contributing to the risk of CM, very young children also lack language or the ability to express themselves verbally. Further, in some communities there are restrictions on the persons with whom children may associate. As a consequence, a child may not have the ability to report abuse when it occurs and also may lack the power to access supportive outsiders. Very young or isolated children thus may be most at risk for CM. All of these factors have implications for how we measure abuse and detect levels of abuse in a community.

If a child does not label the behavior as maltreatment or as wrong, there may be a failure to identify CM unless it is observed and reported by another person. Even if children do recognize behavior as maltreatment, the experience must be encoded in their memory so they can either report it directly or respond to an adult's or a clinician's inquiry or to a later survey about childhood experiences. Of course, the adult (e.g., a clinician or helping person or the researcher) must be able to cue a child's memory about the behaviors, and the affected individual must be able and willing to disclose what has occurred. When definitions between these parties are not in accord, incidents may be missed. Of course, the person to whom the child reports must identify the behavior as a reportable case of child maltreatment and subsequently make such a report. Finally, the recipient of the report must assess the report's validity in order for it to "count" in the official records of CM.

In most countries, official records of criminal activities or crimes reported to the police do not provide adequate measurement of CM because even when the behavior is defined as a crime by the relevant local law, often the CM is not reported. Even in cases in which the CM results in a fatality, it remains difficult to get accurate counts via the police records.

The World Perspectives on Child Abuse survey is conducted by the International Society for the Prevention of Child Abuse and Neglect (ISPCAN). Since 1992, the organization has conducted 10 surveys. The survey is a mail survey that relies on key informants across the globe from different countries. The respondents are responsible for indicating what types of CM occur in their countries and the overall prevalence of such CM. One of the important findings regarding CM is how countries differ in their capacities to establish formal surveillance systems.

In the United States, the National Child Abuse and Neglect Data System (NCANDS) relies on this "official reporting" method of measuring and counting CM. It collects case-level data from all 50 states, the District of Columbia, and Puerto Rico on all children who received a CPS agency response in the form of an investigation response or an alternative response (U.S. Department of Health and Human Services, 2012). NCANDS case-level data consist of CPS investigation of reports of child maltreatment. Only reports that receive an investigation or assessment response from a CPS agency are included. States that are unable to provide case-level data submit aggregated counts of key indicators. The limitations of these data are, of course, that they only reflect CM that has been reported to CPS agencies.

Another approach in the United States, the National Incidence Survey (NIS) (Sedlak et al., 2010) attempts to go beyond estimates provided by CPS agencies in a method that extends the scope of ISPCAN's World Perspectives Survey. The NIS includes information from a variety of professionals mandated to report child maltreatment, but who perhaps had not reported it. It includes professionals such as school staff, hospitals, police, probation officers, and public health workers. Uniform definitions of child maltreatment were developed in order to standardize the abuse label. The NIS employs both the Harm Standard (which counts children as maltreated only if they were harmed) and the Endangerment Standard (which counts children as maltreated who experienced abuse and neglect that put them at risk of harm). NIS is a national survey, the goal of which is to obtain an overall measure of the prevalence of CM at the national level. The reporters are referred to as "sentinels," and the children who are included in the NIS only represent the small fraction of children who are known to these "sentinels." The definitions used in the study are standardized, and a representative sample of 122 counties covers the necessary geographic areas. The sample is then weighted to allow for the creation of prevalence rates. Overall, for the NIS-4 (Sedlak et al., 2010) covering the period 2005–2006, 10,000 professionals were surveyed from about 1,000 agencies.

The main goal of these official informant surveys is to obtain system-level measures of CM and assess changes in prevalence rates. These "macro-level" estimates rely on standardized definitions, and in the case of the World Perspectives survey, permit variations in some definitions between countries. However, one of the main limitations of these surveys is the amount of unreported CM that fails to be captured when CPS data are used or when children are excluded from reporting (Runyan & English, 2006). For example, the NIS refers to the known cases as "the tip of the iceberg." In order to more closely examine CM and explore at the individual level how children are being harmed, self-report surveys can offer more detailed, in-depth information.

In the United States, one example of a self-report survey, the National Crime Victimization Survey (NCVS)—a national-level, weighted estimate of crime based on reports of crime incidents including those not reported to the police—introduces an important technique for measuring CM (direct surveys of individuals impacted by the behavior). The survey design is a complex, probability-based, rolling panel design of about 49,000 residential households within the United States who are interviewed every six months for a limited time frame and then replaced. The survey was originally implemented in the 1970s as a way to estimate the prevalence of unreported crime in the country as compared to the FBI's Unified Crime Report (UCR), which does not provide a way to identify the CM crimes. But NCVS also provides little good data on CM crimes. It does not include respondents under the age of 12, and the interviewed individual represents the household and could possibly be unaware of criminal behavior, or withhold a report because he or she does not want to implicate someone in the household in the abuse of a child. But the NCVS does, however, lead us to an important critical method for measuring CM—the self-report survey.

Self-Report Surveys of Child Maltreatment

Cases that are not known to CPS or other service providers can be included in research by use of community epidemiological surveys of the general population. But it is clear that these surveys require child self-report as well as parent report measures (see also Milner, 1989). Standardized measures have been used not only in the United States but across the globe. This approach is critical for all types of CM to bring cases that are not known to CPS into research (Portwood, 2006; Straus & Kantor, 2005).

Straus and colleagues at the Family Research Laboratory have developed and reviewed many self-report measures of CM, including the

Conflict Tactics Scale (Straus 1995, 1997) and the revised scale (CTS2) (Straus et al., 1996, 1998). This work also has been expanded to surveys of neglect (Straus, Kinard, & Williams, 1995; Straus & Kantor, 2005). Other useful scales provide critical measures of parent caregiving (Polansky et al., 1981) and child abuse and neglect (Bernstein et al., 1994; Harrington et al., 2002). One of the problems with self-report measures is that due to time limitations and interviewee fatigue, the survey scales are often unable to include the full range of behaviors that might injure children or be considered CM. Another complication that arises is that CM usually does not occur in isolated "silos." A child who has been sexually abused very often has experienced psychological and emotional abuse. Often our research (see Saunders, 2003), our measures, and our self-report surveys do not capture this complexity. In addition, the need to increase the cultural relevance of the measures has been noted.

In response, we have witnessed the development of the ISPCAN Child Abuse Screening Tools (ICAST). Since its creation in 1977, the International Society for the Prevention of Child Abuse and Neglect (ISPCAN) has worked to bring professionals together who are committed to preventing and treating CM on a global scale. Defining and measuring CM on a global scale presents a challenge because many countries do not have access to the resources that are available to many western, English-speaking countries (Dunne et al., 2009). In addition, as we have seen, definitions of the words "abuse" and "molested" vary among cultures and languages (Dunne et al., 2009). Regardless of countries' resources, researchers have learned to focus on identifying key sources of the CM knowledge that will be measured. ISPCAN has utilized retrospective self-report information from surveys that are administered to children, parents, and adults (Dunne et al., 2009; Runyan et al., 2009; Zolotor et al., 2009). It is important to ask adults and offenders as well as victims because the adults (e.g., parents) may bias their responses when answering questions about their discipline practices or the CM in which they have engaged, while both adults and children may have difficulty recalling their past abuse experiences. The self-report information is retrospective, meaning that it asks parents, adults, and adolescents about their past experiences with the behaviors that comprise our definition of abuse and neglect. Because past measurement tools were often limited due to lack of cross-cultural generalizability and difficulty of comparing across studies (Dunne et al., 2009), to obtain a valid measurement system, the ISPCAN consulted with CM professionals who work in many countries across various cultures (Zolotor et al., 2009).

The Child Abuse Retrospective Screening Tools (ICAST), developed in 2004, sought to build a consensus or intersubjective agreement on CM, which would allow for the comparison across cultures. They started a priori with agreement that the focus would *not* be on past definitions, standards, or thresholds of CM, but rather would consider harmful actions that affect children and also where the abuse took place (e.g., home, school, workplace). The included acts were determined to be common and harmful (Zolotor et al., 2009). By focusing on specific acts, it could be argued that the vagueness of pre-established western definitions and harm standards would pose less of a threat to the internal validity of the measure when administered cross-culturally. For example, a question administered to a child asking if he or she has had to go to the doctor as a result of discipline, when used as a way to measure the seriousness of physical abuse, is biased to detection in countries with adequate medical care and availability of medical doctors. ICAST also departed from the common Western approach of focusing solely on caretaker abuse. ICAST includes abuse by other adults and children (i.e., bullying). The main categories of CM experiences in the ICAST are violence exposure, psychological victimization, neglect, physical punishment, and sexual abuse (Zolotor et al., 2009). Here is an example of the violence-exposure items from the ICAST-C (child) survey:

Violence exposure
- Adult used drugs
- Adults shouted in frightening way
- Witnessed adults in home hit, kick, slap
- Witnessed adults in home use weapons
- Someone close got killed near home
- Saw people being shot, bombs, fighting, or rioting
- Something stolen from home

The ICAST-R or retrospective survey not only focuses on past CM, but also on who the perpetrator was. Perpetrator categories include adult male, adult female, male peers, and female peers. Within those categories, the specific relationship and type of abuse are identified (Dunne et al., 2009). By including more than the parental caretaker, the measurement of CM was broadened and the ability to examine harm caused to a child by a peer or sibling as well as by parents was enhanced (Dunne et al., 2009). The ICAST does recognize the importance of the parental caretaker relationship and has developed a specific survey to address parental discipline that has occurred in the previous year and over the child's lifetime.

The ICAST-P seeks to measure CM that is perpetrated by parents and harm to children due to discipline or neglectful actions. It also inquires about sexual abuse. Similar to the ICAST-C and ICAST-R, the designers emphasized the focus on parental actions. Parents were also asked about disciplinary actions and about positive and negative reinforcement that they had used with their children. By including nonviolent discipline in addition to beating and other harsh discipline, researchers can establish a more full range of parental disciplinary actions (Runyan et al., 2009). In addition, the parental survey asks whether the parent ever shook a child who was under the age of two. Shaking a child or baby can result in severe long-term injury or death (Runyan, 2008). The parental survey is needed as it is difficult to measure abuse completely from solely the victim's self-reports. The categories of discipline are nonviolent, moderate physical, severe physical, psychological, neglect, and sexual abuse. Below are the items for moderate versus severe physical discipline:

Physical discipline (moderate)
- Shook child (> 2 years)
- Hit on buttocks with object
- Hit elsewhere with object
- Twisted ear
- Knuckled back of head
- Pulled hair
- Painful kneel/stand
- Chili pepper in mouth
- Spanked
- Pinched
- Slapped back of head

Severe physical discipline
- Shook child (< 2 years)
- Kicked
- Choked
- Smothered
- Burned
- Beat up
- Threatened with knife or gun
- Gave drug or alcohol

Overall, the current ICAST survey has sought to provide a cross-culturally sensitive way of measuring and comparing CM on a global scale with the focus on specific, commonly occurring harmful actions. Defining the harmful actions was a consensus-building process that included CM professionals across the globe. Thus far, the ICAST survey has achieved valid reliability scores in the countries in which it has been administered (Dunne et al., 2009; Runyan et al., 2009; Zolotor et al., 2009).

The ISPCAN organization has built on existing measures, such as the Conflict Tactics Scale, to cover a more diverse global population. It is important to understand that such surveys need updating and improvement both to keep up with social and cultural changes as well as to improve their psychometric properties. Such revision is critical for redesign of measures of CM or when incorporating (with permission) some of the existing surveys into a new survey tailored to a specific community.

We have discussed the need for clear conceptual and operational definitions of CM and some of the self-report measures commonly used by the field, but how do we utilize the best approach to elicit valid and reliable information on CM? The balance of this chapter is devoted to discussion of these issues.

As a general principle for any survey, it is critical to provide a contextually orienting preface (for the survey as a whole and also for the CM questions). For example, in a question designed to ask parents about their behaviors toward a child, one can introduce this as follows:

> Sometimes a physical interaction with a child can lead to the child getting injured. This could happen when punishing a child, when hitting a child by mistake, or when playing with a child, by accident. Has there ever been any physical interaction between you and [name of child] that resulted in. . . .

When a respondent responds "yes," a specified behavior occurred, often it is best to ask the detailed follow-up questions for these "hits" on screening questions only after *all* the screening questions have been asked. If one follows up after the first "yes" response, the person may be reluctant to say yes again (see Williams, Siegel, & Pomeroy, 2000).

Question Content and Structure

In addition, one needs to assure that questions are clear and meaningful. To accomplish this, it is important to avoid confusing phrasing, vagueness, negatives and double negatives, and double-barreled questions. (A double-barreled question is usually two questions rolled into one. For example, "When you were with your family did you misbehave and did they hit you for this behavior?" This question needs to be broken down into several simple questions. It is important to break complex ideas into several questions and address each component separately.) Therefore, a question (like a variable) should be about only one thing.

Interview Setting and Context

Many factors may impact the identification of CM and the validity of responses. To increase the likelihood that CM will be reported, the context of the setting in which the questions are being asked should be private and comfortable, and appropriate for the population surveyed. Respondents need assurances of confidentiality, or clear discussion of any limits of confidentiality.

Interviewer Training and Demeanor

To address these sensitive issues, it is important that the interviewer be trained in and have confidence in his or her own use of proper assessment techniques; have dealt with his or her own fear of being too invasive and with any concern about alienating the child or family; and know how to minimize distress without closing down the interview and take an approach that is empathetic and relaxed, with a calm demeanor, and that reflects normalization of the interview process. In addition, it is important that the interviewer not reflect biases, especially interviewer condemnation of behaviors, revealing distaste, disgust, or surprise at answers provided. A successful interviewer has learned how to put the respondent at ease by being open and concerned without being overly familiar or personal.

Problems with Nondisclosure

There are a number of factors that can increase the likelihood that CM will *not* be disclosed to an interviewer or in a survey. For example, if the definitions are not clear and are not commonly shared, there may be few endorsements. Also, if the person being interviewed fears retribution by an abuser or others, or has been instructed by someone to not tell about the CM, then a disclosure is less likely. The person interviewed may fear other negative consequences to self, family, or friends if one reports CM. In addition, if the person interviewed has a sense of stigma or shame or is afraid of being blamed, or has feelings of guilt, he or she may not report experiences of CM. This is one of the reasons why it is important to use behaviorally specific questions that do not label the behavior as "abuse."

Approaches to Elicit Recall and Reporting

Of course, a difficulty could arise in getting valid measures of CM if the respondent does not immediately recall the experiences (Williams, 1994). Experiences not recalled and not accessible result in no report (false negative). However, sometimes experiences may be partially forgotten, but retrievable with the right cueing (Williams, Siegel, & Pomeroy, 2000). For that reason, it is important for surveys on CM to use an approach that cues recall by asking behaviorally specific questions and getting the respondent to consider different possible experiences. Recall can be enhanced by using face-to-face interview methods; a structured, systematic set of screening questions; questions designed to elicit closed-ended responses initially; and repeated measures (series of Qs) and multiple screening questions. Most importantly, behaviorally specific questions that clearly describe experiences of interest without labeling them as abuse are needed.

In our work on retrospective reporting of experiences of child sexual abuse, we found that it was important to ask questions that directed the respondent's attention to specific kinds of behaviors (touching, kissing, penetrating, photographing) or relationships (family members, neighbors, employers, friends) salient to his or her experiences (Williams et al., 2000). Our research also found that asking behaviorally specific questions may help to provide a definitional framework for the respondent by providing detail on the definitions and types of experiences that are of interest. In addition to different behaviors, it is likely to help if new questions add considerations of the caregiver relationship of interest (Is the caregiver a biological parent? Stepparent? Adoptive parent? Extended kinship caregiver?). Such questions likely help the respondent apply the definitions to his or her own experiences. Finally, the opportunity to revisit questions later in the interview is also critical, and may give a respondent an opportunity to report experiences recalled as the interview progressed.

An approach that asks all screening questions first and follow-up questions last, and provides opportunity for the respondent to add additional experiences; that avoids questions that apply labels to behaviors that may not reflect the respondent's definition of what occurred; that avoids labeling behaviors as "abuse," "rape," or "neglect"; and that avoids vague terms such as "fondled," "molested," or "punished" is needed.

Using Cognitive Interviewing to Develop Quality New Measures of CM in Your Locality

When designing new measures of CM (in addition to translation and back translation if the survey will be used in languages other than the one in which it was developed and tested), one helpful step would be to conduct "cognitive interviews" with individuals who have completed the questions to ask them about their answers. The aim of cognitive interviewing is to understand what the person answering the question was thinking and figure out how that might impact the validity of the data you will be collecting. So you might ask a "test" respondent what he or she believes the question was asking. What do specific words and phrases in the question mean to the respondent? For example, if we ask, "Did your parent ever leave you alone without an adult when you were too young for that?" we would want to later ask the respondent what he or she thought we were asking. We would also be interested in how easy it was for the respondent to retrieve the answer from memory and if he or she was able to recall the information. What types of information did the respondent need to recall in order to answer the question? And what strategies did he or she use to retrieve information? If we ask a young person, "How many times did you run away from home?" did the respondent try to recall specific elements and count them, or did he or she use an estimation strategy? We also would look at the decision process. Here we want to try to figure out if the respondent was motivated to devote sufficient mental effort to answer the question accurately and thoughtfully. Did he or she just become inclined to toss out an answer without really thinking? Or counting? We also have to be concerned about sensitivity and social desirability: Did the respondent want to tell the truth? Is this a situation in which the individual may say something that makes him or her look "better"? How can we address this? Then, we are also interested in response processes. We need to find out if the respondent was able to match his or her internally generated answer to the response categories we provide in the survey question. Did we give the respondent the correct number and type of choices from which to select a response?

This method of cognitive interviewing can help us to identify many types of problems. It is critical that the individuals interviewed to test the measures of CM reflect the population to be surveyed. So while it may help at first to do a trial run of a survey on your colleagues and others in the field, if they do not reflect the characteristics of the group you will have as respondents, you need to conduct cognitive interviews with a more representative sample.

CONCLUSION

This chapter has highlighted how specific behaviors or lack of behavior, such as neglect, becomes defined as CM. CM has existed for a very long time, but only relatively recently has it received focused attention from citizens, state officials, and governing bodies. In addition, CM is not limited to Western nations; it can be considered a significant worldwide phenomenon. While some consensus has been reached on what constitutes CM, international surveys indicate that many cultural variations exist. These variations are known to add complexity to the study of CM. The chapter also addresses how we measure CM. Child maltreatment can be measured by summarizing the official report data or through representative samples of different groups of people. Of course, conducting a survey depends on available resources, so numerous areas of the globe are underrepresented in the overall picture of CM. Self-report surveys are an important component of measuring CM, and they are becoming more widely used because they can access maltreatment that often goes unreported. Multiple measures of complex experiences are clearly needed. Combining proven self-report measures, such as ICAST and the Conflict Tactics Scale, as well as cognitive interviewing, with official report data will enhance our ability to support our findings and provide a deeper understanding of child maltreatment.

REFERENCES

Bernstein, D. P., Fink, L., Handelsman, L., Foote, J., Lovejoy, M., & Wenzel, K. (1994). Initial reliability and validity of a new retrospective measure of child abuse and neglect. *American Journal of Psychiatry, 151*(8), 1132–1136.

Chalk, R. (2006). Defining child abuse and neglect. In M. M. Feerick, J. F. Knutson, P. K. Trickett, & S. M. Flanzer (Eds.), *Child abuse and neglect: Definitions, classifications, & a framework for research* (pp. 29–48). Baltimore, MD: Paul H. Brooks.

Department for Children, School and Families (DCSF). (2010). *Working together to safeguard children: A guide to inter-agency working to safeguard and promote the welfare of children.* London, UK: DCSF.

Dunne, M. P., Zolotor, A. J., Runyan, D. K., Andreva-Miller, I., Choo, W. Y., Dunne, S. K., . . . & Youssef, R. (2009). ISPCAN child abuse screening tools retrospective version (ICAST-R): Delphi study and field testing in seven countries. *Child Abuse & Neglect, 33*(11), 815.

Gilbert, R., Kemp, A., et al. (2009). Recognising and responding to child maltreatment. *The Lancet, 373*, 167–180.

Greenstein, T. N. (2006). *Methods of family research* (2nd ed.). New York, NY: Guilford Press.

Haberland, N., Chong, E., & Bracken, H. (2004). *Married adolescents: An overview.* Geneva: WHO/UNFPA/Population Council.

Hamby, S. L., & Finkelhor, D. (2000). The victimization of children: Recommendations for assessment and instrument development. *Journal of the American Academy of Child and Adolescent Psychiatry, 39,* 829–840.

Harrington, D., Zuravin, S., DePanfilis, D., Ting, L., & Dubowitz, H. (2002). The neglect scale: Confirmatory factor analysis in a low-income sample. *Child Maltreatment, 7*(4), 359–368.

ISPCAN. (2008). *World perspectives on child abuse* (8th ed.), D. Daro (Ed.). Chicago, IL: ISPCAN.

Korbin, J. E., & Spilsbury, J. C. (1999). Cultural competence and child neglect. In H. Dubowitz (Ed.), *Neglected children: Research, practice, and policy* (pp. 69–88). Thousand Oaks, CA: Sage.

Krug, A., Dahlberg, L. L., Mercy, J. A., Zwi, A. B., & Lo, R. (Eds.). (2002). *World report on violence and health.* Geneva: World Health Organization. Retrieved from http://www.who.int/violence_injury_prevention/violence/world_report/en/introduction.pdf

Milner, J. S. (1989). Applications and limitations of the child abuse potential inventory. *Early Child Development and Care, 42,* 85–97.

National Research Council. (1993). *Understanding child abuse and neglect.* Washington, DC: National Academies Press.

Polansky, N. A., Chalmers, M. A., Buttenweiser, E., & Williams, D. (1981). Assessing adequacy of child caring: An urban scale. *Child Welfare, 57*(7), 439–449.

Portwood, S. G. (2006). Self-report approaches. In M. M. Feerick, J. F. Knutson, P. K. Trickett, & S. M. Flanzer (Eds.), *Child abuse and neglect: Definitions, classifications, & a framework for research* (pp. 233–253). Baltimore, MD: Paul H. Brooks.

Runyan, D. K. (2008). The challenges of assessing the incidence of inflicted traumatic brain injury: A world perspective. *American Journal of Preventive Medicine, 34* (4 Suppl), S112–S115. doi:10.1016/j.amepre.2008.01.011

Runyan, D. K., Dunne, M. P., Zolotor, A. J., Madrid, B., Jain, D., Gerbaka, B., . . . & Youssef, R. M. (2009). The development and piloting of the ISPCAN Child Abuse Screening Tool—Parent version (ICAST-P). *Child Abuse & Neglect, 33*(11), 826–832.

Runyan, D. K., & English, D. J. (2006). Measuring child abuse and neglect using child protective services records. In M. M. Feerick, J. F. Knutson, P. K. Trickett, & S. M. Flanzer (Eds.), *Child abuse and neglect: Definitions, classifications, & a framework for research* (pp. 255–292). Baltimore, MD: Paul H. Brooks.

Saunders, B. E. (2003). Understanding children exposed to violence: Toward an integration of overlapping fields. *Journal of Interpersonal Violence, 18*(4), 356–376.

Sedlak, A. J., & Broadhurst, D. D. (1996). *Third national incidence study of child abuse and neglect: Final report.* Washington, DC: U.S. Department of Health and Human Services.

Sedlak, A. J., Mettenburg, J., Basena, M., Petta, I., McPherson, K., Greene, A., and Li, S. (2010). *Fourth national incidence study of child abuse and neglect (NIS–4): Report to Congress, executive summary.* Washington, DC: U.S. Department of Health and Human Services, Administration for Children and Families.

Sedlak, A. J., Mettenburg, J., Brown, J., Basena, M., & Madden, K. (2010). *Fourth national incidence study of child abuse and neglect (NIS–4) public use file manual.* Prepared under contract to the U.S. Department of Health and Human Services. Rockville, MD: Westat, Inc. Retrieved from http://www.acf.hhs.gov/programs/opre/abuse_neglect/natl_incid/index.html#nisreports

Straus, M. A. (1995). *Manual for the conflict tactics scales.* Durham, NH: Family Research Laboratory, University of New Hampshire.

Straus, M. A. (1997). Measuring physical and psychological maltreatment of children with the conflict tactics scales. In G. Kaufman Kantor & J. L. Jasinski (Eds.), *Out of the darkness: Contemporary perspectives on family violence* (pp. 119–135). Thousand Oaks, CA: Sage.

Straus, M. A. (2001). *Beating the devil out of them: Corporal punishment in American families and its effects on children.* New Brunswick, NJ: Transaction Publishers.

Straus, M. A., Hamby, S. L., Boney-McCoy, S., & Sugarman, D. B. (1996). The revised conflict tactics scales (CTS2). *Journal of Family Issues, 17*(3), 283–316.

Straus, M. A., Hamby, S. L., Finkelhor, D., Moore, D. W., & Runyan, D. (1998). Identification of child maltreatment with the parent-child conflict tactics scales. *Child Abuse and Neglect, 22*(4), 249–270.

Straus, M. A., & Kaufman Kantor, G. (2005). Definition and measurement of neglectful behavior: Some general principles and guidelines. *Child Abuse & Neglect, 29,* 19–29.

Straus, M. A., Kinard, E. M., & Williams, L. M. (1995). *The multidimensional neglectful behavior scale, form A: Adolescent and adult-recall version.* Durham, NH: Family Research Laboratory.

U.S. Department of Health and Human Services (US-DHHS), Administration for Children and Families, Administration on Children, Youth and Families, Children's Bureau. (2012). *Child maltreatment 2011.* Retrieved from http://www.acf.hhs.gov/programs/cb/research-data-technology/statistics-research/child-maltreatment, http://www.acf.hhs.gov/programs/cb/resource/child-maltreatment-2011

WHO. (1999). *Report of the consultation on child abuse prevention, 29–31 March 1999* (WHO/HSC/PVI/99.1). Geneva: World Health Organization. Retrieved from http://whqlibdoc.who.int/hq/1999/aaa00302.pdf

WHO. (2012). Geneva: World Health Organization. Retrieved from www.who.int/mediacentre/factsheets/fs241/en/

WHO & ISPCAN. (2006). *Preventing child maltreatment: A guide to taking action and generating evidence.* Geneva: World Health Organization and International Society for Prevention of Child Abuse and Neglect. Retrieved from http://c.ymcdn.com/sites/www.ispcan.org/resource/resmgr/docs/prevent ing_child_maltreatment.pdf

Williams, L. M. (1994). Recall of childhood trauma: A prospective study of women's memories of child sexual abuse. *Journal of Consulting and Clinical Psychology, 62*(6): 1167–1176.

Williams, L. M., Siegel, J. A., & Pomeroy, J. J. (2000). Validity of women's self-reports of documented child sexual abuse. In A. Stone, J. S. Turkkan, C. A. Bachrach, J. B. Jobe, H. S. Kurtzman, & V. S. Cain (Eds.), *The science of self-report: Implications for research and practice* (pp. 211–226). Mahwah, NJ: Lawrence Erlbaum.

Zolotor, A. J., & Puzia, M. E. (2010). Bans against corporal punishment: A systematic review of the laws, changes in attitudes and behaviors. *Child Abuse Review, 19,* 229–227.

Zolotor, A. J., Runyan, D. K., Dunne, M. P., Jain, D., Péturs, H. R., Ramirez, C., & Isaeva, O. (2009). ISPCAN child abuse screening tool children's version (ICAST-C): Instrument development and multi-national pilot testing. *Child Abuse & Neglect, 33*(11), 833–841.

ADDITIONAL RESOURCES

For more information and guides for translating the Conflict Tactics Scale into another language, see http://pubpages.unh.edu/~mas2/ctsb.htm

For more information and access to the various forms of the Sexual Experiences Survey, see http://www.midss.ie/tools/search?body_value=sexual+experiences +survey &title=

For more information and resources and publications from the World Health Organization, see http://www.who.int/topics/child_abuse/en/

For more information, resources, publications, and prevention guides from the International Society for Prevention of Child Abuse and Neglect (ISPCAN), see http://www.ispcan.org

3

Cultural, Environmental, and Psychosocial Risk Factors for Child Maltreatment

Todd I. Herrenkohl, Sheryl A. Hemphill, Ariane Florent, and Tamara Dee

Child maltreatment (CM) is a costly but preventable problem. To effectively prevent maltreatment, the World Health Organization (WHO, 2006) recommends the following: 1) define the problem; 2) identify the causes and risk factors; 3) design interventions; and 4) disseminate information. In this chapter, we focus primarily on underlying risk factors related to the occurrence of child maltreatment, particularly those factors in the general categories of cultural, environmental, and psychosocial risks. We review the literature on these topics and comment on future research needs and implications for practice. Additional information on risk factors and interventions can be found in a number of recent publications, including the WHO (2006) report.

DEFINING CHILD MALTREATMENT

CM is a subcategory of interpersonal violence that includes physical, sexual, and emotional abuse, as well as neglect (WHO, 2006). According to the WHO report:

  i. *Physical abuse* involves the intentional use of physical force (e.g., hitting, shaking, throwing, burning, strangling, poisoning) that results in a high likelihood of harm to a child.
 ii. *Sexual abuse* involves sexual acts perpetrated on a child, including fondling, oral sex, penetration, and indecent exposure.

iii. *Emotional or psychological abuse* involves a failure to provide a developmentally appropriate and supportive environment and includes another's blaming, belittling, threatening, and ridiculing a child.

iv. *Neglect* involves the failure of a caregiver to provide basic physical needs (safe and clean housing, food, healthcare, and adequate clothing), emotional/psychological needs (warmth, nurturance, and support); educational needs, and environmental needs (shelter, safety).

Although not included in the WHO definitional framework, there has been increasing attention focused on children's witnessing of domestic violence as yet another source of child maltreatment (Christoffel, Scheidt, et al., 1992; Bromfield, 2005; Herrenkohl, 2011). As are other forms of adversity and adverse childhood events (Felitti, Anda, et al., 1998), abuse, neglect, and childhood exposure to domestic violence are known risk factors for a range of problems in children and adults (Herrenkohl, 2011), several of which are mentioned below. A risk factor is a variable that increases the likelihood of an undesired outcome, such as mental illness or violence, whereas a protective factor is a variable that reduces risk and increases the likelihood of a desired or positive outcome, such as succeeding in school or earning a college degree. A more general discussion of the concepts of risk and protection in relation to CM and other forms of interpersonal violence can be found elsewhere (Herrenkohl, 2011).

In a report of the National Research Council (1993) published almost 20 years ago, it was noted that few studies had compared the etiologies and outcomes of different forms of CM. The report defined child maltreatment as a general phenomenon and category of risk exposure in children. While there has been considerable progress in research since that earlier report was written, it remains the case that most research still focuses on CM as if the underlying risks, experiences, and consequences of the different maltreatment types are much the same (Herrenkohl & Herrenkohl, 2009). With sexual abuse as a possible exception, prevention and intervention efforts also are generally similar, suggesting that theories of change related to the different CM types are themselves undifferentiated. Further discussion of prevention and intervention goals is provided in the concluding section of this chapter.

Research shows that CM types often co-occur at a relatively high rate. Although limited to a relative few published studies, Herrenkohl and Herrenkohl (2009) found as much as 90 percent overlap in abuse types, depending on the data sources that were used and methods of obtaining data for each study. Whether overlapping or experienced alone, all types of CM—physical, sexual, and emotional abuse, neglect, and exposure to domestic violence—are highly detrimental to a developing child (Herrenkohl, Sousa, et al., 2008). Common among each form of maltreatment is a violation of basic human rights, now afforded to children, that the United States and other Western societies accept as inviolable (Barnett, Miller-Perrin, et al., 2011). As described in their historical overview of the policy and practice responses to the maltreatment of children, Barnett et al. (2011) note that the move to define child abuse as a social problem took place more than 100 years ago, as advocates began to vocalize and act on their concerns, leading eventually to the passage of state statutes that now limit the authority given to parents to treat their children in any way they choose. With the backing of the medical community, and with the discovery of battered child syndrome in the 1960s, efforts to protect children from physical harm were further advanced, leading in turn to more focused efforts at prevention. This move has prompted researchers to investigate the risk factors and correlates of CM in an effort to identify malleable targets for intervention.

Sexual abuse of children is perhaps the least well understood type of child maltreatment. One question at issue is whether a minor is capable of a consensual sexual relationship with someone older (Barnett, Miller-Perrin, et al., 2011). However, it is assumed that most adults in Western countries recognize the emotional and physical harm that is caused to children by the adults who abuse them sexually—and most, if not all, stand in support of current laws that forbid sexual contact of any form between an adult and child, whether or not the adult considers it consensual (Barnett, Miller-Perrin, et al., 2011).

The consequences of CM vary to some extent on the basis of how severely a child is maltreated and for how long the abuse and/or neglect is endured. Generally speaking, the consequences of CM are typically long lasting and sometimes disabling, particularly for those who are severely and chronically abused (Margolin & Gordis, 2000; Lansford, Dodge, et al., 2002; Herrenkohl, 2011). Consequences for the child subjected to chronic abuse and neglect include low self-esteem, depression, anxiety, physical aggression, peer rejection, school failure, and substance use (Hughes, 1988; McCloskey, Figueredo, et al., 1995; Fantuzzo, Boruch, et al., 1997; Sudermann & Jaffe, 1997; Graham Bermann, 1998; Edleson, 1999; Litrownik, Newton, et al., 2003; McCloskey & Lichter, 2003; Moffitt & Caspi, 2003; Lichter & McCloskey, 2004). In particularly severe cases, abused children can experience symptoms of post-traumatic stress disorder (PTSD), which include difficulty concentrating, sleep problems, severe emotional distress, and frequent upsetting thoughts and memories of the events that were experienced (Lynch & Cicchetti, 2003). Further, children who are abused and neglected are at a higher risk for becoming violent criminals, entering prostitution, committing suicide, and becoming victims of rape (WHO, 2002). Retrospective and some prospective studies also show a relationship between CM and poor physical health, stress-related illnesses, and health risk behaviors, such as smoking and drug abuse (Felitti, Anda, et al., 1998; Goldman, Salus, et al., 2003). The costs of child maltreatment, estimated at over $100 billion annually in the United States (Wang & Houlton, 2007), are massive.

With possible exceptions, studies show that the consequences of child maltreatment are generally similar across racial and ethnic groups (Lansford, Dodge, et al., 2005; Durrant, 2008). At the same time it is understood that rates and consequences of CM can differ according to other risks within the family and the surrounding environment, and possibly culture, depending on how it is defined (Korbin, 2002; Aisenberg & Herrenkohl, 2008; Herrenkohl, 2011). The primary focus of this chapter is on the cultural, environmental, and psychosocial risks for child maltreatment. We review the literature on these topics and conclude the chapter with a brief discussion of the implications for future research and practice that emerge from current research findings. First, we touch briefly on the scope of the problem in the United States and Australia, two countries that have similar approaches to the prevention and amelioration of CM risk factors.

RATES OF CHILD MALTREATMENT

As noted in other sources, estimating the prevalence of child maltreatment worldwide poses major challenges due to variation in definitions, reporting laws, and data gathering systems (WHO, 2002). However, estimates from countries like the United States and Australia can be made to at least begin to comprehend the enormity of the problem.

According to statistics compiled by the U.S. Children's Bureau in the Administration on Children, Youth, and Families using the National Child Abuse and Neglect Data System (NCANDS) data, 3.3 million referrals for alleged maltreatment were made to U.S. child protective service (CPS) agencies in 2010 (DHHS, 2011). These referrals involved approximately 5.9 million children. Nearly 2 million cases were screened by CPS and 436,321 reports were substantiated. The largest percentage of child maltreatment victims were in the age range of birth to one year, and just slightly more than half (51.2 percent) were female. The NCANDS data also revealed that neglect was the most common form of child maltreatment, accounting for more than 75 percent of all maltreatment cases. It is estimated that there were over 1,500 child fatalities in 2010 that resulted from child maltreatment. According to a WHO (2002) report, there were 57,000 child fatalities worldwide in 2000 attributable to some form of direct victimization.

In Australia, national figures from the Australian Institute of Health and Welfare (AIHW) for 2009–2010 were summarized in a report by Lamont (2011). According to the report, 286,437 notifications for abuse and neglect concerning 187,314 children were recorded for that span of time. The total number of finalized investigations in the same year recorded across Australia was 131,689, and the total number of substantiations exceeded 46,000. Similar to the situation in the United States, Australian children aged less than one year were the most reported subjects of substantiated abuse or neglect cases. The most commonly substantiated form of maltreatment in Australia in 2009–2010 was emotional abuse (17,092 cases), followed by neglect (13,275 cases). In all parts of Australia, girls were much more likely than boys to be sexually abused.

These statistics are humbling and underscore the need for effective screening tools and protocols (Gilbert, Kemp, et al., 2009), as well as systems-wide prevention goals and evidence-based approaches (MacMillan, Wathen, et al., 2009). The need and urgency are even greater if one considers the number of maltreatment cases that go unreported to authorities in any given year.

CULTURAL, ENVIRONMENTAL, AND PSYCHOSOCIAL RISK FACTORS FOR CHILD MALTREATMENT

Cultural Influences

There is considerable interest in the role of culture as both a risk and a possibly protective factor for CM (Korbin, 2002). A challenge, however, is that some researchers treat findings on racial and ethnic differences as if they are consistent with culture (Elliott & Urquiza, 2006). Importantly, Elliott and Urquiza (2006) caution that "culture is not synonymous with ethnicity [and that] studies highlighting ethnic differences may obscure the salient underlying cultural factors." Culture, according to Korbin (2002), "is not monolithic or stable but variable and dynamic" (638). She notes that there is considerable cultural variability within racial and ethnic groups and that it is inappropriate to assume that all individuals of a particular ethnicity share the same culture. Her comments suggest that there may be little value in trying to study culture as an extension of ethnicity and that it is instead more productive to focus within particular groups on individual values and beliefs that distinguish abusers from nonabusers. Even still, it has been common practice to talk about culture and ethnicity interchangeably—and research has at times shown that CM rates and developmental findings can vary between ethnic groups (Ferrari, 2002). In these instances it is unclear whether differences are attributable to ethnicity or to other variables, such as reporting bias or measurement error (Ferrari, 2002).

If it is assumed that ethnic and racial group differences in CM are possible, then it is important to understand when and how they come into play. Durrant's (2008) review of literature points to several potential explanations for what some view as a higher tolerance of physical punishment among African American parents and their children. Scholars who have researched the topic refer to evidence showing that while both African American and European American parents use physical punishment as an approach to discipline children, European American children are more negatively impacted (e.g., show higher levels of externalizing behaviors) by the physical punishment they receive. This difference is thought to show a higher tolerance and greater instrumental use of physical punishment within African American families because it is part of the "cultural normative context" of the family. Parents and children view physical punishment as a common practice, not something aberrant or intended to humiliate or harm (Lansford, Deater-Deckard, et al., 2004). There is also a presumption that the use of physical punishment among African American parents is often coupled with warm and nurturing behaviors, which can serve to buffer the effects of the punishment on children (Ferrari, 2002). Because some research shows equally strong adverse effects of physical punishment for children of all racial and ethnic groups, there is a need for more research and careful investigation of where and under which conditions physical punishment is perceived and experienced negatively (Durrant, 2008).

Several studies have investigated the role of culture as defined by values and beliefs about family (e.g., familism) and gender roles (e.g., machismo) (Ferrari, 2002). Familism emphasizes the importance of family, sense of obligation to the family, and respect among family members (Ferrari, 2002; Elliott & Urquiza, 2006). Machismo is characterized by male dominance, authoritarian parenting, and strict adherence to traditional gender roles (Ferrari, 2002). According to Elliott and Urquiza's (2006) review, there is some research that shows higher levels of familism are associated with less risk of child abuse, whereas strict adherence to gender roles and conservative beliefs about authority and respect elevate the risk of abuse.

A study by Ferrari (2002) of 150 Hispanic, African American, and European American parents found that familism and machismo were predictive of physical punishment by fathers, but not mothers, after accounting for ethnicity and parents' history of child maltreatment. Yet the small group sizes and cross-sectional design of the study limit the extent to which findings can be generalized.

In sum, research on culture points to certain values and beliefs that may increase the risk of CM within families. While research has focused on ethnic group differences in CM risk (rather than culture per se), there continues to be confusion about what research actually reveals about the role of culture in the abuse and neglect of children. Generally, evidence does not favor a perspective that elevates the role of culture in CM etiology, and findings on ethnic and racial group differences require further investigation.

Environmental Risk Factors

Studies on social and environmental risk factors for CM typically refer to an ecological framework in which risk and protective factors outside the family are organized more and less proximally to the family microsystem (Bronfenbrenner, 1979; Belsky, 1980; Belsky, 1981; Cicchetti & Lynch, 1993; Black, Heyman, et al., 2001; WHO, 2006; Coulton, Crampton, et al., 2007). Belsky's (1980) "Ecological Integration" is one of the frequently cited examples of this ecological framework and an adaptation of Bronfenbrenner's (1979) more general model of human development. Belsky's framework relies on the notion that child maltreatment is "multiple determined" by characteristics of individuals, of the family, and of the surrounding community and broader society. Cicchetti and Lynch (1993) followed Belsky's model with a version of their own. They similarly proposed that at the broadest (macro-cultural) level, social risks for child maltreatment include society's willingness to tolerate violence and the use of physical punishment in disciplining children. At the exosystem level, risk factors include chronic stress (from high levels of unemployment and other forms of disadvantage) and dangers (from community violence) in the surrounding community. Lack of resources and support in the community (neighborhood) also can impinge on the functioning of families, particularly those with resources of their own.

Community Influences

According to a review by Coulton and colleagues (2007), several neighborhood characteristics have been consistently linked to variation in officially recorded child maltreatment statistics. These include census measures of neighborhood social and economic deprivation and disadvantage (e.g., poverty status), unemployment, and residential turnover and instability. Their review of 25 studies showed general consistency in reported findings on structural influences despite differences in the measures used and the populations that were studied. Measures of neighborhood overcrowding, high child care burden, and density of alcohol outlets have also been investigated as risks for CM occurrence (WHO, 2006).

As noted in the Coulton et al. (2007) report, evidence of neighborhood variation and structural predictors in maltreatment rates is well documented, but the processes through which structural factors impinge on family functioning (leading to higher rates of child maltreatment) are less clear. Some evidence suggests that variables like low social integration and social impoverishment are related to CM risk, yet these findings are from relatively few studies and require replication. Coulton and colleagues argue, in addition, for more attention to common frameworks to help incorporate relevant theory and research. A framework they propose includes both neighborhood (e.g., social organization) and transactional (e.g., environmental stressors) processes to help explain the connection between neighborhood structure and CM reports.

Related to the question of risk processes, Aisenberg and Herrenkohl (2008) discussed the hypothesis that families living in dangerous and violent neighborhoods are at higher risk of child maltreatment because parents, under considerable stress, have less capacity to "parent" well; that is, environmental stressors reduce parents' ability to appropriately discipline, monitor, and supervise their children. Evidence favoring this hypothesis, while documented in some qualitative, ethnographic studies—such as that of Furstenberg (1993), focused on inner-city neighborhoods of Philadelphia—remains somewhat tentative. However, research has shown that stress on families, both social and economic, does increase risk for child maltreatment generally (Li et al., 2011).

Measurement in neighborhood and social context studies of maltreatment risk is a primary consideration and a topic investigated by Ben-Arieh (2010) in his study of small towns in Israel. As noted by the author, researchers have relied heavily on census data to investigate neighborhood influences, while the unit of analysis provided by the census (e.g., census tract, block group) often fails to correspond to a geographic area of a particular neighborhood, as typically defined by its residents. Consequently, data are imprecise and do not provide an accurate assessment of the conditions surrounding individual families. Further, because the census does not contain information on neighborhood processes, what can be learned about social and environmental risks is somewhat limited (Coulton, Crampton, et al., 2007; Aisenberg & Herrenkohl, 2008). This is an issue raised by Aisenberg and Herrenkohl (2008) in their review. The authors of that article note that more qualitative and observational research within an identified locale could add to what is learned from census studies.

Responding to the need for more focused research on community influences at a scale where local variation in child maltreatment rates can be accurately and somewhat more easily discerned, Ben-Arieh (2010) studied data (from various indexes and local records) from small, defined towns of no more than 10,000 people in Israel. He found that the following community-level variables were correlated with child maltreatment investigations: adult unemployment rate (indicative of low income/family poverty), rate of new immigrants, proportion of children in single-parent families, population loss, and geographic (centrality) location. Interestingly, findings of this analysis, although defined by location, not census unit, are quite similar to those of other (census) studies (Coulton, Crampton, et al., 2007). In the Ben-Arieh investigation, nationality (Jewish, Arab, mixed) and religion were not associated with child maltreatment rates, nor was socioeconomic status of families. However, previous research in Israel and elsewhere has shown these or similar variables to be important predictors (risks) of child maltreatment.

It is important to briefly mention social and contextual variables that research has shown to lessen risk or to promote protection from child maltreatment (Aisenberg & Herrenkohl, 2008). As noted in Aisenberg and Herrenkohl's review, children of vulnerable families can often benefit from a supportive community environment in which there is access to mentoring by adults outside the family, as well as to positive, youth-focused community organizations and service systems (e.g., arts and recreational programs, religious organizations, and health and social services). Other reviews of the literature also underscore the important role of social support as a protective factor for vulnerable families (Stith, Liu, et al., 2009) and the benefits that come from extended caregiving and collective action on the part of neighborhood residents (Sampson, Raudenbush, et al., 1997; Sampson, Morenoff, et al., 2002).

Psychosocial Risk Factors

By far, the most research on psychosocial risk factors for child maltreatment has focused on physical abuse. Within this literature are studies on the characteristics of abused children. Although it is difficult to determine whether distinguishing characteristics of these children contribute to, or extend from, the abuse they experience, evidence does appear to suggest that certain qualities and behaviors correlate consistently with reports and documented accounts of abuse. For example, research shows that children who are physically abused exhibit more conduct disorder symptoms than do non-abused children (Knutson, 1995), and both physically abused and neglected children are more aggressive and have more attention problems than do others, according to mothers' reports and observations (Burgess & Conger, 1978; George & Main, 1979; Reid, Taplin, et al., 1981). Additionally, analyses of data from the National Family Violence Survey (Black, Smith Slep, et al., 2001) show that psychologically abused children engage in more fights with other children and have interpersonal difficulties in making and maintaining friends (Vissing, Straus, et al., 1991). Further, studies of parent-child interactions have found that maltreated children are generally less compliant (George & Main, 1979; Schindler & Arkowitz, 1986) or overcompliant to their parents' demands (Crittenden & DiLalla, 1988).

Attempts to link the psychological characteristics of parents to their use of abusive practices has been slowed by the lack of standardized measures (Black, Smith Slep, et al., 2001). Yet studies have shown associations between CM and measures of parents' emotional state, including anxiety, depression, and interpersonal problems, as well as parenting stress and coping styles (Black et al., 2001 [CPA paper]). Moderate to strong correlations between child abuse and parental depression are reported in several studies (Lahey, Conger, et al., 1984; Pianta, Egeland, et al., 1989; Whipple & Webster-Stratton, 1991; Straus, 1994; Chaffin, Kelleher, et al., 1996). Additionally, there is some evidence from early studies like that of Helfer et al. (1977) that suggests parents who engage in physical abuse are more lonely and isolated, angry, easily upset, and quicker to feel threatened.

In a study by Pianta et al. (1989), mothers of children who were sexually abused experienced more life stress, were more tense, angry, confused, and depressed, and were more calculating, skeptical, and restless. In a study of 44 Dutch parents whose children had been admitted to local hospitals, Lesnik-Oberstein et al. (1995) found that mothers who were psychologically abusive, compared to those who were not, received less affection from their husbands and gave less affection to them, and were more physically and verbally aggressive in their marital relationships. Psychologically abusive mothers also were more socially anxious, neurotic, dysthymic, and hostile—and they had lower self-esteem and were less socially engaged (Lesnik-Oberstein, Koers, et al., 1995). In that same study, psychologically abusive mothers had lower verbal reasoning scores than nonabusive mothers.

Indeed, the likelihood of abuse is greater when parents lack the tools to parent nonaggressively and without hostility, such as in the use of name-calling and emotional manipulation (e.g., threatening to leave or abandon the child). Evidence also exists that abusive parents tend to attribute more negative qualities to their children and to generally view their children's behaviors less positively (Larrance & Twentyman, 1983). For example, maltreating parents may perceive their young children's misbehavior in a supermarket as a deliberate attempt to embarrass the parent or to make the parent look bad in public when, in fact, the behavior is a reflection of the child's feeling hungry, bored, or physically uncomfortable. Abusive parents are also more inclined to categorize their children as either "good" or "bad," failing to recognize the nuances in behaviors and actions of the child.

Important differences have been found in the parenting practices of those who abuse. Compared to nonabusive parents, those who physically abuse their children are more inclined to spank, to use isolation, and to reason less to get their children to comply (Trickett & Kuczynski, 1986; Whipple & Webster-Stratton, 1991). Additionally, mothers of physically abused children can appear more verbally and physically aggressive and tend to use more negative commands and criticism in dialogue with their children (Reid, Taplin, et al., 1981; Bousha & Twentyman, 1984; Lahey, Conger, et al., 1984; Whipple & Webster-Stratton, 1991). Bousha and Twentyman (1984) reported that, compared to abusive mothers, mothers who were abusive used fewer positive nonverbal and verbal behaviors. Of note, however, is that some studies have failed to find these differences (Burgess & Conger, 1978; Mash, Johnston, et al., 1983; Silber, Bermann, et al., 1993). Findings on child maltreatment and the quality of the parent-child relationship extend to China, where evidence resembles that found by studies in the United States and other Western countries (Chen, Dunne, & Han, 2007; Leung, Wong, Chen, & Tang, 2008).

Child Neglect

Summarizing the child and parent psychosocial risk factors for neglect is challenging because, although it is a common form of maltreatment, limited research has been conducted on neglect specifically (Schumacher, Smith Slep, et al., 2001). Studies examining mother-child interactions suggest that neglectful mothers engage less with their children and are generally less positive in their interactions. Polansky et al. (1992) found that mothers who engaged in neglectful behavior toward their children had lower scores than did controls on verbal accessibility, which includes warmth when talking with children, warmth when discussing children, giving direct opinions, and responding to questions in sentences rather than in a word or two. Additionally, strong associations have been found between child neglect and maternal impulsivity, low self-esteem, substance abuse, and low social support (Schumacher, Smith Slep, et al., 2001). The research also suggests that the presence of high-level daily stressors (rather than major life stressors) may increase the risk of child neglect (Schumacher, Smith Slep, et al., 2001). Relatedly, McCubbin et al. (1985) showed that neglected children tended to live in families with higher levels of stress.

In sum, there is a range of factors related to children and parent caregivers that have been linked to child maltreatment. In general, abused and neglected children show more conduct problems, including antisocial and aggressive behavior, than do children who are not maltreated, based on mothers' and teachers' reports and observational studies. Studies of the interactions between mothers and children show maltreated children to be less compliant or overcompliant in response to parents' requests. Such children may also have difficulties interacting with peers and other adults. An important caveat, however, is that studies to date have failed to solidly differentiate between antecedents and consequences of maltreatment with respect to parent and child conduct (Knutson, 1995). Thus, it is important to interpret results with some caution and at the same time take steps to potentially lessen CM occurrence using prevention programs that target parents and children together. Without question, there is a need for more rigorously designed studies that can help advance knowledge of these important issues. In future studies, it is also necessary to examine the accuracy of mothers' reports of problem behaviors in their children, which are likely shaped by levels of stress in the surrounding environment (Knutson, 1995).

Research on child and parent characteristics related to maltreatment is somewhat constrained by the use of unstandardized and sometimes poorly defined measures. Without clear, agreed-upon definitions and psychometrically established measures, it is difficult to discern true substantive differences from measurement error. Additionally, the relatively few studies conducted on correlates of certain forms of maltreatment, particularly neglect, make it difficult to draw solid conclusions. Reliance on cross-sectional designs and small sample sizes also renders results somewhat questionable. Overall, there is a need for larger scale and higher quality studies on the topics reviewed. Additionally, much of the research reviewed in this section was conducted in Western countries, and it is unclear how well findings generalize to the broader global community. Studies of child maltreatment in countries like China (Chen, Dunne, et al., 2007; Leung, Wong, et al., 2008) appear to show similar patterns in CM risks, although research involving a range of countries is needed to gain a more global perspective on the psychosocial risk factors for child maltreatment.

CONCLUSIONS AND IMPLICATIONS FOR PRACTICE AND POLICY

As noted at the beginning of this chapter, child maltreatment represents a major public health concern and a costly social problem worldwide, for which prevention programs are desperately needed. Rates of abuse and neglect remain very high in countries around the globe, although the full extent of the problem cannot be fully understood until definitions, reporting laws, and data gathering systems are made more uniform (WHO, 2002). It is assumed that rates of CM in other countries are as high or higher than those of the United States and Australia, where there have been major advances in CM surveillance and prevention. In their review of literature, Mikton and Butchart (2009) note that recent increasing attention to CM in low- and middle-income countries has helped established CM as a "truly global phenomenon." Even in countries where advances have helped to bring about changes in public awareness and actions to reduce CM, statistics show that far too many children are still being physically and emotionally harmed each year by parent caregivers and other adults.

Studies reviewed in this chapter on the cultural, environmental, and psychosocial risk factors for child maltreatment point to a number of important targets for prevention. These include very broad and less well-defined targets, such as gender roles and societal values that promote male dominance and authoritarian parenting, as well as risks in the community and family, and those associated with individuals, both parents and children. For example, research has found parents who abuse their children perceive their children and their behavior more negatively and are more apt to use abusive discipline practices of various forms, including physical punishment. Although some research points to variation in the use of physical punishment that is associated with ethnic and racial group membership, the most likely determinants of whether a parent will discipline a child physically and harshly are the environmental stressors that impinge on the functioning of families, the beliefs parents hold about the use of physical punishment (i.e., whether or not it is considered appropriate and children deserving of such punishment), how they perceive the actions of their children (e.g., acts of defiance versus normative or justified behaviors), and whether they were themselves disciplined severely when they were children (Herrenkohl, 2011). Abuse and neglect of children have also been linked to mental health problems in parents, and to their low self-esteem, anger, and social isolation. Conduct problems on the part of children are also associated with various forms of CM, although it is unclear whether the behaviors precede or follow parents' behaviors toward them.

The damage of CM inflicted on children is evident in studies of short-term and long-term consequences of individual and overlapping forms of abuse and neglect (Herrenkohl, 2011). Studies have linked child maltreatment to a wide range of risk behaviors, problems, and disorders later in life—and to the repetition of abuse across generations (Pears & Capaldi, 2001). Unfortunately, the quality of research on risk factors and consequences is somewhat mixed and there has been a tendency to rely too much on cross-sectional data collection and retrospective reporting of CM from adulthood. This is mainly due to the lower cost and easier administration of cross-sectional studies, but there is a tradeoff between cost and quality, and findings from cross-sectional research for practice and policy are not as compelling. Nevertheless, a substantial evidence base now exists from which to move the field systematically forward toward broad-scale prevention of CM.

Research has shown that there are considerable costs savings associated with preventing CM before it occurs rather than trying to act on the consequences after the fact (Wang & Houlton, 2007; Mikton & Butchart, 2009). For that and other reasons, the U.S. Centers for Disease Control and Prevention (CDC) developed its Essentials for Childhood framework for the prevention of child abuse and neglect that includes the following priorities: 1) measuring impact; 2) creating and evaluating new prevention approaches; 3) applying and adapting effective practices; and 4) building community readiness. The framework emphasizes primary prevention and surveillance of risk and protective factors, and the promotion of safe, stable, and nurturing relationships (U.S. Department of Health and Human Services et al., 2012). The CDC is actively engaged in activities to expand surveillance, to improve technology to ease the transfer of information to help guide prevention efforts (such as home visiting programs and parenting interventions), and to broadly disseminate research findings in real time. The efforts underway at CDC provide a model for how to address CM risks, using science to guide practice. Although developed for the U.S. context, where prevention of CM and other childhood risks has gained momentum, it is quite likely that a similar public health model of primary prevention could be tailored and adapted for other countries where social, cultural, and economic conditions differ. However, that has yet to be shown.

Prevention programs that show promise for reducing CM occurrence are those that target empirically documented risk and protective factors, such as those reviewed in this chapter. An extensive "review of reviews" on child maltreatment prevention conducted by Mikton and Butchart (2009) found that home visiting programs appear to reduce various risk factors and thus hold promise for preventing CM, although some research has not been sufficiently rigorous. Parent training and education programs also appear promising, although reductions in CM occurrence have not been consistently documented. These programs seek to increase parents' knowledge of child development and caregiving skills, which were identified in our current review as important predictors of CM. Multicomponent programs, which include parent education, family support, and preschool child education, also appear promising, but again, findings are somewhat inconsistent and not uniformly positive. Further, child sexual abuse prevention programs are mentioned in the report and appear to show some capacity to lessen risks and enhance protection against sexual abuse in particular. Of all the evaluations conducted on programs included in the Mikton and Butchart review, a large majority (about 83 percent) were conducted in the United States and nearly all (over 99 percent) were conducted in high-income countries. Consequently, it is hard to determine whether the findings of these studies pertain to lower-income countries, where circumstances surrounding child maltreatment can be more extreme.

Programs in the United States that have shown effects in lowering risk for child maltreatment have mostly focused on risk factors within the family domain, such as with Nurse Family Partnership (NFP) (Olds, Sadler, et al., 2007) and the Triple Parenting program (Sanders, 1999; Prinz, Sanders, et al., 2009), although the reach of these programs can extend into the surrounding community. Evidence of rigorous evaluation studies and cost-benefit reports show that programs like NFP can both reduce maltreatment and save sizable sums of money over an extended period, both in costs that are incurred for injuries and services provided to victims and their caregivers (MacMillan, Wathen, et al., 2009). Multilevel and multifaceted prevention programs that are aligned with an ecological framework (Belsky, 1981; Black, Heyman, et al., 2001) are worthy of particularly strong consideration and are most necessary to attend to the full range of risk and protective factors that have been documented in the child maltreatment literature (Herrenkohl, 2011). Also needed is a broad view of programming and policy development that uses empirical findings to bring about large-scale systems change to improve services for the most vulnerable families.

In conclusion, a considerable amount of information on the cultural, environmental, and psychosocial risk factors for child maltreatment has been generated to help spur practice innovation and policy change. Further well-designed longitudinal studies on the underlying risk (and protective) factors for child maltreatment will advance the field beyond this point and provide an even stronger base for empirically supported prevention and intervention programs. However, as noted in the WHO (2006) report, it is only when child maltreatment prevention becomes a political priority that we will begin to see sizable annual reductions in the number of reported and suspected cases of abuse and neglect in Western countries and possibly worldwide. It has long been assumed, and it has been increasingly well documented, that child abuse and neglect can be prevented—but up to this point, sufficient resources to support the implementation of tested programs over many years have not been secured.

REFERENCES

Aisenberg, E., & Herrenkohl, T. I. (2008). Community violence in context: Risk and resilience in children and families. *Journal of Interpersonal Violence, 23,* 296–315.

Barnett, O. A., Miller-Perrin, C. L., et al. (2011). *Family violence across the lifespan.* Los Angeles, CA: Sage.

Belsky, J. (1980). Child maltreatment: An ecological integration. *American Psychologist, 35*(4), 320–335.

Belsky, J. (1981). Child maltreatment: An ecological integration. *Annual Progress in Child Psychiatry and Development,* 637–665.

Ben-Arieh, A. (2010). Socioeconomic correlates of rates of child maltreatment in small communities. *American Journal of Orthopsychiatry, 80*(1), 109–114.

Black, D. A., Heyman, R. E., et al. (2001). Risk factors for child physical abuse. *Aggression and Violent Behavior, 6,* 121–188.

Black, D. A., Smith Slep, A. M., et al. (2001). Risk factors for child psychological abuse. *Aggression and Violent Behavior, 6,* 189–201.

Bousha, D. M., & Twentyman, C. T. (1984). Mother-child interactional style in abuse, neglect, and groups: Naturalistic observations in the home. *Journal of Abnormal Psychology, 93,* 106–114.

Bromfield, L. M. (2005). *Chronic child maltreatment in an Australian statutory child protection sample.* Unpublished doctoral dissertation. Deakin University, Geelong, Victoria, Australia.

Bronfenbrenner, U. (1979). *The ecology of human development: Experiments by nature and design.* Cambridge, MA: Harvard University Press.

Burgess, R. L., & Conger, R. D. (1978). Family interaction in abusive, neglectful, and normal families. *Child Development, 49,* 1163–1173.

Chaffin, M., Kelleher, K., et al. (1996). Onset of physical abuse and neglect: Psychiatric, substance abuse, and social risk factors from prospective community data. *Child Abuse & Neglect, 20,* 191–203.

Chen, J. Q., Dunne, M. P., et al. (2007). Prevention of child sexual abuse in China: Knowledge, attitudes, and communication practices of parents of elementary school children. *Child Abuse & Neglect, 31,* 747–755.

Christoffel, K. K., Scheidt, P. C., et al. (1992). Standard definitions for child injury research—excerpts of a conference report. *Pediatrics, 89*(6), 1027–1034.

Cicchetti, D., & Lynch, M. (1993). Toward an ecological/transactional model of community violence and child maltreatment: Consequences for child development. *Psychiatry, 56,* 96–117.

Coulton, C. J., Crampton, D. S., et al. (2007). How neighborhoods influence child maltreatment: A review of the literature and alternative pathways. *Child Abuse & Neglect, 31,* 1117–1142.

Crittenden, P. M., & DiLalla, D. (1988). Compulsive compliance: The development of an inhibitory coping strategy in infancy. *Journal of Abnormal Child Psychology, 16,* 585–599.

DHHS. (2011). *Child Maltreatment 2010.* Washington, DC: U.S. Department of Health and Human Services, Administration for Children and Families, Administration on Children, Youth and Families, Children's Bureau.

Durrant, J. E. (2008). Physical punishment, culture, and rights: Current issues for professionals. *Journal of Developmental and Behavioral Pediatrics, 29*(1), 55–66.

Edleson, J. L. (1999). Problems associated with children's witnessing domestic violence. *Violence against Women Online Resources.* Retrieved from www.vaw.umn.edu

Elliott, K., & Urquiza, A. (2006). Ethnicity, culture, and child maltreatment. *Journal of Social Issues, 62*(4), 787–809.

Fantuzzo, J., Boruch, R., et al. (1997). Domestic violence and children: Prevalence and risk in five major U.S. cities. *Journal of the American Academy of Child and Adolescent Psychiatry, 36*(1), 116–122.

Felitti, V. J., Anda, R. F., et al. (1998). Relationship of childhood abuse and household dysfunction to many of the leading causes of death in adults: The adverse childhood experiences (ACE) study. *American Journal of Preventive Medicine, 14*(4), 245–258.

Ferrari, A. M. (2002). The impact of culture upon child rearing practices and definitions of child maltreatment. *Child Abuse & Neglect, 26,* 793–813.

Furstenberg, F. F. (1993). How families manage risk and opportunity in dangerous neighborhoods. In W. J. Wilson (Ed.), *Sociology and the public agenda* (pp. 231–258). Newbury Park, CA: Sage.

George, C., & Main, M. (1979). Social interactions of young abused children: Approach, avoidance, and aggression. *Child Development, 50,* 306–318.

Gilbert, R., Kemp, A., et al. (2009). Recognising and responding to child maltreatment. *The Lancet, 373,* 167–80.

Goldman, J., Salus, M. K., et al. (2003). *A coordinated response to child abuse and neglect: The foundation for practice.* Washington, DC: U.S. Department of Health and Human Services.

Graham Bermann, S. A. (1998). The impact of woman abuse on children's social development: Research and theoretical perspectives. In G. W. Holden, R. Geffner, & E. N. Jouriles (Eds.), *Children exposed to marital violence: Theory, research, and applied issues* (pp. 21–54). Washington, DC: American Psychological Association.

Helfer, R. E., Schneider, C., et al. (1977). *Manual for use of the Michigan screening profile of parenting.* East Lansing, MI: Michigan State University Press.

Herrenkohl, R. C., & Herrenkohl, T. I. (2009). Assessing a child's experience of multiple maltreatment types: Some unfinished business. *Journal of Family Violence, 24,* 485–496.

Herrenkohl, T. I. (2011). Family violence and co-occurring risk factors for children exposed to violence. In T. I. Herrenkohl, E. Aisenberg, J. H. Williams, & J. M. Jenson (Eds.), *Violence in context: Current evidence on risk, protection, and prevention* (pp. 73–91). New York, NY: Oxford University Press.

Herrenkohl, T. I., Sousa, C., et al. (2008). Intersection of child abuse and children's exposure to domestic violence. *Trauma, Violence, & Abuse, 9*(2), 84–99.

Hughes, H. M. (1988). Psychological and behavioral correlates of family violence in child witnesses and victims. *American Journal of Orthopsychiatry, 58*(1), 77–90.

Knutson, J. F. (1995). Psychological characteristics of maltreated children: Putative risk factors and consequences. *Annual Review of Psychology, 46,* 401–431.

Korbin, J. E. (2002). Culture and child maltreatment: Cultural competence and beyond. *Child Abuse & Neglect, 26,* 637–644.

Lahey, B. B., Conger, R. D., et al. (1984). Parenting behavior and emotional status of physically abusive mothers. *Journal of Consulting and Clinical Psychology, 52,* 1062–1071.

Lamont, A. (2011). *Child abuse and neglect statistics: National Child Protection Clearinghouse resource sheet.* Melbourne: Commonwealth of Australia.

Lansford, J. E., Deater-Deckard, K., et al. (2004). Ethnic differences in the link between physical discipline and later adolescent externalizing behaviors. *Journal of Child Psychology & Psychiatry, 45*(4), 810–812.

Lansford, J. E., Dodge, K. A., et al. (2002). A 12-year prospective study of the long-term effects of early child maltreatment on psychological, behavioral, and academic problems. *Archives of Pediatrics & Adolescent Medicine, 156*, 824–830.

Lansford, J. E., Dodge, K. A., et al. (2005). Physical discipline and children's adjustment: Cultural normativeness as a moderator. *Child Development, 76*, 1234–1246.

Larrance, D. T., & Twentyman, C. T. (1983). Maternal attributions and child abuse. *Journal of Abnormal Psychology, 92*, 449–457.

Lesnik-Oberstein, M., Koers, A. J., et al. (1995). Parental hostility and its sources in psychologically abusive mothers: A test of the three-factor theory. *Child Abuse & Neglect, 19*, 33–49.

Leung, P. W. S., Wong, W. C. W., et al. (2008). Prevalence and determinants of child maltreatment among high school students in southern China: A large-scale school-based survey. *Child and Adolescent Psychiatry and Mental Health, 2*, 27–48.

Li, F., Godinet, M. T., et al. (2011). Protective factors among families with children at risk of maltreatment: Follow up early school years. *Children and Youth Services Review, 33*, 139–148.

Lichter, E. L., & McCloskey, L. A. (2004). The effects of childhood exposure to marital violence on adolescent gender-role beliefs and dating violence. *Psychology of Women Quarterly, 28*, 344–357.

Litrownik, A. J., Newton, R., et al. (2003). Exposure to family violence in young at-risk children: A longitudinal look at the effects of victimization and witnessed physical and psychological aggression. *Journal of Family Violence, 18*(1), 59–73.

Lynch, M., & Cicchetti, D. (2003). Links between community violence and the family system: Evidence from children's feelings of relatedness and perceptions of parent behavior. *Family Process, 41*(3), 519–532.

MacMillan, H. L., Wathen, C. N., et al. (2009). Interventions to prevent child maltreatment and associated impairment. *The Lancet, 373*(9659), 250–266.

Margolin, G., & Gordis, E. B. (2000). The effects of family and community violence on children. *Annual Review of Psychology, 51*, 445–479.

Mash, E. J., Johnston, C., et al. (1983). A comparison of the mother-child interactions of physically abused and non-abused children during play and task situations. *Journal of Clinical Child Psychology, 12*, 337–346.

McCloskey, L. A., Figueredo, A. J., et al. (1995). The effects of systemic family violence on children's mental health. *Child Development, 66*(5), 1239–1261.

McCloskey, L. A., & Lichter, E. L. (2003). The contribution of marital violence to adolescent aggression across different relationships. *Journal of Interpersonal Violence, 18*(4), 390–412.

McCubbin, H. I., Patterson, J. M., et al. (1985). Adolescent-family inventory of life events and changes. In D. H. Olson, H. I. McCubbin, H. L. Barnes et al. (Eds.), *Family Inventories* (pp. 109–119). St. Paul, MN: Department of Family Social Science, University of Minnesota.

McMorris, B. J., Hemphill, S. A., et al. (2007). Prevalence of substance use and delinquent behaviour in adolescents from Victoria, Australia and Washington State, United States. *Health Education & Behavior, 34*(4), 634–650.

Mikton, C., & Butchart, A. (2009). Child maltreatment prevention: A systematic review of reviews. *Bulletin of the World Health Organization, 5*(87). Geneva: World Health Organization.

Moffitt, T. E., & Caspi, A. (2003). Preventing the intergenerational continuity of antisocial behaviour: Implications of partner violence. In D. P. Farrington & J. W. Coid (Eds.), *Early prevention of adult antisocial behaviour* (pp. 109–129). Cambridge, UK: Cambridge University Press.

National Research Council. (1993). *Understanding Child Abuse and Neglect.* Washington, DC: National Academic Press.

Olds, D. L., Sadler, L., et al. (2007). Programs for parents and infants and toddlers: Recent evidence from randomized trials. *Journal of Child Psychology and Psychiatry, 48*, 355–391.

Pears, K. C., & Capaldi, D. M. (2001). Intergenerational transmission of abuse: A two-generational prospective study of an at-risk sample. *Child Abuse & Neglect, 25*, 1439–1461.

Pianta, R., Egeland, B., et al. (1989). The antecedents of maltreatment: Results of the mother-child interaction project. In D. Cicchetti & V. Carlson (Eds.), *Child maltreatment: Theory and research on the causes and consequences of child abuse and neglect* (pp. 203–253). New York, NY: Cambridge University Press.

Polansky, N. A., Gaudin, J. M., et al. (1992). The maternal characteristics scale: A cross validation. *Child Welfare League of America, 71*, 271–280.

Prinz, R. J., Sanders, M. R., et al. (2009). Population-based prevention of child maltreatment: The U.S. triple P system population trial. *Prevention Science, 10*, 1–12.

Reid, J. B., Taplin, P. S., et al. (1981). A social interactional approach to the treatment of abusive families. In R. B. Stuart (Ed.), *Violent behavior: Social learning approaches to prediction, management, and treatment* (pp. 83–101). New York, NY: Brunner/Mazel.

Sampson, R. J., Morenoff, J. D., et al. (2002). Assessing neighborhood effects: Social processes and new directions in research. *Annual Review of Sociology, 28*, 443–478.

Sampson, R. J., Raudenbush, S. W., et al. (1997). Neighborhoods and violent crime: A multilevel study of collective efficacy. *Science, 277*, 918–924.

Sanders, M. R. (1999). Triple P-positive parenting program: Towards an empirically validated multilevel parenting and family support strategy for the prevention of behavior and emotional problems in children. *Clinical Child and Family Psychology Review, 2*(2), 71–90.

Schindler, F., & Arkowitz H. (1986). The assessment of mother-child interactions in physically abusive and nonabusive families. *Journal of Family Violence, 1*, 247–257.

Schumacher, J. A., Smith Slep, A. M., et al. (2001). Risk factors for child neglect. *Aggression and Violent Behavior, 6,* 231–254.

Silber, S., Bermann, E., et al. (1993). Patterns of influence and response in abusing and nonabusing families. *Journal of Family Violence, 8,* 27–38.

Stith, S. M., Liu, T., et al. (2009). Risk factors in child maltreatment: A meta-analytic review of the literature. *Aggression and Violent Behavior 14,* 13–29.

Straus, M. A. (1994). *Beating the devil out of them: Corporal punishment in American families.* New York, NY: Lexington Books.

Sudermann, M., & Jaffe, P. (1997). Children and youth who witness violence: New directions in intervention and prevention. In D. A. Wolfe, R. J. McMahon, & R. D. Peters (Eds.), *Child abuse: New directions in prevention and treatment across the lifespan* (pp. 55–78). Thousand Oaks, CA: Sage.

Trickett, P. K., & Kuczynski, L. (1986). Children's misbehaviors and parental discipline strategies in abusive and nonabusive families. *Developmental Psychology, 22,* 115–123.

U.S. Department of Health and Human Services, Administration for Children and Families, Administration on Children, Youth and Families, Children's Bureau. (2012). Essentials for Childhood: Steps to Create Safe, Stable, and Nurturing Relationships. Washington, DC: U.S. Department of Health and Human Services.

Vissing, Y. M., Straus, M. A., et al. (1991). Verbal aggression by parents and psychosocial problems of children. *Child Abuse & Neglect, 15,* 223–238.

Wang, C.-T., & Houlton, J. (2007). *Total estimated costs of child abuse and neglect in the United States: Economic impact study.* Chicago, IL: Prevent Child Abuse America.

Whipple, E. E., & Webster-Stratton, C. (1991). The role of parental stress in physically abusive families. *Child Abuse & Neglect, 15,* 279–291.

WHO. (2002). *World report on violence and health.* Geneva: World Health Organization.

WHO. (2006). *Preventing child maltreatment: A guide to taking action and generating evidence.* Geneva: World Health Organization.

4

Child Sexual Abuse

Rebecca M. Bolen and Kellie B. Gergely

DEFINITION

Child sexual abuse (CSA) is the willful sexual violation of an underage child. The age at which the child is considered underage—that is, the age at which the child is considered incapable of giving consent to the sexual activity—is set by state and national statutes and typically varies by type of abuse and relationship of perpetrator. For example, molestation tends to be defined as the sexual touching of the child, whereas rape or attempted rape is typically defined as any object passing through any orifice in the body. In the United States, this legal age of consent is usually between ages 14 and 18 (Berliner, 2011). Teens older than the age of consent can also experience unwanted sexual violation, but unless these unwanted violations are perpetrated by someone in the immediate family, they tend to be covered by laws pertaining to sexual assault or statutory rape. For example, in Zambia it is illegal to "carnally know" any girl under the age of 16 (Fleischman, 2002; UNICEF, 2012), whereas in Tonga this age of consent is 12, after which the Sexual Offences Act is activated (CBC News, 2006; UNICEF, 2012). This act is similar to statutory rape laws in the United States, in which it is illegal to engage in sexual intercourse with a youth under a given age when the offender is not within a certain age range. The age of consent also varies in the United States. In Tennessee and Arizona, the age of consent is 18 (Glosser, Gardiner, & Fishman, 2004). However, the minimum age at which a youth can give consent under certain circumstances differs. In Arizona, the age of consent is 15, with an age differential of two (i.e., the two teens can be no more than two years apart). For example, a 17-year-old teen may have sex with a 15-year-old, but an 18-year-old may not have sex with a 15-year-old because it exceeds the age differential and therefore is considered statutory rape. In Tennessee the minimum age of consent is 13, with an age differential of 4. Another important parameter of the definition of sexual abuse is whether it is non-contact or contact. Noncontact abuse may include exposure or voyeurism, whereas contact abuse may range from sexual touching of the breasts or genitals to rape.

Other abusive events that are sexual in nature are sexual exploitation, trafficking of children, and prostitution of children. These events tend to be treated as special categories, sometimes falling within the statutes of CSA and sometimes falling outside these statutes. For purposes of this review, they are considered as being a special category and will only be reviewed briefly.

The remainder of this chapter reviews what is known about CSA in the United States and internationally. The first section discusses the scope of the problem of CSA, including its incidence and prevalence. The chapter then turns to the physical, psychological, and neurophysiological effects of sexual abuse on children and adults.

THE SCOPE OF THE PROBLEM

Prevalence and incidence are measures of the scope of the problem of CSA. Prevalence captures whether individuals were ever abused in child-hood, whereas incidence captures whether individuals were abused during a specific time period, usually a year (Russell & Bolen, 2000).

Incidence of CSA

Incidence is typically reported as the number of individuals per 1,000 who experienced sexual abuse during that time frame. Incidence studies are important for depicting how well cases of CSA are being identified.

United States

In the United States, one of the most important attempts to gather data on incidence of CSA is the annual Child Maltreatment report collected by the Children's Bureau. This report includes all cases of child maltreatment identified by CPS during a given year. Typically, the only cases investigated by CPS are those in which the abuse is perpetrated by a caregiver of the child.

The latest Child Maltreatment report, for 2010, stated that 63,527 children in the United States had a substantiated or indicated case of CSA (U.S. Department of Health and Human Services, 2012). This was down from 65,964 cases in 2009. Substantiated cases are those identified by CPS as definitely having occurred, whereas in indicated cases, the suspicion of abuse is high but not definitive. CSA cases accounted for 9.2 percent of all cases of abuse and neglect substantiated by CPS in 2010. Substantiated sexual abuse is considered a significant under-representation of child sexual abuse, even when indicated abuse is included. Most children do not disclose their abuse. When mandated reporters in the United States suspect abuse, only 40 to 44 percent consistently report known suspicions of abuse (Finkelhor, 1990; Zelman & Antler, 1990). Of those cases of suspected abuse reported to CPS, only 42 to 44 percent of abuse is investigated (Sedlak & Broadhurst, 1996). Of those cases investigated, only one-third are substantiated. Further, this refers only to intrafamilial abuse, which accounts for only 30 percent of all abuse. In another example, of the 1,251,445 referrals to CPS over a seven-year period, 51 percent were unfounded, 16 percent were substantiated (i.e., they met the state's standard for abuse) and 33 percent were indicated (i.e., there was some evidence of abuse but they did not meet the state's standard for abuse) (Weitzel, Yampolskaya, & McCann, 2009).

The other major attempt to capture incidence of CSA in the United States is the National Incidence Study (NIS), which is commissioned by Congress and completed every few years. It was last conducted in 2008 (Sedlak et al., 2010). This study, the NIS 4, attempts to capture CSA cases identified by CPS as well as those known to other community professionals serving children and families. Incidents of sexual abuse had to meet either the harm or endangerment standard. The more stringent harm standard requires that the child be a) abused by a parent or his or her substitute and b) moderately harmed by the incident. The endangerment standard includes all children who meet the harm criterion, as well as children in danger of being harmed. All cases of penetration are assumed to fit the harm standard, with cases in which sexual touching occurred fitting the endangerment standard (Sedlak & Broadhurst, 1996). Using these criteria, 135,300 cases of CSA were identified, for a rate of 1.8 per 1,000 children. This rate was down from a rate of 3.2 per 1,000 children in the NIS done in 1993, and the rates of physical abuse and neglect were also down. The decrease in abuse has been a topic of much conversation among professionals working with victims of child maltreatment. It is true that cases of suspected CSA have become increasingly difficult to substantiate. For example, many more cases are now screened out so are never investigated by CPS (Finkelhor & Jones, 2004). After accounting for this and other possible reasons for the decline, however, some of the decrease found in the number of children sexually abused could be a result of a legitimate decrease in the number of children who experience sexual abuse.

Risk Factors—U.S. Incidence Studies

For the Harm Standard in the NIS 4, 0.6 out of 1,000 boys in the United States were sexually abused in 2010, as compared to 3.0 out of 1,000 girls (Sedlak et al., 2010). Black children also had a higher rate of sexual abuse (2.6 out of 1,000) than did whites (1.4 out of 1,000), and children not enrolled in school had a greater rate of sexual abuse than did children enrolled in public school. Children with no parents in the labor force were also more likely to be sexually abused than children with at least one unemployed parent or a parent not consistently employed. The incidence rate was also greater when children lived in families low on the socioeconomic scale. Children were least likely to have an identified case of CSA if they had both biological parents (0.5 out of 1,000), and were most likely to have an identified case (9.9 out of 1000) when children had a single parent with a partner.

Whereas all abuse declined from the previous study done in 1993 (Sedlak & Broadhurst, 1996), sexual abuse declined more for white children (down 56 percent) than for Hispanic children (down 39 percent) or black children (down 25 percent) (Sedlak et al., 2010). Further, substantiated cases in two-parent families decreased 62 percent, whereas substantiated cases in single-parent families increased by 49 percent. Children were at greater risk of CSA as well when they lived in rural versus urban counties. Of most concern is the increase of substantiated abuse in single-parent families. Such a sizeable increase during a period of declining rates begs the question of *why* such an increase is occurring. No known analyses have addressed this question.

Whereas the majority of all perpetrators were male, 22 percent of all perpetrators were female biological parents and 3 percent were female non-biological parents. It is likely that some of these females were categorized as sexual offenders because of their purported failure to protect. Finally, the most likely perpetrator was a biological parent (Sedlak et al., 2010), which is most likely an artifact of the methodology of incidence studies in the United States, in which suspected CSA by a member of the household is prioritized.

Canadian Incidence Study

The Canadian Incidence Study (Trocmé, Tourigny, MacLaurin, & Fallon, 2003; Trocmé et al., 2005) captured cases of child maltreatment reported to and screened by its child welfare system. The methodology was very similar to that of the United States' National Incidence Study as well as an earlier study done in Canada. Sexual abuse accounted for 10 percent of all cases of child maltreatment, or 5,900 of the 61,200 substantiated cases of child maltreatment, for an incidence rate of 0.93 out of 1,000. Sexual abuse constituted 24 percent of cases meeting the Harm Standard.

Child Protection in Australia 2010–2011

Australia also gathers yearly statistics from their child welfare system. As in the United States, the multiple jurisdictions report to a central authority, which gathers the data for the annual report. Of 40,466 substantiated cases of maltreatment in 2010 and 2011, 14 percent (N = 5,665) were of sexual abuse, with a range of 5 to 23 percent across jurisdictions. For Aboriginal and Torres Strait Islander children, 10 percent of all substantiated child maltreatment was CSA, representing a lesser proportion of sexual abuse to all child maltreatment than for nonindigenous children (Australian Institute of Health and Welfare, 2012).

England's Child Protection Plan, 2009

Finally, England captures yearly information on children and youth who receive a Child Protection Plan. In a one-year period ending in March 2009, 37,900 children became the subject of a Child Protection Plan, 9 percent of whom were sexually abused (Department for Children, Schools and Families, 2009). Of all girls subject to a Child Protection Plan ending in March 2007, 9 percent had substantiated sexual abuse, whereas 6 percent of boys referred for such a plan had substantiated sexual abuse (Department for Children, Schools and Families, 2007). Respective incidence rates were 0.2 out of 1,000 for girls and 0.1 out of 1,000 for boys.

Summary

Consistent across all incidence studies was the ratio of CSA to all child maltreatment, at just 9 to 14 percent of all child maltreatment. Of the incidence rates across studies, the NIS 4 in the United States had the highest incidence (1.8 out of 1,000 for boys and girls combined) (Sedlak et al., 2010), with England having the lowest (0.1 out of 1,000 for boys) (Department for Children, Schools and Families, 2007). Also consistent across these studies, the most significant risk factor appeared to be gender, with females at heightened risk in all countries.

Importantly, incidence studies only provide information about *identified* cases of CSA; they do not provide an accurate representation of the scope of the problem of CSA. Indeed, identified sexual abuse is considered only the tip of the iceberg (Sedlak & Broadhurst, 1996) of all sexual abuse that occurs.

Prevalence of CSA

Prevalence studies provide an estimate of the percentage of persons in the sample who have experienced sexual abuse. The best of these are random prevalence studies that can be generalized to the larger population from which the study was drawn.

United States

Several studies with rigorous methodologies have been done in the United States. The first random prevalence study, albeit a community study of women living in the San Francisco area, was done by Russell and published in 1983. Thirty-eight percent of females reported they experienced contact sexual abuse prior to the age of 18. This was an important study not simply because of its seminal position, but because of the rigorous methodology that then informed methodologies of future studies.

Since Russell's study, a few important random national prevalence studies have been done, primary among them the National Women's Study (NWS) (Kilpatrick, Edmunds, & Seymour, 1992), the National Violence against Women Survey (NVAW) (Tjaden & Thoennes, 2000), and a study by Vogeltanz and colleagues (1999) that sampled 1099 women, with oversampling of heavy drinkers. The latter study utilized the definitions of CSA from both Russell's (1983) and Wyatt's (1985) survey and screened for a sexual abuse history using eight behaviorally specific questions. Wyatt's definition of CSA was somewhat broader than Russell's, which captured contact abuse only. Using these definitions, 23 and 17 percent respectively of the women in the study experienced sexual abuse during childhood.

The other two prevalence studies—the NWS and NVAW, although important, have more narrow definitions of sexual abuse, restricting their definitions to child and adolescent rape (Saunders, Kilpatrick, Hanson, Resnick, & Walker, 1999; Tjaden & Thoennes, 2000). As a comparison point, for completed rapes, 6.6 percent of adult women in Russell's (1983) sample experienced forcible completed childhood rape. A total of 18.8 percent experienced forcible completed or attempted childhood rape, and 20.6 percent of adult females experienced forceful and nonforceful, completed and attempted rape before the age of 18. The prevalence of rape was considerably lower in the NWS and NVAW. Of the 4,008 randomly selected women in the NWS (Kilpatrick et al., 1992), 8.5 percent reported experiencing a completed forcible rape before the age of 18 (Saunders et al., 1999). Of the 8,000 women in the NVAW study, 9.5 percent reported experiencing a completed or attempted forcible rape prior to the age of 18 (Russell & Bolen, 2000).

More recently, children and parents have been asked directly whether the child previously experienced sexual abuse (Finkelhor, Ormrod, Turner, & Hamby, 2005; Finkelhor, Turner, Ormrod, Hamby, & Kracke, 2009). The first of these polls, the Moore, Gallup, and Schussel Poll (1995), asked 1,000 parents nationwide whether they knew if their children had been sexually abused. Parents reported that within the previous year, 2 percent of children had been abused; 6 percent had been abused over their lifetime. Conversely, 30 percent of mothers and 9 percent of fathers reported they had experienced childhood sexual abuse.

The most recent study of this type, a national survey of children's exposure to a variety of types of violence including sexual assault, was completed by Finkelhor and his colleagues (2009). In this study, the National Survey of Children's Exposure to Violence, 6 percent of children and adolescents had experienced sexual victimization (i.e., contact and noncontact sexual abuse and sexual harassment) within the last year, with a lifetime prevalence of about 10 percent (Finkelhor et al., 2009). Sixteen percent of adolescents ages 14 to 17 experienced sexual victimization in the previous year, and 28 percent had experienced lifetime sexual victimization.

International

Finkelhor (1994) was the first to qualitatively review and compare prevalence studies of CSA done internationally. He located at least one epidemiological study in 21 different countries. In countries with more than one study, the study with the largest sample size was chosen. He found that the prevalence of CSA for women ranged from 7 to 36 percent, and for men from 3 to 29 percent. Finkelhor suggested that methodological factors across studies probably explained the extreme variability in prevalence.

Pereda and colleagues followed this study in 2009 with two reviews of prevalence studies across nations (Pereda, Guilera, Forns, & Gómez-Benito, 2009a; Pereda, Guilera, Forns, & Gómez-Benito, 2009b). In the first review (Pereda et al., 2009a), 39 prevalence studies across 21 countries were located. Pereda and colleagues found CSA prevalences of 0 to 53 percent for women and 0 to 60 percent for men. However, in most studies the prevalence for women was between 10 and 20 percent, whereas the prevalence for men tended to be below 10 percent.

The other study by Pareda and colleagues (2009b) was a meta-analysis of 65 studies across 22 countries. Its purpose was to establish empirically the international prevalence of CSA in men and women as well as to assess potential methodological factors that could account for some of the variation in the prevalence of CSA across studies. Inclusion criteria were that the studies had to measure prevalence, use a nonclinical sample, identify the sample size, and be reported in English. Across countries and studies, 7.9 percent of males were sexually abused prior to the age of 18, along with 19.2 percent of women. There were important differences in prevalence across countries. Prevalence of the sexual abuse of male children was below 4 percent in France, Malaysia, Norway, and Portugal, as compared to 25 percent in Tanzania, 27 percent in Jordan, and 60.9 percent in South Africa. For women, the prevalence was below 4 percent in Finland, France, and Portugal, and above 30 percent in Australia, Costa Rica, Israel, and Tanzania. It was above 40 percent in South Africa. Prevalence of CSA was lowest in Europe and highest in Africa.

Factors that accounted for some of the variation in prevalence were the continent, type of sample, geographical area of the sample, age range for abuse, type of data gathering, abuse definition, whether the country was economically developed or developing, and whether the sample was random (Pareda et al., 2009b). The larger prevalences were in studies in which children up to the age of 13 could be included in the sample as victims of sexual abuse. Otherwise there was a generally linear increase in prevalence as the age of abuse allowed increased. Prevalence was also somewhat higher when the study used a broad versus narrow definition of abuse; data were gathered using interviews versus questionnaires; the study was nonrandom versus random, local versus national, and a general population study versus student study; and the country was developing versus developed.

Stoltenborgh et al., Meta-Analysis of International Sexual Abuse

Another meta-analysis of CSA committed across countries was done by Stoltenborgh, van IJzendoorn, Euser, and Bakersman-Kranenburg (2011). They located 217 publications internationally published from 1982 to 2008 that assessed the prevalence of CSA. These publications included 331 independent samples with a total of 9,911,748 participants. The prevalence was 11.8 percent, with a prevalence of 7.6 percent for male samples and 18.0 percent for female samples. Study samples in Africa, Australia, and North America had the highest prevalences, as did those countries considered high resource. African American and Hispanic samples had higher prevalences than did white samples, and studies using questionnaires or face-to-face interviews had higher prevalences than did those using a telephone interview or computer-assisted questionnaire format.

Summary

Although well-done studies conducted in the 1980s on United States samples found a high prevalence of sexual abuse, later studies and meta-analyses have not been able to replicate these high prevalences. Therefore, a conservative estimate of the prevalence of CSA for girls is 18 to 22 percent for females and 5 to 10 percent for males, with higher estimates in Africa, Australia, and North America. Given the propensity of sexual abuse survivors to under-report their own victimization, the prevalence of sexual abuse could be somewhat higher.

Attorney General's United Nations Report on Violence against Children

In 2006, the United Nations issued a report on world violence, both physical and sexual, against children (Pinhiero, 2006, 2007). This report combined the findings of various studies into a single report. For example, it was reported that the World Health Organization (WHO) estimated that 150 million girls and 73 million boys worldwide have experienced a rape or some other type of contact sexual abuse, although they considered this an underestimate. Of this abuse, much of it was reported to occur within the home by someone the child trusted. It was reported that, like in the United States, children disclosed the abuse only occasionally, and in some countries children risked being beaten or even killed if they disclosed the sexual abuse. In other countries, the child was thought to be culpable for the abuse, even when the abuse was forced. In still other countries, children who experienced rape were thought to dishonor the family name, leading to honor killings. This WHO document also reported that children in some parts of the world were being sold into forced marriages, sometimes at a very young age, where they endured unwanted and often forced intercourse. In another form of extreme sexual abuse, 100 to 140 million girls or young women worldwide had experienced some type of female genital mutilation. Another approximately 1.8 million children worked in prostitution or pornography, and 1.2 million children worldwide were trafficked each year. Smaller in scope but equally as serious, approximately 4 percent of all priests have molested children, mostly boys (Fay, 2004).

In Africa, different types of sexual abuse are much more prevalent than in developed countries. Sexual abuse by teachers, who sometimes trade grades for sex, is common, as is sexual abuse of children working as domestic laborers, who may start work as young as seven or eight years of age (Lalor, 2004). Being in the roles of servitude and bonded laborers places children at high risk for sexual abuse. Sometimes these children are kidnapped, tortured, and killed. Child prostitution, trafficking internationally (Lalor, 2004; Raymond, 2002; Snell, 2003; Zimmerman, Hossain, & Watts, 2011) and child brides (Hampton, 2010) are other realities.

RISK FACTORS FOR SEXUAL ABUSE

Drawing on random prevalence studies, Bolen (2001) reviewed risk factors for sexual abuse victimization. By far the single biggest risk factor in the United States (Bolen, 2001) and throughout the world (Pereda et al., 2009b; Stoltenborgh et al., 2011) is gender, with females being at greatly increased risk of sexual abuse victimization. Age of the child acted as a risk factor, with children ages 11 to 13 being at increased risk and children from the ages of 7 to 10 at a somewhat increased risk (Bolen, 2001). Conversely, too little or conflicting information makes it impossible at this time to determine whether race/ethnicity or developmental delays of the child act as risk factors.[1] The same is true with problems within the family, religion, and income, although two studies suggest that alcohol use in the family increases risk of sexual abuse for these children (Hernandez, 1992; Moore, Nord, & Peterson, 1989). Both maternal employment and separation from parents may also have some relationship to victimization history, although it is probably complex. Maternal employment may interact with family structure (Bolen, 1998), and type of separation from parents may interact with gender to predict victimization (Bolen, 1998; Finkelhor, Hotaling, Lewis, & Smith, 1990).

International studies also contribute to the study of cross-national risk factors. Using the Danish Civil Registration System, Elklit and Shevlin (2010) compared 214 females coming into a rape crisis center over a two-year period with 4,343 controls matched for age and residential location. They found that single women with children at home had a significantly increased likelihood of having visited the rape crisis center. In another survey of 3,005 adolescents ages 12 to 18 living in Mexico City, a few risk factors were associated with sexual abuse (Benjet et al., 2009). Being female, being ages 15 to 17 as compared to 12 to 14, and having three or more siblings as compared to two or less were risk factors for victimization. In addition, children whose parents had a high school education or less as compared to those with a university degree, and those children with mothers who were less than 21 years of age when that child was born had an increased risk of sexual abuse. Of equal interest, parental monitoring was not a risk factor for sexual abuse.

Other international studies have focused on risk factors for committing sexual abuse. In Sweden, a school-based random survey of 1,933 males compared those who were sexually coercive (5.2 percent of the sample), those with a nonsexual conduct problem, and normal controls (Kjellgren, Priebe, Svedin, & Långström, 2010). The sexually coercive and nonsexual conduct disorder males shared many characteristics apart from those of normal controls, including increased depressive symptoms, substance abuse, aggressiveness, sexual victimization, and sexual preoccupation, among others. Having pro-rape attitudes and sexual preoccupation were the only variables that separated sexually coercive from nonsexual conduct problem males.

Bolen (2001) also reviewed characteristics of offenders based on random prevalence studies. From these studies, it is clear that the large majority of offenders are male, 20 to 50 percent of all offenders are juveniles, and about 70 percent of all offenders are *not* relatives of the child. Only about 6 to 16 percent of all abuse is by a parent figure, typically the father. A small percentage of offenders are strangers to the child, with most abuse being perpetrated by acquaintances.

Finally, a qualitative study done in Africa of women and children infected with HIV suggests another particularly tragic risk factor. Some of these children had been infected when they were raped by an adult male infected with HIV, who falsely believed that having sex with a young virgin girl would cure him of his HIV (Lalor, 2004; Murray, Haworth, Semrau, Aldrovandi, Sinkala, et al., 2006).

Taken together, these sections suggest a profound risk of sexual victimization, especially for girls but also for boys. Although this chapter reviewed only studies of CSA, it was clear that multiple types of sexual victimization are serious problems internationally. These studies also suggest that approximately 20 percent of females worldwide are victims of sexual abuse, but many millions more are victims of other types of sexual victimization. Boys are also sexually abused, prostituted, trafficked, and otherwise victimized, but at perhaps half the rate of females. Several factors place children at greater risk for sexual abuse. Children living with single parents are at greater risk, perhaps because of the presumed access by sex offenders to these children. The single biggest factor placing individuals at risk for abuse also appears to be gender, with females at greatly increased risk.

Risk factors do not stop here. Other cultural factors place certain children at higher risk of CSA. Cultural rituals and patterns across countries account for such acts as genital mutilation of girls in some countries, especially in Africa, or having sex with a girl purportedly to rid oneself of AIDS. Another important dynamic across countries is the objectification and oppression of females. Again in certain countries in Africa, this plays out in the abuse of girls by teachers, sometimes as "payment" for a grade.

Another concern is that the United States and indeed most countries remain male-dominated. For example, 95 percent of decisions made at the level of the world are made by men (Mayor-Zaragoza, 2008). When the balance of power is held by men, an apparently inevitable corollary is the sexualization of females. One has only to watch television to recognize the high level of sexualization and objectification of girls and women. Until there is greater gender equality, girls will be at elevated risk for sexual victimization.

Sexual exploitation of children remains an enormous problem worldwide, with primarily females being trafficked (United Nations Office on Drugs and Crime, 2010). Further, globalization makes it easier to transport children across boundaries, especially into countries where children are commodities, frequently as prostitutes or slaves. Human trafficking, some of which includes the trafficking of children for child prostitution, is also a global problem. At least 137 countries have reported detecting victims of trafficking. A third of these victims are female, although not necessarily children or adolescents, and 79 percent of those trafficked are victims of sexual exploitation. Approximately half are from the Balkans and the former Soviet Union. In Europe alone there are approximately 140,000 victims of sexual exploitation each year (United Nations Office on Drugs and Crime, 2010).

Poverty is also a risk factor, as it sometimes drives parents to sell a child so the family can survive. As the world population rises, poverty is expected to rise with it, with a concomitant movement of people from villages to larger communities, and often to large urban areas (Skeldon, 2003). As families move into the city, they may lose informal systems of child care available in small communities or tribes. If parents cannot afford child care, these children may be at greater risk for sexual abuse.

Finally, one of the revolutions in the late twentieth and early twenty-first centuries has been the development of the Internet and Web-based methods of communication across countries. While the Internet has great benefits, it also comes with costs, especially to children who may not be old enough to understand its dangers. Other problems are the exposure of children to hardcore pornography, the intentional use of the Internet by pedophiles to try to lure children or adolescents to meet with them, and the risk of pedophiles potentially posing on the Internet as friends in children's social networks. As technology continues to develop at an incredible pace, security software to protect children may lag, especially on newer types of technology such as smart phones and tablets, which may also be vulnerable. Advances in technology also now allow sexual offenders to transmit encrypted pornography, making the pool of potential buyers much larger. Because of the fast turnover in new technology, officers of the law will likely remain one step behind in attempting to respond. The next section turns to a review of the effects of CSA.

EFFECTS OF SEXUAL ABUSE

CSA can have short- and long-term psychological, behavioral, physical, and neurophysiological effects that are exacerbated by the accumulation of multiple traumas throughout childhood. To review these effects we use national and international meta-analyses as well as important studies from South America, Australia, Canada, Europe, Asia, and Africa. We review this literature by the type of effect, including trauma-specific, internalizing, externalizing, nonspecific, and neurophysiological effects.

Trauma-Specific Disorders

Post-Traumatic Stress Disorder (PTSD)

As compared to their nonabused peers, sexually abused children are at an increased risk of suffering from PTSD, with approximately one-third of these children having PTSD (Kendall-Tackett et al., 1993). This risk is further elevated when children experience both physical and sexual abuse (Wechsler-Zimring & Kearney, 2011). A study by Ackerman and colleagues (Ackerman, Newton, McPherson, Jones, & Dykman, 1998) found in their clinical sample of 204 abused children 7 to 13 years of age that 62 percent of the children had been sexually abused. Of those sexually abused, 23 percent of boys and 42 percent of girls presented with clinical findings of PTSD. In other samples, PTSD is often not the most common diagnosis given to children, as they frequently lack the full symptom profile of PTSD (van der Kolk, 2005).

Sexually Transmitted Infections (STIs)

STIs are considered diagnostic of genital contact and thus of sexual abuse in young children. Studies offer varying rates of STIs diagnosed in children who have been sexually abused, though the rates of infection appear low in most parts of the world (Finkel, 2011; Girardet, Lemme, Biason, Bolton, & Lahoti, 2009; Kelly & Koh, 2006). For example, in a retrospective review of medical records in New Zealand, Kelly and colleagues (2006) found that of 2,162 patients examined for suspected sexual abuse, 112 cases of STIs and 13 cases of pelvic inflammatory disease were discovered. Little research has been done regarding CSA in Africa, and what is available is information gleaned from varied professionals in the course of their work. However, Meursing and her colleagues (1995) noted concerns regarding the high number of sexually abused children in Zimbabwe diagnosed with sexually transmitted diseases, suggesting that 8 of 10 victims of incest and half of rape victims were diagnosed with sexually transmitted diseases.

Adolescent Pregnancy

Pregnancy itself may be an effect of sexual abuse. More often, however, CSA appears to increase the risk of adolescent pregnancy (Young, Deardorff,

Ozer, & Lahiff, 2011). In a study by Young and colleagues, women who experienced sexual abuse prior to 12 years of age were at 20 percent greater risk of early pregnancy than the nonabused controls. Women sexually abused after 12 years of age had a 30 percent greater risk of early pregnancy, and women who experienced sexual abuse in childhood *and* adolescence had an 80 percent greater risk of early pregnancy. In another well-constructed meta-analysis of the relationship between childhood sexual abuse and pregnancy, 4.5 of every 10 pregnant adolescents had experienced CSA (Noll, Shenk, & Putnam, 2009). The odds of adolescent pregnancy given a history of childhood sexual abuse were 2.2 times greater. Finally, Pallitto and Murillo (2008) reported that 40 percent of women in El Salvador give birth to their first child before the age of 20. Based on a large survey sample (N = 3,753) of women between the ages of 15 and 24, a relationship between childhood sexual abuse and adolescent pregnancy was found. Specifically, childhood sexual abuse increased a woman's risk of adolescent pregnancy by 48 percent. Pallitto and Murillo also noted that other Latin American countries, such as Honduras, Guatemala, and Nicaragua, experience even higher rates of adolescent pregnancies.

Sexualized Behaviors

Sexualized behaviors are also found in sexually abused children. In young children this sexualized behavior might take the form of sexual precociousness or sexual knowledge beyond the age level of the child, sexual preoccupation, sexualized behaviors with others, or excessive masturbation (Friedrich, 1993). Sexualized behaviors increase as the severity of the abuse, the use of force, and the number of perpetrators increase (Friedrich, 1993). Older sexually abused adolescents may increase their participation in risky sexual behaviors (Negriff, Noll, Shenk, Putnam, & Trickett, 2010; Widom & Kuhns, 1996; Young et al., 2011), as might adults sexually abused in childhood (Beck-Sagué & Solomon, 1999; Wilson & Widom, 2009). Probability of involvement in risky sexual behaviors is highest when sexual abuse occurs only in childhood or in childhood *and* adolescence (Parillo, Freeman, Collier, & Young, 2001). Finally, victims of childhood sexual abuse are more likely than their nonabused counterparts to have arrests for prostitution (Widom & Ames, 1994).

Sexualized behaviors have also been studied internationally. A study of Chinese female sexual abuse victims reported that victims were younger at first sexual intercourse than the nonabused control group (Chen, Dunne, & Han, 2004). Based on a nationally representative household survey of

South African youths, Speizer and colleagues (2009) found that female youths who had experienced sexual contact by threat or force were 41 percent less likely to use condoms as compared to their peers who had never been threatened or forced to have sex. These findings support continuity of sexualized behaviors among different cultures.

Poly-Victimization

Repeated abuse is termed *poly-victimization* (Finkelhor, Ormrod, & Turner, 2007). A majority of children experience more than one traumatic event in their lives, and repeated exposures to trauma/abuse can compound the effects of abuse. A child experiencing one victimization is at increased risk of experiencing another during the same year (Finkelhor, Ormrod, Turner, & Hambry, 2005). In a 15-year prospective study, adult survivors of childhood sexual abuse had a twofold increase in risk of being a victim of physical or sexual violence at a later time as compared to a nonabused control group (Barnes, Noll, Putnam, & Trickett, 2009).

Internalizing Effects

Sexually abused children experience many psychological symptoms non-specific to trauma. To present this information we divide these symptoms into the categories of internalizing and externalizing.

Mood and Anxiety Disorders

A number of studies have assessed the relationship between CSA and both the short- and long-term mood and anxiety symptoms. In both childhood and adolescence, depression is a common psychological symptom following CSA (Ackerman et al., 1998; Feiring, Taska, & Lewis, 1999; Kendall-Tackett, Williams, & Finkelhor, 1993; Tyler, 2002). This finding has stood up through a series of meta-analyses on the short- and long-term effects of CSA (Jumper, 1995; Maniglio, 2010; Neumann, Houskamp, Pollock, & Briere, 1996; Paolucci, Genius, & Violato, 2001) and has also been replicated internationally. Chen, Dunne, and Han (2004), in a large sample (N = 2,300) of adolescents in China, reported that those experiencing childhood sexual abuse were more likely to be depressed and suicidal than their nonabused peers. In a study completed in Puerto Rico, inpatients experiencing higher rates of sexual abuse also had higher levels of dissociative and depressive symptoms as compared to inpatients who did not report sexual abuse (Francia-Martinez et al., 2003). In a comparison study between United States and Singapore survivors, college women in the United States reported more severe forms of CSA than did Singapore women but had fewer symptoms (Back, Jackson, Fitzgerald, Shaffer, Salstrom, & Osman, 2003). Finally, a study of 2,023 female and 1,955 male Israelis found that mood and anxiety disorders in adulthood were related to childhood sexual abuse and that abuse in childhood was a stronger predictor than abuse in adolescence (Gal, Levav, & Gross, 2011).

Shame and Guilt

Many sexually abused children experience shame and guilt following the abuse. In a study completed by Mannarino and Cohen (1996), sexually abused females were more likely than their nonabused controls to experience heightened self-blame and to feel different from their peers. They also experienced reduced feelings of interpersonal trust. Shame also contributes to adjustment, as children experiencing high levels of shame are at increased risk of adjustment issues (Feiring, Taska, & Lewis, 2002). Shame coupled with pessimistic attributional style is related to even higher levels of symptoms. Survivors of sexual assault from different cultures also appear to be at differential risk of experiencing significant emotional distress. In a review of this literature, La Flair, Franko, and Herzog (2008) reported that Asian female survivors of sexual assault were at increased risk of experiencing significant emotional distress, shame, and embarrassment due to the culture's conservative attitude towards survivors of sexual assault.

Externalizing Effects

Sexually abused children are also at an increased risk of behavioral problems when compared to children who have not been sexually abused (Dubowitz, Black, Harrington, & Verschoore, 1993). Anger issues in sexually abused children may be a result of the intensely negative and arousing experiences they may not be able to modulate (Berliner, 2011). Their unbridled emotional responses may then erupt in angry tantrums, outbursts, and other expressions of extreme anger. As these children age, these responses may take the form of more aggressive and delinquent behaviors. Indeed, children who have been sexually abused report higher rates of antisocial and adolescent delinquent behaviors and are at increased risk of arrest as juvenile runaways (Bensley, Van Eenwyk, Spieker, & Schoder, 1999; Widom & Ames, 1994). Similarly, in a study of adolescents in China, males who experienced CSA were more likely to engage in violent behavior, including carrying weapons and fighting, than those not abused. Chinese female sexual abuse victims similarly reported externalizing effects of abuse (Chen et al., 2006).

Substance Abuse

In addition to other externalizing behaviors, substance use is routinely reported in those with a CSA history. Such a history occurs with both adolescent samples (Danielson, Macdonald, Amstadter, Hanson, de Arellano, et al., 2010) and adult samples (Polusny & Follette, 1995). Sexual abuse increases the risk of abuse of and dependence on alcohol, marijuana, and hard drugs in children and adolescents. Victimized youth also use substances at an earlier age than their nonvictimized peers (Kilpatrick, Acierno, Saunders, Resnick, Best, & Schnurr, 2000) and have a higher use pattern for tobacco and marijuana (Chandy, Blum, & Resnick, 1997; Garnefski & Arends, 1998). Adults who experienced childhood sexual abuse are also more likely to abuse or become dependent on substances and to have adult arrests for alcohol and/or drug-related offenses (Bensley, Van Eenwyk, Spieker, & Schoder, 1999; Polusny & Follette, 1995), as compared to nonabused women. Finally, Chen and colleagues (2006) reported that Chinese female sexual abuse victims also report increased alcohol use and smoking.

Nonspecific Effects

Eating Disorders

Eating disorders can serve a few functions. They may play a part in the dissociation and emotional numbing of survivors of childhood sexual abuse, help victims allay the painful feelings associated with the abuse, and even alter the body's appearance to make it less attractive to potential offenders (La Flair, Franko, & Herzog, 2008). In a meta-analysis of 53 studies examining the relationship between CSA and eating disorders, Smolak and Murnen (2002) found a small relationship between the two. Fuemmeler, Dedert, McClernon, and Beckham (2009) also found that, compared to their nonabused counterparts, men who experienced childhood sexual abuse were at an increased risk of being overweight. Women with a history of childhood sexual abuse, as compared to those with no history of sexual abuse, had higher rates of problematic eating behaviors and possible eating disorder histories.

In a sample (N = 77) of females from an inpatient eating disorders unit at a Toronto hospital, Carter and colleagues (2006) found that 48 percent of the women reported childhood sexual abuse prior to the onset of their eating disorder. In addition, binge-purge anorexia nervosa patients were more likely to report childhood sexual abuse (65 percent) compared to patients diagnosed with restricting anorexia nervosa (37 percent). Brewerton (2007) reviewed the literature regarding the relationships between eating disorders, trauma, and comorbid psychiatric disorders. It was concluded that whereas childhood sexual abuse is a nonspecific risk factor, trauma is more common in persons with bulimic eating disorders than in those without bulimic eating disorders. It was also concluded that multiple episodes or forms of trauma are associated with eating disorders, and trauma is associated with greater comorbidity (often mediated by PTSD) in eating disorders. La Flair and colleagues (2008) note the cross-cultural differences in eating disorder symptoms and how culture influences the development of eating disorders. Unlike Western countries, Asian countries do not have the same body issues and concerns for becoming overweight. Thus a diagnosis of an eating disorder among the Asian population is atypical, though researchers are finding that these rates are increasing.

Self-Injury

Sexually abused children report higher rates of suicidal ideation and injurious suicide attempts than their nonabused peers (Bensley, Van Eenwyk, Spieker, & Schoder, 1999). Indeed, a systematic review found that only one of 21 studies regarding the relationship between CSA and self-injury did not show a relationship (Fliege, Lee, Grimm, & Klapp, 2009). CSA by a caretaker (Dubo et al., 1997), injury experienced during incest, and age of incest (Weaver, 2004) are also related to a history of self-injury. Further, this relationship between CSA and self-injury is found in adolescent samples (Glassman et al., 2007), in outpatient samples of adult survivors of CSA (Bolen, Winter, & Hodges, 2013), samples of psychiatric emergency room patients (Briere & Zaidi, 1989), and in samples of adults with a personality disorder or bipolar II disorder (van der Kolk, 2005). In each case, those experiencing CSA engaged in greater self-injury.

Academic

Because of the emotional and behavioral issues associated with CSA, it has been hypothesized that these children may have poor outcomes in school, increasing the risk of dropping out. Instead, findings appear to be mixed. Daignault and Hébert (2009) found that approximately half of the sexually abused girls in their sample of French-speaking Canadian girls experienced postdisclosure social, behavioral, academic, or cognitive difficulties that could negatively influence their ability to adapt in an academic environment. Thompson and colleagues (Thompson, Wiley, Lewis, English, Dubowitz, et al., 2012) found that children who experienced child maltreatment, including sexual abuse, reported less expected academic and employment success in their future and higher expected employment instability.

Though abused or neglected children in some studies have experienced decreased school performance and increased disciplinary problems, Eckenrode, Laird, and Doris (1993) found that sexually abused children were similar in school performance and disciplinary problems to their nonabused peers. When sexual abuse was coupled with neglect, though, children were at increased risk of grade repetition and decreased test scores in math and reading. In a longitudinal study of abused and neglected children, Perez and Widom (1994) found that maltreated children showed lower levels of intellectual ability and academic outcomes when compared to the matched control children. However, sexual abuse itself was not a significant predictor of IQ scores or reading ability scores, indicating that intellectual ability and academic outcomes may depend on the form of abuse or neglect.

Parenting Deficits and Relationship Issues

Adults sexually abused as children may have deficits in parenting their own children. This may be because women with histories of childhood sexual abuse are more likely to have insecure attachments and to report higher levels of attachment-related anxiety than their nonabused counterparts (Kwako, Noll, Putnam, & Trickett, 2010). Mothers with a history of CSA are more likely than those without a history to engage in abusive parenting with their own children, to be more permissive as parents (DiLillo & Damashek, 2003; DiLillo, Tremblay, & Peterson, 2000), and to suffer from more maternal depressive symptoms (Dubowitz, Black, Kerr, Hussey, Morrel, & Everson, 2001). Banyard (1997) found that, after controlling for negative family-of-origin experiences (physical abuse, neglect, negative relationship with primary caregivers), mothers with a history of childhood sexual abuse were also more likely to use physical strategies for handling parent-child conflict and had higher levels of dissatisfaction with themselves as parents. Not only did childhood abuse experiences influence future parenting behaviors, but when combined with adult traumas (intimate partner violence, sexual assault), self-reported parenting behaviors and perceptions of oneself as a parent became increasingly negative (Banyard, Williams, & Siegel, 2003). Finally, Finkelhor, Hotaling, and Smith (1989) found that men and women who experienced childhood sexual abuse were more likely to experience marital disruption as compared to the nonabused adults.

Adverse Childhood Experiences

The Adverse Childhood Experiences (ACEs) survey asked over 17,000 adult members of a health plan about the presence of 10 ACEs, including: childhood abuse (emotional, physical, and sexual); neglect (emotional and physical); witnessing domestic violence; parental marital discord; and living with substance-abusing, mentally ill, or criminal household members (Anda et al., 2006; Dong et al., 2004). According to the ACEs study, a greater number of adverse childhood experiences are related to a greater number of psychological, social, and health problems later in life. These outcomes include an increase in mental health problems, somatic disturbances, and substance use and abuse, increased probability of risky sexual behaviors, difficulty controlling anger, and risk of intimate partner violence.

There is also a cumulative effect. For example, persons experiencing one ACE are 2 to 18 times more likely to experience another ACE as compared to those reporting no ACEs (Anda et al., 2006; Dong et al., 2004). In regard to CSA, 21 percent of respondents (25 percent of women and 16 percent of men) in the ACEs study reported childhood sexual abuse. Compared to participants who were not sexually abused, sexually abused respondents had a 2- to 3.4-fold (for women) and a 1.6- to 2.5-fold (for men) increase in experiencing each of the remaining nine ACE categories. This risk of experiencing multiple ACEs increased as the severity of the sexual abuse increased (Dong, Anda, Dube, Giles, & Felitti, 2003). Further, as incidents of maltreatment to which a child was exposed increased, the risk of negative long-term effects also increased (Anda et al., 2006; Barnes, Noll, Putnam, & Trickett, 2009; Dong et al., 2004; Finkelhor, Ormrod, & Turner, 2007).

In another interesting study, adverse outcomes of childhood sexual abuse were assessed in twins living in Australia. One twin had a history of CSA whereas the other did not. The twin reporting childhood sexual abuse was at an increased risk of experiencing adverse outcomes such as depression, suicide attempts, conduct disorder, alcohol and/or nicotine dependence, social anxiety, rape after the age of 18 years of age, and divorce, as compared to the twin not reporting childhood sexual abuse (Nelson, Heath, Madden, Cooper, Dinwiddie, et al., 2002).

Neurophysiological Effects

One important concern of professionals in more recent years is the effect sexual abuse and other traumas have on the brain. When abused or when experiencing a significant trauma, the victim experiences fear, which sets in motion a number of other processes. One of the central processes is found in the hypothalamus-pituitary-adrenal (HPA) axis. When one is frightened, a chemical—corticotropin releasing factor (CRF)—is released from the hypothalamus, which in turn triggers the pituitary gland to release adrenocorticotropic hormone (ACTH), which in turn triggers the adrenal glands to release cortisol. Almost simultaneously, norepinephrine is released from the brain stem, and the sympathetic nervous system (SNS) is activated (Bremner, 2006; Gunnar & Vasquez, 2006; van der Kolk, 2003). Taken together, these and other processes prepare the individual to fight or flee by increasing cardiac output, shunting blood from the skin and digestive organs to the muscles, and providing more fuel by releasing glucose from fat stored in the body to power muscles and provide fuel to the brain (Gunnar & Vasquez, 2006; van der Kolk, 2003). Sweat glands are also activated to cool the body and keep it from overheating (van der Kolk, 2003). Once the danger has passed, cortisol acts as a feedback mechanism to turn the stress response off and return the body to a normal state (Nunes, Watanabe, Morimoto, Moria, & Reiche, 2010).

For children who live in chaotic households, who have other types of victimization or multiple episodes of sexual abuse, this fear response is experienced repeatedly. Because of the toxic effect of too much cortisol on the brain, this repeated experiencing of the fear response can be at great cost. First, cortisol can damage certain structures in the brain, including the corpus callosum, prefrontal cortex, and hippocampus (Bremner, 2006; Teicher, Anderson, & Polcari, 2011; van der Kolk, 2003). Reduction in volume of the hippocampus may be related to poorer explicit memory, impairment of memory recall, and inhibition of cell neurogenesis (i.e., the creation of new neurons) (Teicher et al., 2011; van der Kolk, 2003).

A second consequence of repeated experiences of the fear response is that the victim becomes sensitized to the fear response, which becomes progressively easier to experience (Bremner, 2006; van der Kolk, 2003). Now the victim may not have to experience the sexual abuse. Thinking about it or seeing, smelling, or touching something reminiscent of the abuse may be sufficient to initiate the fear response. Over time, the fear response may also become generalized to situations not reminiscent of the abuse. This long-term sensitization, or long-term potentiation, means that the child not only comes to experience this fear response more quickly but also over a larger number of abuse and nonabuse situations. Children who experience a sensitized fear response may have higher resting heart rates, blood flow, and respiration (Perry, 2008), enhanced likelihood of temporal-lobe seizures (Bob, Susta, Gregusova, Jasova, & Raboch, 2010), reduced brain weight, and suppressed neuronal cell growth (Anderson, Teicher, Polcari, & Renshaw, 2002; van der Kolk, 2003). Therefore, chronic stress or trauma comes at greater and greater cost to the child.

This fear response of hyperarousal is only one of two primary responses to trauma. The other primary response is dissociation. Sexual abuse victims, those abused at a younger age, and females are more likely to experience dissociation than hyperarousal in response to a trauma (Perry, 2008). Unique to this response, the brain's endogenous opioids are released. Like the hyperarousal response, dissociation becomes more sensitized as the abuse becomes chronic. When dissociated, child victims and adult survivors may experience altered pain perception, sense of time, place, and reality, providing a sense of neuropsychological space between the child and the abuse (Pain, Bluhm, & Lanius, 2009).

Victims of sexual abuse may also experience changes in brain architecture. The corpus callosum, the part of the brain that connects the two hemispheres of the brain, is reduced in size and has less density in comparison to nonsexually abused controls (Teicher, Dumont, Ito, Vaituzis, Giedd, et al., 2004). Further, the left hemisphere of the brain is underdeveloped in comparison to the right hemisphere (van der Kolk, 2003). Symptoms of ADHD are related to impairment in the connections of the corpus callosum. The prefrontal cortex (i.e., the executive part of the brain) is also damaged by increased cortisol (Bremner, 2006; van der Kolk, 2003). Indeed, the prefrontal cortex is the most likely of the cortices to be damaged by trauma and the resultant chemical and hormonal responses in the brain. The prefrontal cortex is the area of the brain that determines whether the fear response is needed given the stimulus. With this process impaired, the survivor of trauma may experience hyperarousal or dissociation more frequently and may stay in that state longer.

Other costs associated with the overproduction of cortisol in the fear response are an inability to relax, difficulty in sleeping, problems with self-regulation (van der Kolk, 2003), and greater irritability of the limbic system (Anderson, Teicher, Polcari, & Renshaw, 2002). This greater limbic irritability is also higher in those with temporal lobe epilepsy, making victims of CSA at greater risk for this type of disorder. Further, cortisol increases the release of glucose in the body, which can make the person susceptible to diabetes and other such disorders (Rich-Edwards et al., 2010). Other physical effects may be indirectly related to the trauma, which increases the allostatic load on the body (i.e., the cumulative wear and tear on the body and brain caused by previous traumas, stressors, and chronic stressors). As the allostatic load increases, children are at greater risk for a number of different stress-induced disorders (Lupien et al., 2006; McEwen, 2007).

Cultural Differences in Effects

As the previous review of effects of child sexual abuse indicates, there is remarkable consistency across the few studies that have reported on effects cross-culturally. A relationship between child sexual abuse and PTSD exists in the United States (Ackerman et al., 1998) and in Cambodia (Carlson & Rosser-Hogan, 1994). Sexually transmitted diseases are related to CSA in the United States (Finkel, 2011), New Zealand (Kelly & Koh, 2006), and Zimbabwe (Meursing et al., 1995). The same can be said of adolescent pregnancy in the United States (Young et al., 2011) and El Salvador (Pallitto & Murillo, 2008), as well as several other symptoms, with little variation. There are some differences, however. Asians experiencing childhood sexual abuse (La Flair, 2008) are less likely to experience eating disorders than North American individuals experiencing childhood sexual abuse (Carter et al., 2006) but are at increased risk of experiencing significant emotional embarrassment and shame (La Flair, 2008). These changes were attributed to different cultural norms.

To end the discussion by comparing effects of CSA across countries, however, is to end it prematurely. Whereas it appears that there are universal symptom sets, such as internalizing and externalizing disorders or substance abuse, that are related to CSA, it is difficult to discern differences among cultures when measures used have been designed within and for Western cultures. These measures may not easily capture differences in cultures, especially between developed and developing nations where cultural norms are so different. They may capture the broad category of symptoms, such as depression or anxiety, but not capture the symptoms specific to different cultures. The DSM-IV™ (2004) has a list of culturally bound syndromes that more or less typify Western mental health disorders. These culturally bound symptoms are widely familiar to persons in the west and are recognized as a disease within that culture, but are unfamiliar in other cultures, where they are frequently treated with folk medicine. For example, the condition *brain fag* used in West Africa has a symptom set of vague somatic symptoms, difficulty concentrating, depression, and mental fatigue (American Psychiatric Association, 2004; Peltzer, Cherian, & Cherian, 1998).

What may be more likely is that a general set of neurophysiologically mediated symptom sets exist, such as affect dysregulation disorders (mood disorders/other internalizing symptoms and externalizing symptoms), hyperarousal (PTSD) and hypoarousal (dissociation), sexualized symptoms, cognitive symptoms (reflecting areas of the brain damaged or changed by the abuse), and others. What might change across cultures, however, is the manner in which the symptom set presents. We know this to be true of attachment, as all individuals experience attachment relationships and about one-third experience insecure attachment (Belsky, 2009). The type of insecure attachment (e.g., ambivalent, avoidant, and disorganized), however, differs across cultures. For example, insecurely attached children raised in the kibbutzes in Israel are more likely to be ambivalent, whereas insecurely attached children raised in Germany are more likely to be avoidant (van IJzendoorn & Kroonenberg, 1988).

One of the important principles of attachment is that it is the meaning of the behavior that is relevant—not the actual behavior (Sroufe & Waters, 1977). Perhaps the same applies to symptom formation across cultures. The fear response leads to a neurophysiological experience of hyperarousal or dissociation. Perhaps that experience is universal, but whether the victim experiences greater hyperarousal or dissociation, and the manner in which that is displayed, may be sensitive to cultural norms. Another important principle that derives from neurophysiological development is that development occurs as a result of both nature *and* nurture, that is, a gene-environment interaction. Clearly, culture is a significant part of one's environment. Therefore, following this principle, it could be that the environment profoundly affects the eventual symptom presentation, as certain symptoms in different cultures are more acceptable.

Fontes (2005) states that components of shame, or a feeling of being permanently damaged, are shared by most victims, but the manner in which victims experience this feeling and the manner in which it is received vary from culture to culture. For example, females in many cultures are raised to believe that male identity is wrapped up in how many conquests they have, whereas female identity is dependent on how chaste they are. That females are still being stoned to death when raped is a gruesome example of how much some cultures buy into this belief system.

Summary

To summarize this literature, sexually abused children are at great risk for a variety of stress-related physical, psychological, and neuropsychological problems as a result of the effect of the abuse on the brain. When exposed to more chronic sexual abuse and dysfunctional homes, young children are at greater risk for more enduring and pervasive effects of the abuse, as the brain is more vulnerable and malleable during this time. Further, the manner in which the brain develops is use-dependent; that is, it is dependent upon the environment. Therefore, for younger children, the experience of the sexual abuse and its effects are central in *organizing* the developing brain (Perry, 2008). This may be the most tragic of all the effects of sexual abuse.

CONCLUSION

Across the United States, North America, Europe, and the remaining continents, CSA is occurring in epidemic proportions. Perhaps it is not as prevalent as it was 30 years ago, but it is still occurring at an unacceptably high rate, with approximately 10 percent of males and 20 percent of females sexually abused prior to the age of 18. Much of this sexual abuse of children goes undisclosed, unreported, uninvestigated, unsubstantiated, or unprosecuted (Bolen, 2001), however, allowing too many sex offenders to roam free. Prevention programs can only do so much when the large majority of child sex offenders remain free.

Ten years ago, professionals rued the psychological toll that sexual abuse took on children and adult survivors. Today, however, it is apparent that the psychological toll is just a small part of the cost children and adult survivors pay when sexually abused. Now the devastating effect of sexual abuse on the brain, on its architecture and processes, has become apparent. Yet this type of research is in its infancy and what we know now may be just a small representation of the knowledge to come. Even though this knowledge seems to get only worse over time, it can be hoped that with new knowledge will come new ways to treat, and perhaps even to heal, some of the core trauma that child victims and adult survivors of sexual abuse experience.

NOTE

1. Although some studies indicate race/ethnicity is not a risk factor (Bolen, 2001), certain of these studies (Wyatt, 1985; Wyatt, Loeb, Solis, Carmona, & Romero, 1999) may not have large enough sample sizes and, hence, sufficient power.

REFERENCES

Ackerman, P. T., Newton, J. E. O., McPherson, W. B., Jones, J. G., & Dykman, R. A. (1998). Prevalence of posttraumatic stress disorder and other psychiatric diagnoses in three groups of abused children (sexual, physical, and both). *Child Abuse & Neglect, 22*(8), 759–774.

Anda, R. F., Felitti, V. J., Bremner, J. D., Walker, J. D., Whitfield, C., Perry, B. D., Dube, S. R., & Giles, W. H. (2006). The enduring effects of abuse and related adverse experiences in childhood: A convergence of evidence from neurobiology and epidemiology. *European Archives of Psychiatry and Clinical Neuroscience, 256*, 174–186.

Anderson, C. M., Teicher, M. H., Polcari, A., & Renshaw, P. F. (2002). Abnormal T2 relaxation time in the cerebellar vermis of adults sexually abused in childhood: Potential role of the vermis in stress-enhanced risk for drug abuse. *Psychoneuroendocrinology, 27*, 231–244.

Australian Institute of Health and Welfare. (2012). *Child protection Australia 2010–11*. Child Welfare Series no. 53. Canberra: AIHW.

Back, S. E., Jackson, J. L., Fitzgerald, M., Shaffer, A., Salstrom, S., & Osman, M. M. (2003). Child sexual and physical abuse among college students in Singapore and the United States. *Child Abuse & Neglect, 27*, 1259–1275.

Banyard, V. L. (1997). The impact of childhood sexual abuse and family functioning on four dimensions of women's later parenting. *Child Abuse & Neglect, 21*(11), 1095–1107.

Banyard, V. L., Williams, L. M., & Siegel, J. A. (2003). The impact of complex trauma and depression on parenting: An exploration of mediating risk and protective factors. *Child Maltreatment, 8*, 334–349.

Barnes, J. E., Noll, J. G., Putnam, F. W., & Trickett, P. K. (2009). Sexual and physical revictimization among victims of severe childhood sexual abuse. *Child Abuse & Neglect, 33*, 412–420.

Beck-Sagué, C. M., & Solomon, F. (1999). Sexually transmitted diseases in abused children and adolescent and adult victims of rape: Review of selected literature. *Clinical Infectious Diseases, 28*(S1), S74–83.

Belsky, J. (2009). *Experiencing the lifespan* (2nd ed.). New York, NY: Worth Publishers.

Benjet, C., Borges, G., Medina-Mora, M., Zambrano, J., Cruz, C., & Méndez, E. (2009). Descriptive epidemiology of chronic childhood adversity in Mexican adolescents. *Journal of Adolescent Health, 45*, 483–489.

Bensley, L. S., Van Eenwyk, J., Spieker, S. J., & Schoder, J. (1999). Self-reported abuse history and adolescent problem behaviors. I. Antisocial and suicidal behaviors. *Journal of Adolescent Health, 24*, 163–172.

Berliner, L. (2011). CSA: Definitions, prevalence, and consequences. In J. E. B. Myers (Ed.), *The APSAC handbook on child maltreatment* (3rd ed.) (pp. 215–232). Thousand Oaks, CA: Sage.

Bob, P., Susta, M., Gregusova, A., Jasova, D., & Raboch, J. (2010). Traumatic stress, dissociation, and limbic irritability in patients with unipolar depression being treated with SSRIs. *Psychological Reports, 107*, 685–696.

Bolen, R. M. (1998). Predicting risk to be sexually abused: A comparison of logistic regression analysis. *Child Maltreatment, 3*(2), 157–170.

Bolen, R. M. (2001). *CSA: Its scope and our failure.* New York, NY: Kluwer Academic/Plenum Publishers.

Bolen, R. M., Ramsayer Winter, G. R., & Hodges, L. (2013). Affect and state dysregulation as moderators of the relationship between childhood sexual abuse and nonsuicidal self-injury. *Journal of Interpersonal Violence, 28*(1), 201–228.

Bolen, R. M., & Scannapieco, M. (1998). Prevalence of CSA: A corrective met-analysis. *Social Service Review, 73*(3), 281–313.

Bremner, J. D. (2006). Traumatic stress from a multiple-levels-of-analysis perspective. In D. Cicchetti & D. J. Cohen (Eds.), *Developmental psychopathology:* Vol. 2. *Developmental neuroscience* (pp. 656–676). Hoboken, NJ: Wiley & Sons.

Brewerton, T. D. (2007). Eating disorders, trauma, and comorbidity: Focus on PTSD. *Eating Disorders: The Journal of Treatment and Prevention, 15*(4), 285–304.

Briere, J., & Zaidi, L. Y. (1989). Sexual abuse histories in female psychiatric patients. *American Journal of Psychiatry, 146*(12), 1602–1606.

Carlson, E. B., & Rosser-Hogan, R. (1994). Cross-cultural response to trauma: A study of traumatic experiences and posttraumatic symptoms in Cambodian refugees. *Journal of Traumatic Stress, 7*(1), 43–58.

Carter, J. C., Bewell, C., Blackmore, E., & Woodside, D. B. (2006). The impact of childhood sexual abuse in anorexia nervosa. *Child Abuse and Neglect, 30*, 257–269.

CBC News. (2006, June 26). *Age of consent FAQ.* Retrieved from http://www.cbc.ca/news/background/crime/ageofconsent-faq.html

Chandy, J. M., Blum, R. W., & Resnick, M. D. (1997). Sexually abused male adolescents: How vulnerable are they? *Journal of CSA, 6*(2), 1–16.

Chen, J., Dunne, M. P., & Han, P. (2004). Child sexual abuse in China: A study of adolescents in four provinces. *Child Abuse & Neglect, 28*(11), 1171–1186.

Chen, J., Dunne, M. P., & Han, P. (2006). CSA in Henan province, China: Associations with sadness, suicidality, and risk behaviors among adolescent girls. *Journal of Adolescent Health, 38*, 544–549.

Daignault, I. V., & Hébert, M. (2009). Profiles of school adaptation: Social, academic, and behavioral functioning in sexually abused girls. *Child Abuse & Neglect, 33*(2), 102–115.

Danielson, C. K., Macdonald, A., Amstadter, A. B., Hanson, R., De Arellano, M. A., Saunders, B. E., et al. (2010). Risky behaviors and depression in conjunction with—or in the absence of—lifetime history of PTSD among sexually abused adolescents. *Child Maltreatment, 15*(1), 101–107.

Department for Children, Schools, and Families. (2007). *Referrals, assessments and children and young people who are the subject of a child protection plan or are on child protection registers.* London, UK: Department for Children, Schools, and Families. http://www.education.gov.uk/rsgateway/DB/SFR/s000742/sfr28-2007 comment.pdf

Department for Children, Schools, and Families. (2009). *Referrals, assessments and children and young people who are the subject of a child protection plan or are on child protection registers.* London, UK: Department for Children, Schools, and Families. Retrieved from http://www.education.gov.uk/rsgateway/DB/SFR/s000873/sfr22-2009.pdf

DiLillo, D., & Damashek, A. (2003). Parenting characteristics of women reporting a history of childhood sexual abuse. *Child Maltreatment, 8*(4), 319–333.

DiLillo, D., Tremblay, G. C., & Peterson, L. (2000). Linking childhood sexual abuse and abusive parenting: The mediating role of maternal anger. *Child Abuse & Neglect, 24*(6), 767–779.

Dong, M., Anda, R. F., Dube, S. R., Giles, W. H., & Felitti, V. J. (2003). The relationship of exposure to other forms of abuse, neglect, and household dysfunction during childhood. *Child Abuse & Neglect, 27*, 625–639.

Dong, M., Anda, R. F., Felitti, V. J., Dube, S. R., Williamson, D. F., Thompson, T. J., et al. (2004). The interrelatedness of multiple forms of childhood abuse, neglect, and household dysfunction. *Child Abuse & Neglect, 28*, 771–784.

Dubo, E. D., Zanarini, M. C., Lewis, R. E., & Williams, A. A. (1997). Relationship between lifetime self-destructiveness and pathological childhood experiences. In M. C. Zanarini (Ed.), *Role of sexual abuse in the etiology of borderline personality disorder* (pp. 107–129). Washington, DC: American Psychiatric Association.

Dubowitz, H., Black, M., Harrington, D., & Verschoore, A. (1993). A follow-up study of behavior problems associated with CSA. *Child Abuse & Neglect, 17*, 743–754.

Dubowitz, H., Black, M. M., Kerr, M. A., Hussey, J. M., Morrel, T. M., Everson, M. D., et al. (2001). Type and timing of mother's victimization: Effects on mothers and children. *Pediatrics, 107*(4), 728–735.

Eckenrode, J., Laird, M., & Doris, J. (1993). School performance and disciplinary problems among abused and neglected children. *Developmental Psychology, 29*(1), 53–62.

Elklit, A., & Shevlin, M. (2010). Family structure as a risk factor for women's sexual victimization: A study using the Danish Registry System. *Archives of Sexual Behavior, 39*(6), 1375–1379.

Fay, W. P. (2004). *The nature and scope of the problem of sexual abuse by Catholic priests and deacons in the United States.* John Jay College of Criminal Justice. Retrieved from http://www.philvaz.com/apologetics/PriestAbuseScandal.htm

Feiring, C., Taska, L., & Lewis, M. (1999). Age and gender differences in children's and adolescents' adaptation to sexual abuse. *Child Abuse & Neglect, 23*(2), 115–128.

Feiring, C., Taska, L., & Lewis, M. (2002). Adjustment following sexual abuse discovery: The role of shame and attributional style. *Developmental Psychology, 38*(1), 79–92.

Finkel, M. A. (2011). Medical issues in CSA. In J. E. B. Myers (Ed.), *The APSAC handbook of child maltreatment* (3rd ed.) (pp. 253–266). Thousand Oaks, CA: Sage.

Finkelhor, D. (1990). Is child abuse overreported? *Public Welfare,* Winter, 22–29.

Finkelhor, D. (1994). The international epidemiology of CSA. *Child Abuse & Neglect, 18*(5), 409–417.

Finkelhor, D., Hotaling, G., Lewis, I. A., & Smith, C. (1990). Sexual abuse in a national survey of adult men and women: Prevalence, characteristics, and risk factors. *Child Abuse & Neglect, 14*(9), 19–28.

Finkelhor, D., Hotaling, G. T., & Smith, C. (1989). Sexual abuse and its relationship to later sexual satisfaction, marital status, religion and attitudes. *Journal of Interpersonal Violence, 4,* 379–398.

Finkelhor, D., & Jones, L. M. (2004). Explanations for the decline in sexual abuse cases. *Juvenile Justice Bulletin,* January, 1–12. Washington, DC: U.S. Department of Justice.

Finkelhor, D., Ormond, R., & Turner, H. A. (2007). Poly-victimization: A neglected component in child victimization. *Child Abuse & Neglect, 31,* 7–26.

Finkelhor, D., Ormrod, R., Turner, H., & Hamby, S. L. (2005). The victimization of children and youth: A comprehensive, national survey. *Child Maltreatment, 10*(1), 5–25. doi:10.1177/1077559504271287

Finkelhor, D., Turner, H., Ormrod, R., Hamby, S., & Kracke, K. (2009). *Children's exposure to violence: A comprehensive national survey.* Washington, DC: U.S. Department of Justice.

Fleischman, J. (2002). *Suffering in silence: The links between human rights abuses and HIV transmission in Zambia.* New York, NY: Human Rights Watch.

Fliege, H., Lee, J., Grimm, A., & Klapp, B. F. (2009). Risk factors and correlates of deliberate self-harm behavior: A systematic review. *Journal of Psychosomatic Research, 66,* 477–493.

Follette, V. M., & Polusny, M. A. (1995). Long-term correlates of child sexual abuse. *Applied & Preventive Psychology, 4*(3), 145–166.

Fontes, L. A. (2005). *Child abuse and culture: Working with diverse families.* New York, NY: Guilford Press.

Francia-Martinez, M., De Torres, I. R., Alvarado, C. S., Martinez-Taboas, A., & Sayers, S. (2003). Dissociation, depression and trauma in psychiatric inpatients in Puerto Rico. *Journal of Trauma & Dissociation, 4*(4), 47–61.

Friedrich, W. N. (1993). Sexual victimization and sexual behavior in children: A review of recent literature. *Child Abuse & Neglect, 17,* 59–66.

Fuemmeler, B. F., Dedert, E., McClernon, F. J., & Beckham, J. C. (2009). Adverse childhood events are associated with obesity and disordered eating: Results from a U.S. population-based survey of young adults. *Journal of Traumatic Stress, 22*(4), 329–333.

Gal, G., Levav, I., & Gross, R. (2011). Psychopathology among adults abused during childhood or adolescence: Results from the Israel-based World Mental Health Survey. *The Journal of Nervous and Mental Disease, 199*(4), 222–229.

Garnefski, N., & Arends, E. (1998). Sexual abuse and adolescent maladjustment: Differences between male and female victims. *Journal of Adolescence, 21,* 99–107.

Girardet, R. G., Lemme, S., Biason, T. A., Bolton, K., & Lahoti, S. (2009). HIV post-exposure prophylaxis in children and adolescents presenting for reported sexual assault. *Child Abuse & Neglect, 33,* 173–178.

Glassman, L., Weierich, M., Holley, J., Deliberto, T., & Nock, M. (2007). Child maltreatment, non-suicidal self-injury, and the mediating role of self-criticism. *Behaviour Research and Therapy, 45,* 2483–2490.

Glosser, A., Gardiner, K., & Fishman, M. (2004). *Statutory rape: A guide to state laws and reporting requirements.* U.S. Department of Health and Human Services. Retrieved from http://aspe.hhs.gov/hsp/08/SR/StateLaws/

Gunnar, M. R., & Vazquez, D. (2006). Stress neurobiology and developmental psychopathology. In D. Cicchetti & D. J. Cohen (Eds.), *Developmental psychopathology:* Vol. 2. *Developmental neuroscience* (pp. 533–577). Hoboken, NJ: Wiley & Sons.

Hampton, T. (2010). Child marriage threatens girls' health. *JAMA, 304*(5), 509–510.

Hernandez, J. T. (1992). Substance abuse among sexually abused adolescents and their families. *Journal of Adolescent Health, 13,* 658–662.

Jumper, S. A. (1995). A meta-analysis of the relationship of CSA to adult psychological adjustment. *Child Abuse & Neglect, 19*(6), 715–728.

Kelly, P., & Koh, J. (2006). Sexually transmitted infections in alleged sexual abuse of children and adolescents. *Journal of Paediatrics and Child Health, 42,* 434–440.

Kendall-Tackett, K. A., Williams, L. M., & Finkelhor, D. (1993). Impact of sexual abuse on children: A review and synthesis of recent empirical studies. *Psychological Bulletin, 113*(1), 164–180.

Kilpatrick, D. G., Acierno, R., Saunders, B., Resnick, H. S., Best, C. L., & Schnurr, P. P. (2000). Risk factors for adolescent substance abuse and dependence: Data from a national sample. *Journal of Consulting and Clinical Psychology, 68*(1), 19–30.

Kilpatrick, D. G., Edmunds, C. N., & Seymour, A. (1992). *Rape in America: A report to the nation.* Arlington, VA: National Victim Center; Charleston, SC: Crime Victims Research and Treatment Center.

Kjellgren, C., Priebe, G., Svedin, C. G., & Långström, N. (2010). Sexually coercive behavior in male youth: Population survey of general and specific risk factors. *Archives of Sexual Behavior, 39*, 1161–1169.

Kwako, L. E., Noll, J. G., Putnam, F. W., & Trickett, P. K. (2010). Childhood sexual abuse and attachment: An intergenerational perspective. *Clinical Child Psychology and Psychiatry, 15*(3), 407–422.

La Flair, L. N., Franko, D. L., & Herzog, D. B. (2008). Sexual assault and disordered eating in Asian women. *Harvard Review of Psychiatry, 16*, 248–257.

Lalor, K. (2004). Child sexual abuse in sub-Saharan Africa: A literature review. *Child Abuse & Neglect, 28*(4), 439–460.

Lalor, K., & McElvaney, R. (2010). Child sexual abuse, links to later sexual exploitation/high risk sexual behavior, and prevention/treatment programs. *Trauma, Violence and Abuse, 11*(4), 159–177.

Lupien, S. J., Ouellet-Morin, I., Hupbach, A., Tu, M. T., Buss, C., et al. (2006). Beyond the stress concept: Allostatic load—a developmental biological and cognitive perspective. In *Developmental Psychopathology,* Vol. 2: *Developmental neuroscience* (2nd ed.) (pp. 578–628). Hoboken, NJ: Wiley & Sons.

Maniglio, R. (2010). Child sexual abuse in the etiology of depression: A systematic review of reviews. *Depression and Anxiety, 27*, 631–642. doi: 10.1002/da.20687

Mannarino, A. P., & Cohen, J. A. (1996). Family-related variables and psychological symptom formation in sexually abused girls. *Journal of Child Sexual Abuse, 5(1)*, 105–120.

Mayor-Zaragoza, F. (2008). The university of the 21st century: Political and social trends of globalization—challenges for higher education. *Higher Education in the World, 3*, 20–27.

McEwen, B., & Lasley, E. N. (2007). Allostatic load: When protection gives way to damage. In B. McEwen & I. N. Lasley (Eds.), *The Praeger handbook on stress and coping,* Vol. 1 (pp. 99–109). Westport, CT: Praeger Publishers.

Meursing, K., Vos, T., Coutinho, O., Moyo, M., Mpofu, S., Oneko, O., Mundy, V., Dube, S., Mahlangu, T., & Sibindi, F. (1995). CSA in Matabeleland, Zimbabwe. *Social Science & Medicine, 41*(12), 1693–1704.

Moore, D. W., Gallup, G. H., & Schussel, R. (1995). *Disciplining children in America: A Gallup poll report.* Princeton, NJ: The Gallup Organization.

Moore, K. A., Nord, C. W., & Peterson, J. L. (1989). Nonvoluntary sexual activity among adolescents. *Family Planning Perspectives, 21*(3), 110–114.

Murray, L. K., Haworth, A, Semrau, K., Aldrovandi, G. M., Sinkala, M., et al. (2006). Violence and abuse among HIV-infected women and their children in Zambia: A qualitative study. *Journal of Nervous & Mental Disorders, 194*(8), 610–615.

Negriff, S., Noll, J. G., Shenk, C. E., Putnam, F. W., & Trickett, P. K. (2010). Associations between nonverbal behaviors and subsequent sexual attitudes and behaviors of sexually abused and comparison girls. *Child Maltreatment, 15,* 180–189.

Nelson, E. C., Heath, A. C., Madden, P. A. F., Cooper, M. L., Dinwiddie, S. H., Bucholz, K. K., Glowinski, A., McLaughlin, T., Dunne, M. P., Statham, D. J., & Martin, N. G. (2002). Association between self-reported childhood sexual abuse and adverse psychosocial outcomes. *Archives of General Psychiatry, 59,* 139–145.

Neumann, D. A., Houskamp, B. M., Pollock, V. E., & Briere, J. (1996). The long-term sequelae of childhood sexual abuse in women: A meta-analytic review. *Child Maltreatment, 1*(1), 6–16.

Noll, J. G., Shenk, C. E., Putnam, K. T. (2009). Childhood sexual abuse and adolescent pregnancy. A meta-analytic update. *Journal of Pediatric Psychology, 34*(4), 366–378.

Nunes, S. O. V., Watanabe, M. A. E., Morimoto, H. K., Moria, R., & Reiche, E. M. V. (2010). The impact of childhood sexual abuse on activation of immunological and neuroendocrine response. *Aggression and Violent Behavior, 15,* 440–445.

Pain, C., Bluhm, R. L., Lanius, R. A. (2009). Dissociation in patients with chronic PTSD: Hyperactivation and hypoactivation patterns, clinical and neuroimaging perspectives. In C. Pain, R. L. Bluhm, & R. A. Lanius (Eds.), *Dissociation and the dissociative disorders: DSM-V and beyond* (pp. 373–380). New York, NY: Routledge/Taylor & Francis.

Pallitto, C. C., & Murillo, V. (2008). Childhood abuse as a risk factor for adolescent pregnancy in El Salvador. *Journal of Adolescent Health, 42,* 580–586.

Paolucci, E. O., Genius, M. L., & Violato, C. (2001). Meta-analysis of the published research on the effects of child sexual abuse. *The Journal of Psychology, 135*(1), 17–36.

Parillo, K. M., Freeman, R. C., Collier, K., & Young, P. (2001). Association between early sexual abuse and adult HIV-risky sexual behaviors among community recruited women. *Child Abuse & Neglect, 25,* 335–346.

Peltzer, K., Cherian, V. I., & Cherian, L. (1998). Brain fag symptoms in rural South African secondary school pupils. *Psychological Reports, 83*(3, Pt 2), 1187–1196.

Pereda, N., Guilera, G., Forns, M., & Gómez-Benito, J. (2009a). The prevalence of CSA in community and student samples: A meta-analysis. *Clinical Psychology Review, 29,* 328–338.

Pereda, N., Guilera, G., Forns, M., & Gómez-Benito, J. (2009b). The international epidemiology of child sexual abuse. A continuation of Finkelhor (1994). *Child Abuse & Neglect, 33*(6), 331–342.

Perez, C. M., & Widom, C. S. (1994). Childhood victimization and long-term intellectual and academic outcomes. *Child Abuse and Neglect, 18*(8), 617–633.

Perry, B. D. (2008). Child maltreatment: A neurodevelopmental perspective on the role of trauma and neglect in psychopathology. In T. P. Beauchaine & S. P. Hinshaw (Eds.), *Child and adolescent psychopathology* (pp. 93–128). Hoboken, NJ: Wiley & Sons.

Pinheiro, P. S. (2006). *Report of the independent expert for the United Nations study on violence against children.* New York, NY: United Nations. http://www.unicef.org/violencestudy/reports/SG_violencestudy_en.pdf

Pinheiro, P. S. (2007). *World report on violence against children.* New York, NY: United Nations. http://www.unicef.org/violencestudy/reports.html

Polusny, M. A., & Follette, V. M. (1995). Long-term correlates of child sexual abuse: Theory and review of the empirical literature. *Applied and Preventive Psychology, 4*(3), 143–166.

Raymond, J. G. (2002). The new UN trafficking protocol. *Women's Studies International Forum, 25*(5), 491–502.

Rich-Edwards, J. W., Spiegelman, D., Hibert, E. N., Jun, H., Todd, T., et al. (2010). Abuse in childhood and adolescence as a predictor of type 2 diabetes in adult women. *American Journal of Preventive Medicine, 39*(6), 529–536.

Russell, D. E. H. (1983). The incidence and prevalence of intrafamilial and extrafamilial sexual abuse of female children. *Child Abuse & Neglect, 7*(2), 133–146.

Russell, D. E. H., & Bolen, R. M. (2000). *The epidemic of rape and CSA in the United States.* Thousand Oaks, CA: Sage.

Saunders, B. E., Kilpatrick, D. E., Hanson, R. F., Resnick, H. S., Walker, M. E. (1999). Prevalence, case characteristics, and long-term psychological correlates of child rape among women: A national survey. *Child Maltreatment, 4*(3), 187–200.

Sedlak, A. J., & Broadhurst, D. D. (1996). *Third national incidence study of child abuse and neglect: Final report.* Washington, DC: U.S. Department of Health and Human Services.

Sedlak, A. J., Mettenburg, J., Basena, M., Petta, I., McPherson, K., Greene, A., et al. (2010). *Fourth national incidence study of child abuse and neglect (NIS–4): Report to Congress.* Washington, DC: U.S. Department of Health and Human Services, Administration for Children and Families.

Skeldon, R. (2003). *Migration & poverty.* Paper presented at the Conference on African Migration and Urbanization in Comparative Perspective, Johannesburg, South Africa.

Smolak, L., & Murnen, S. K. (2002). A meta-analytic examination of the relationship between child sexual abuse and eating disorders. *International Journal of Eating Disorders, 31*, 136–150.

Snell, C. L. (2003). Commercial sexual exploitation of youth in South Africa. *The Journal of Negro Education, 72*(4), 506–514.

Speizer, I. S., Pettifor, A., Cummings, S., MacPhall, C., Kleinschmidt, I., & Rees, H. V. (2009). Sexual violence and reproductive health outcomes among South

African female youths: A contextual analysis. *American Journal of Public Health, 99*(S2), S425–S431.

Sroufe, L. A., & Waters, E. (1977). Attachment as an organizational construct. *Child Development, 48,* 1184-1199.

Stoltenborgh, M., van IJzendoorn, M. V., Euser, E. M., & Bakersman-Kranenburg, M. J. (2011). A global perspective on CSA: Meta-analysis of prevalence around the world. *Child Maltreatment, 16*(79), 79–101.

Teicher, M. H., Anderson, C. M., & Polcari, A. (2011). Maltreatment is associated with reduced hippocampal subfields CA3, dentate gyrus, & subiculum. *PNAS: Proceedings of the National Academy of Sciences of the United States of America, 109*(9), 563–572.

Teicher, M. H., Dumont, N. L., Ito, Y., Vaituzis, C., Giedd, J. N., et al. (2004). Childhood neglect is associated with reduced corpus callosum area. *Biological Psychiatry, 56*(2), 80–85.

Thompson, R., Wiley, T. R. A., Lewis, T., English, D. J., Dubowitz, H., Litrownik, A. J., Isbell, P., & Block, S. (2012). Links between traumatic experiences and expectation about the future in high risk youth. *Psychological Trauma: Theory, Research, Practice, and Policy, 4*(3), 293–302.

Tjaden, P., & Thoennes, N. (2000). *Partner violence: Findings from the national violence against women survey.* Washington, DC: U.S. Department of Justice Office of Justice Programs.

Trocmé, N., Fallon, B., MacLaurin, B., Daciuk, J., Felstiner, C., et al. (2005). *Canadian incidence study of reported child abuse and neglect—2003: Major findings.* Minister of Public Works and Government Services, Gatineau, Quebec, Canada. http://www.phac-aspc.gc.ca/cm-vee/csca-ecve/pdf/childabuse_final_e.pdf

Trocmé, N. M, Tourigny, M., MacLaurin, B., & Fallon, B. (2003). Major findings from the Canadian incidence study of reported child abuse and neglect. *Child Abuse and Neglect, 27,* 1427–1439.

Tyler, K. A. (2002). Social and emotional outcomes of childhood sexual abuse: A review of recent research. *Aggression and Violent Behavior, 7,* 567–589.

UNICEF. (2012). *Status on legal frameworks CSEC.* New York, NY: UNICEF. Retrieved from http://www.unicef.org/wcaro/Status_on_legal_frameworks_CSEC_Final_2.pdf

United Nations Office on Drugs and Crime. (2010). *The globalization of crime: A transnational organized crime threat assessment.* New York, NY: UNODC.

U.S. Department of Health and Human Services, Administration on Children, Youth and Families. (2012). *Child maltreatment 2010.* Washington, DC: U.S. Government Printing Office.

van der Kolk, B. A. (2003). The neurobiology of childhood trauma and abuse. *Child & Adolescent Psychiatric Clinic of North America, 12,* 293–317.

van der Kolk, B. A. (2005). Developmental trauma disorder. *Psychiatric Annals, 35*(5), 2–8.

Van IJzendoorn, M. H., & Kroonenberg, P. M. (1988). Cross-cultural patterns of attachment: A meta-analysis of the strange situation. *Child Development, 59*(1), 147–156.

Vogeltanz, N. D., Wilsnack, S. C., Harris, T. R., Wilsnack, R. W., Wonderlich, S. A., & Kristjanson, A. F. (1999). Prevalence and risk factors for childhood sexual abuse in women: National survey findings. *Child Abuse & Neglect, 23*(6), 579–592.

Weaver, T. L., Chard, K. M., Mechanic, M. B., & Etzel, J. C. (2004). Self-injurious behaviors, PTSD arousal, and general health complaints within a treatment-seeking sample of sexually abused women. *Journal of Interpersonal Violence, 19*, 558–575.

Wechsler-Zimring, A., & Kearney, C. A. (2011). Post traumatic stress and related symptoms among neglected and physically and sexually maltreated adolescents. *Journal of Traumatic Stress, 24*(5), 601–604.

Weitzel, S., Yampolskaya, S., & McCann, C. (2009). *Child maltreatment in Florida: A data retrospect.* Tampa, FL: University of South Florida, College of Community and Behavioral Sciences. Retrieved from http://floridakidscount .fmhi.usf.edu/_assets/docs/pubs/ChildMaltreatment2009.pdf

Widom, C. S., & Ames, M. A. (1994). Criminal consequences of childhood sexual abuse. *Child Abuse & Neglect, 18*(4), 303–318.

Widom, C. S., & Kuhns, J. B. (1996). Childhood victimization and subsequent risk for promiscuity, prostitution, and teenage pregnancy: A prospective study. *American Journal of Public Health, 86*(11), 1607–1612.

Wilson, H. W., & Widom, C. S. (2009). Sexually transmitted diseases among adults who had been abused and neglected as children: A 30-year prospective study. *American Journal of Public Health, 99*(S1), S197-S203.

Wyatt, G. E. (1985). The sexual abuse of Afro-American and White-American women in childhood. *Child Abuse & Neglect, 9*(4), 507–519.

Wyatt, G. E., Loeb, T. B., Solis, B., Carmona, J. V., & Romero, G. (1999). The prevalence and circumstances of child sexual abuse: Changes across a decade. *Child Abuse & Neglect, 23*(1), 45–60.

Young, M. D., Deardorff, J., Ozer, E., & Lahiff, M. (2011). Sexual abuse in childhood and adolescence and the risk of early pregnancy among women ages 18–22. *Journal of Adolescent Health, 49*, 287–293.

Zelman, G. L., & Antler, S. (1990). Mandated reporters and CPS: A study in frustration. Misunderstanding and miscommunication threaten the system. *Public Welfare,* Winter, 30–47.

Zimmerman, C., Hossain, M., & Watts, C. (2011). Human trafficking and health: A conceptual model to inform policy, intervention and research. *Social Sciences & Medicine, 73*, 327–335.

5

Child Physical Abuse

David J. Kolko, Amy D. Herschell, Anna Loiterstein,
Wyatt D'Emilia, and Abby J. Reed

INTRODUCTION

The world's population is estimated to be around seven billion people, with approximately 26 percent under the age of 14 years (Central Intelligence Agency, 2012). These early years and the period of adolescence are marked by dramatic growth and a variety of social and environmental experiences that can positively or negatively influence an individual's life course. For some children, maltreatment is one of these life events.

The actual number of children impacted by abuse is difficult to estimate because of inconsistent definitions, data collection, and policies, and an inability to capture every incident.

The United States publishes an annual report on child maltreatment; estimates suggest that between 9.1 and 9.6 percent of U.S. children have been victims of abuse over the last five years (U.S. Department of Health and Human Services et al., 2011). Of all the child victims, 17.6 percent were physically abused. Similarly, recent estimates of Canadian children indicate that 10.7 percent of boys and 9.2 percent of girls reported experiencing physical abuse, defined as getting hit with a fist or an object, or threatened with a knife or gun among other things (Macmillan, Tanaka, Duku, Vaillancourt, & Boyle, 1997). International estimates are much higher. The World Health Organization (2010) estimates that as many as 25 to 50 percent of children worldwide may be physically abused each year. As many as two-thirds of school children in India report facing corporal punishment (CHILDLINE 1098, 2013).

Substantial resources have been invested in preventing and treating child abuse. For example, the U.S. Department of Health and Human Services spent $27 million on child abuse prevention and treatment grants in 2008, and the National Institutes of Health awarded $30 million through grants in 2011 (FindTheData, 2012; National Institutes of Health, 2012). This chapter offers a summary of child physical abuse (CPA) definitions, risk factors including perpetrator characteristics, effects or consequences for victims, intervention and treatment approaches, and prevention programs.

DEFINITIONS

Definitions of CPA vary based on location and policy. In the United States, the Federal Child Abuse Prevention and Treatment Act (CAPTA) provides a general definition of child abuse. Child abuse and neglect is defined as "any recent act or failure to act on the part of a parent or caretaker which results in death, serious physical or emotional harm, sexual abuse, or exploitation or an act or failure to act which presents an imminent risk of serious harm" (Child Welfare Information Gateway, 2008, p. 2). This definition provides the framework for each state to define CPA according to individual state law. States set the standards for state child protective services, defining different forms of abuse and providing numerous examples. Some states (e.g., Arkansas, Florida) have detailed definitions that provide a comprehensive outline of what constitutes physical abuse along with examples (Child Welfare Information Gateway, 2011). For example, in Florida, abuse of a child includes acts or omissions, with harm ranging from inflicting physical, emotional, or mental injury to exposing a child to a controlled substance or alcohol (Child Welfare Information Gateway, 2011). A more explicit definition can eliminate some of the uncertainty around reporting but still does not help to capture all cases. Other states, such as Connecticut, Georgia, and Iowa, adopt the federal definition and do not elaborate further. The variance in definitions can be due to the culture and history of the individual states. States that have agricultural roots may have less comprehensive definitions, possibly due to the notion of children being viewed as another form of personal property. Without a universal definition, reporting an accurate estimate of the number of children abused in the United States is difficult.

Those attempting to gather international estimates of the number of children abused experience the same challenges as we find in the United States. A country's development (industrialized versus third world), cultural influences, and traditions determine how child physical abuse is defined. The World Health Organization (2010) estimates that 25 to 50 percent of children may be physically abused; this wide range reflects the lack of a universal definition.

In terms of variability in definitions, the NSPCC, the United Kingdom's only charity with statutory power that enables it to take action to protect children at risk of abuse, provides examples of what CPA may involve (2010, 2011). Enacted in 2009, Japan's Child Abuse Prevention Law outlines CPA as acts done to a child under the age of 18 years old by a guardian or caretaker; such acts include bodily injury, coercion, prevention of normal physical and mental development, or strong verbal abuse or attitude of rejection (Children's Rainbow Center, 2012). In addition to individual country definitions, international organizations that strive to end child physical abuse in multiple areas define CPA separately and each organization's definition may apply to several countries. Child Safe International, which serves Cambodia, LAO PDR, Thailand, Indonesia, and Switzerland, defines child physical abuse as physical injury, ranging from minor to severe, as a result of a variety of actions such as choking, shaking, beating, or hitting (2007). Clearly, there are a number of different definitions with considerable variability among them. And, not surprisingly, the rates reported across countries vary widely (see Cappa & Khan, 2001).

However a state, country, or organization defines CPA, common elements exist. CPA typically applies to individuals under the age of 18 years old; aggressive acts vary but may include choking, shaking, biting, beating, or hitting; the abuser tends to be a parent, guardian, or caregiver. For the purpose of this chapter, we will consider this broad definition.

As mentioned previously, the definition of child physical abuse depends on the policy makers in a particular state or country, though the topic is rarely a high societal priority. On an international level, the United Nations created the Convention on the Rights of the Child, which outlines basic human rights that every child has, such as protection from harmful influences, abuse, and exploitation (UNICEF, 2005; Zolotor & Puzia, 2010). By ratifying the Convention on the Rights of the Child, 192 countries agreed to protect the rights of children (UNICEF, 2005; Zolotor & Puzia, 2010). Ratification shows a country's support and approval of the convention, but compliance varies. Sweden was one of the first 20 countries to sign and ratify the convention, but a study in 2010 found that 15.2 percent of surveyed children in Sweden reported being hit by a parent or caretaker (Annerbäck, Wingren, Svedin, & Gustafsson, 2010; UNICEF, 2005). The incongruence between policy and practice illustrates the lack of acceptance and compliance in the general population. While country and state officials may be willing to adopt a policy to eliminate child physical abuse, implementation requires the commitment of individual families and caregivers.

RISK FACTORS

Child Characteristics

Several child, adult, family, and community characteristics have been identified as risk factors for either being abused or being a perpetrator of CPA. A meta-analytic review on risk factors of child maltreatment reveals that demographic factors should not be considered in isolation in relation to CPA (Stith et al., 2009); however, some patterns exist between CPA and specific demographic factors (e.g., age, ethnicity, socioeconomic status). Data from the *U.S. Report on Child Maltreatment* (U.S. Department of Health and Human Services et al., 2011) indicate that one-quarter (27.1 percent) of all child abuse victims are younger than three years. Similarly, this age group relative to other age groups appears to be the most vulnerable to CPA, including more severe injuries (Lung & Daro, 1996), increased hospitalization rates, and higher numbers of fatalities (47.9 percent of U.S. child fatalities). A study aimed to provide U.S. estimates on the occurrence of serious injuries due to physical abuse found an incidence of 58.2 per 100,000 children during their first year of life (Leventhal, Martin, & Gaither, 2012).

Some data suggest racial and ethnic differences among CPA cases. For example, Hawkins and colleagues (2010) utilized participants in the National Survey of Adolescents to investigate possible race and ethnicity differences in CPA experiences, focusing on a specific form of CPA (injurious spanking). Their results revealed that Hispanic and African American youth were more likely to report CPA compared to white youth. In the U.S.-based child maltreatment study (Hawkins et al., 2010), rates of victimization per 1,000 children varied by race and ethnicity: African American (14.3), American Indian or Alaska Native (11.4), Asian (1.7), Hispanic (8.6), multiple race (10.1), Pacific Islander (8.5), and white (7.9). These rates remained stable from 2007 through 2011. Consistent with other epidemiological research, these findings may be influenced by reporting bias and cultural differences (Finkelhor, Ormrod, Turner, & Hamby, 2005).

There have been mixed results as to the contribution of the child's health and medical problems to his or her risk for being physically abused.

Belsky and Vondra (1989) found that certain medical, intellectual, or developmental abnormalities, such as low IQ or physical disability, contribute to the child's increased risk of being abused. Additionally, Sullivan and Knutson (1998) found that disabilities were twice as prevalent among the maltreated hospital sample compared to the nonmaltreated sample. In contrast, other research has indicated that these characteristics did not significantly increase the child's risk above and beyond parent characteristics (Azar & Wolfe, 2006; Kolko & Kolko, 2010). Another potential risk factor is a child's difficult temperament or behavioral deviance (Belsky & Vondra, 1989). For example, children with oppositional defiant disorder had much higher rates of early child maltreatment than those with other externalizing or internalizing disorders (Ford et al., 1999), perhaps due to the co-occurrence of child behavior issues and abusive incidents (Herrenkohl, Herrenkohl, & Egolf, 1983; Youngblade & Belsky, 1990).

Adult Characteristics

Just as demographic characteristics alone are unlikely to determine if a child will experience child physical abuse, personal characteristics may not fully predict which individuals will become perpetrators. However, U.S. data suggest that almost 84.6 percent of perpetrators in 2011 were between the ages of 20 and 49 (U.S. Department of Health and Human Services et al., 2011). Perpetrators are highly likely to be a relative of the child; 80.8 percent of perpetrators were parents and 5.9 percent were relatives other than parents. An additional 4.4 percent of perpetrators were the unmarried partner of a parent. Day care workers, foster parents, friends, neighbors, and legal guardians each account for less than 1 percent of perpetrators. Women (53.6 percent) were more likely than men (45.1 percent) to be perpetrators of abuse in the U.S. However, in other countries men are sometimes more likely to perpetrators of CPA. For example, in Canada, fathers were responsible for more abuse than mothers (Macmillan et al., 1997). Racial distributions of perpetrators were similar to the race of their victims (U.S. Department of Health and Human Services et al., 2011). Evidence has shown that among parents, certain demographic characteristics, such as lower educational level, young, and/or single, increase the likelihood that CPA will occur (Cadzow, Armstrong, & Fraser, 1999; Milner, 1998).

Considerable research suggests that a childhood history of abuse is a risk factor for future abusive behavior. Early experiences of harsh punishment or abusive experiences during childhood have been related to the use of physical violence with children (Gelles & Straus, 1987; Pianta, Egeland, & Erickson, 1989; Simons, Whitbeck, Conger, & Wu, 1991; Straus, 1994; Straus, Gelles, & Steinmetz, 1980; Whipple & Webster-Stratton, 1991). Cognitive style has also been associated with CPA, for example, parents perceiving their children in a more negative light than nonabusive parents, attributing responsibility for failure to their children and for success to themselves, and reporting higher levels of behavioral dysfunction among their children than the comparison group even though observations in the home revealed no group differences (Bugental, Mantyla, & Lewis, 1989; Whipple & Webster-Stratton, 1991). In addition, research has indicated that abusive parents are more accepting of physical punishment and have high expectations of their children's behaviors (Kelly, Grace, & Elliot, 1990; Simons et al., 1991).

Family and Community Risk Factors

Among family influences, there are both functional and structural charac-teristics. These characteristics include aggressive or coercive behavior (Azar & Wolfe, 2006; Kolko & Kolko, 2010), and use of ineffective child management techniques such as limited use of positive affect and general discussion (Caliso & Milner, 1992). Some have highlighted the use of con-flict and psychologically hostile communications (Claussen & Crittenden, 1991), including limited family cohesion, expressiveness, and marital sat-isfaction (Mollerstrom, Patchner, & Milner, 1992). Other family context or social-system variables have been suggested, such as family socioeco-nomic disadvantage (e.g., limited income, unemployment, family size, youthful parenthood, single parenthood), that contribute to the expression of violent behavior (Belsky & Vondra, 1989; Whipple & Webster-Stratton, 1991) including domestic violence (Appel & Holden, 1998).

The experience of serious parental stressors in some families (e.g., low parental social support, marital discord) may further restrict parents' abilities to support their children's efforts to cope with adversity (see Pianta, Egeland, & Erickson, 1989; Pianta et al., 1989; Webster-Stratton, 1985; Whipple & Webster-Stratton, 1991). Other contributors to child maltreatment include parental worries, dissatisfaction with children and the parenting role, limited emotional expressiveness, social isolation, and lack of encouragement for the development and autonomy of their children (Trickett, Aber, Carlson, & Cicchetti, 1991). Overall, the experi-ence of few positive relationships and heightened family conflict may influence children's coping and adjustment.

A broad set of variables may contribute to the emergence of CPA (Brown, Cohen, Johnson, & Salzinger, 1998), including low maternal involvement, early separation from mother, and perinatal problems. Two other variables, maternal sociopathology and young maternal age, were associated with risk for CPA, Child Sexual Abuse (CSA), and neglect.

Certain community and family correlates of CPA are evident in both domestic and international studies. For example, in Japan cases of abuse appear among all socioeconomic groups; however, people who report a lower socioeconomic status evidence a higher number of abuse cases (Henry, Ueda, Shinjo, & Yoshikawa, 2003), a finding similar to the United States. Internationally, young girls who experience abuse are more likely to enter relationships with abusive men (Kitamura et al., 1999) just as in the United States.

There also are cultural factors that relate to CPA. For example, the role of the mother as disciplinarian in Japanese culture, as well as societal norms establishing women as passive and mild while men focus on work and income, likely contribute to high rates of unreported abuse in Japan (Kayama, Sagami, Watanabe, Senoo, & Ohara, 2004). The combination of maintaining a perceived mild nature, not seeking necessary support, experiencing multiple stressors, and perceiving children as responsible for their unrelieved stress likely impacts abuse rates (Kayama et al., 2004).

EFFECTS OR CONSEQUENCES

There is a range of psychological consequences that may be experienced by children and adolescents who have experienced CPA. The research findings suggest that these consequences include aggressive or coercive behavior, limited social skills and peer relations, affective disturbances, developmental and academic problems, and psychiatric disorders. Another damaging consequence of CPA is the increased likelihood that victims may later abuse their own children (Straus, 1994). Many of these consequences surface by late childhood and adolescence, although some may be apparent earlier (Mulvaney & Mebert, 2007).

Maladaptive Attribution Patterns

Children who experience CPA often experience maladaptive attribution patterns. For example, girls who have been abused attribute less power to themselves than to parents, and women who were abused as children attribute less power to themselves than to children (Bugental & Shennum, 2002).

These distorted cognitions often lead individuals to accept violence in future relationships (Ponce, Williams, & Allen, 2004). In addition, research has shown that abused children process information relating to emotion differently than nonabused children (Shackman, Shackman, & Pollak, 2007). Specifically, abused children are more attentive to visual and auditory anger cues and potential threats than nonabused children.

Behavioral and Mental Health Problems

Externalizing problems are among the most common consequences of CPA. These externalizing problems include aggression and antisocial behaviors (Grogan-Kaylor, 2005). Additionally, CPA victims are more likely to develop oppositional defiant disorder or abuse alcohol and/or drugs (Steiner, 1997). Externalizing behavior problems related to CPA can occur as early as the late toddler years (Mulvaney & Mebert, 2007). Among the internalizing problems that have been identified, the most widely documented consequence is depression (Fogarty, Fredman, Heeren, & Liebschutz, 2008; Steiner, 1997) followed by anxiety (Mulvaney & Mebert, 2007; Shackman et al., 2007). Some physically abused children may experience post-traumatic stress disorder (PTSD) as a result of exposure to a specific traumatic event or series of events (Kolko, Brown, & Berliner, 2002). In terms of the prevalence of PTSD in victims of CPA, 36 percent of maltreated children and youth met criteria for PTSD (Famularo, Fenton, Kinscherff, Ayoub, & Barnum, 1994), and 33 percent of a subset of those with PTSD were later found to retain the full diagnosis at two-year follow-up (Famularo, Fenton, Augustyn, & Zuckerman, 1996).

The experience of CPA can elicit longstanding consequences for the victim. Cohort studies in New Zealand, for example, show abuse as responsible for 5 percent of subsequent mental disorders (Gilbert et al., 2009) and an increased rate of suicides for abuse victims compared to control cases.

Social/Interpersonal Competence and Relationship Skills

Individuals with a history of CPA tend to have more difficulties with interpersonal relationships than nonabused individuals. For example, abused children may be less communicative, less warm, and more conflicted in their interpersonal relationships than nonabused children, and experience more conflict with peers and partners (Egeland, Yates, Appleyard, & van Dulmen, 2002; Flores, Cicchetti, & Rogosch, 2005). The people who experienced CPA are at a greater risk for continuing the cycle of abuse, either as a perpetrator or a victim (Ponce et al., 2004). Similarly, young girls who experience abuse are more likely to enter relationships with abusive men (Kitamura et al., 1999).

INTERVENTION AND TREATMENT

There are several interventions and treatment approaches for physically abused children and their families that vary in client focus (e.g., child and parent, family), targets (e.g., anger control versus behavior management), and content or methods (skills training, psychoeducation [Barlow, Johnston, Kendrick, Polnay, & Stewart-Brown, 2006; Kolko & Kolko, 2010]). In this section, we offer a brief overview of interventions that have reported worthy outcomes, many of which are described in helpful online sources (see www .NCTSN.org and www.childwelfare.gov).

For children, studies have reported some benefits associated with intensive day and residential treatment programs, mostly for maltreated preschoolers, which include multiple services (e.g., play groups, academic work, family counseling [Culp, Heide, & Richardson, 1987; Sankey, Elmer, Halechko, & Schulberg, 1985]). The inclusion of a therapeutic preschool and home visitation in Australia has been related to better intellectual functioning and receptive language (Oates & Bross, 1995). Other reports have documented benefits from group-based programs that build peer relationships and other adaptive skills using a broad range of methods (e.g., individual and family therapy, group counseling, parent education [Culp, Little, Letts, & Lawrence, 1991]). Relative to a control group, treated children acknowledged several improvements in this program (e.g., cognitive competence, peer and maternal acceptance, academic development). However, these children still experienced numerous deficits, suggesting the potential need for other skills training procedures.

Other interventions for young children have included skills training to enhance peer relations and social adjustment in play buddy sessions that provide exposure to social initiations (resilient peer treatment or RPT [Fantuzzo, Stovall, Schachtel, Goins, & Hall, 1987]). These earlier studies documented benefits for children's social adjustment and peer involvement, which were maintained, highlighting the utility of providing access to peer activities to enhance social adjustment (Fantuzzo et al., 1987; Fantuzzo et al., 1988; Fantuzzo et al., 1996). A cognitive-behavioral group program was reported for physically abused children, which included diverse content (i.e., trauma-specific work, anger management, social skills training [Swenson & Brown, 1999]). Assessments revealed gains in children's anger reactions, post-traumatic symptoms, and behavioral problems after treatment. The use of a group modality can be efficient and promote an enriched understanding of the issues based on the diverse experiences of group members.

Parent-directed services involving training in positive and nonviolent child management practices are a prevalent form of intervention in this area (Azar & Wolfe, 2006; Chaffin & Schmidt, 2006). Parents are often trained in several skills to help them observe and manage their children's behavior (e.g., monitoring, issuing clear instructions, using attending and ignoring, offering praise, using reinforcement, using time-out and response cost). Interventions that incorporate these parenting procedures have found improved parental skill repertoires and family outcomes (e.g., more prosocial interaction, less conflict), and these gains have often been maintained at follow-up. One program that integrated individualized parent training in child management procedures with parent-child stimulation training found improvements in parental functioning (e.g., child abuse potential, parental depression) and child behavior (e.g., behavior problems), though there was less improvement in quality of family interaction (Wolfe, Edwards, Manion, & Koverola, 1988). Other work suggests benefits to providing exposure to a parenting curriculum in enhancing positive child perceptions and reducing child abuse potential (Fennell & Fishel, 1998).

Other interventions for parents have included cognitive-behavioral treatment (CBT) procedures to address parental anger arousal, misattributions and high expectations, and problem-solving skills, to reduce the likelihood of parental aggression (Mammen, Pilkonis, Kolko, & Groff, 2007). These procedures help to replace negative self-statements with coping self-statements and relaxation skills, and to promote the use of effective communication and problem-solving skills (Acton & During, 1992; Barth, Blythe, Schinke, Stevens, & Schilling, 1983; Egan, 1983; Nuris, Lovell, & Edgar, 1988). These CBT methods have shown additive benefits in reducing anger and aggression to children and in reducing child behavior problems, though most of these data reflect short-term assessments (Acton & During, 1992; Whiteman, Fanshel, & Grundy, 1987). Similarly, diverse methods to promote parental education and support with at-risk parents and their young children—respite, support groups, training in discipline and developmental expectations, parent and child sessions—have led to clinical improvements in parental depression and stress, though not in other areas (social support, child misbehavior [Whipple & Wilson, 1996]).

Most current intervention approaches integrate parent and child components due to the importance of targeting parent and child competencies; thus they reflect parent-child or family-based approaches. Some approaches promote greater integration of interventions for caregivers and children/adolescents. On the website maintained by the NCTSN (www.nctsn.org), four interventions have been described as "family-focused interventions." These interventions meet the following criteria: 1) there is a focus on safety and "stopping the abuse"; 2) they work with child and caregiver/family together; 3) they teach specific skills to reduce distress and promote adaptive behavior; and 4) there is a scientific evaluation of outcomes in physical abuse cases that shows clinical benefits. We briefly describe each of these interventions below.

Alternatives for Families: A Cognitive Behavioral Therapy (AF-CBT)

AF-CBT seeks to reduce caregiver/family risk factors for physically abusive or coercive behavior (verbal/physical aggression and abuse, family conflict) and ameliorate the consequences of these experiences for children ages 5 to 17, at both the individual and family-context levels. AF-CBT incorporates individual CBT methods for parents and children with family-system procedures organized in three phases (Engagement and Psychoeducation, Individual Skill-Building, and Family Applications). The content includes abuse-specific and general skills (e.g., orientation and engagement strategies, psychoeducation about force, affect regulation, cognitive restructuring, positive parenting and nonphysical punishment skills, social skills, abuse clarification, imaginal exposure, family communication problem-solving skills). Sessions allow the caregiver and child to meet individually and jointly. Each of these elements has been associated with improvements in child behavior problems, caregiver abuse risk/behavior, and family conflict/cohesion, and with low recidivism rates at follow-up (Kolko, 1996). It is important to note that between 20 and 23 percent of all children and their parents independently reported high levels of physical discipline/force during the early and late phases of treatment, and heightened parental anger and family problems, suggesting the importance of targeting parent-child coercion and use of force (Kolko, 1996). More recent research indicated the maintenance of AF-CBT methods and long-term benefits through a five-year follow-up (e.g., greater child safety, child well-being, respect for peers, child prognosis [Kolko,

Iselin, & Gully, 2011]). A recent controlled study documented benefits related to staff training in the model (Kolko, Baumann, et al., 2012). In this controlled study, staff training in AF-CBT was compared to routine agency training (usual care). Training was associated with enhanced AF-CBT knowledge and use of AF-CBT abuse-specific and general skills. Other controlled studies that include the main content modules of AF-CBT with nonabused populations have reported benefits in terms of greater service use, completion, and satisfaction, as well as improvement in individual target behavior problems (Kolko, Campo, Kilbourne, & Kelleher, 2012; Kolko, Campo, Kelleher, & Cheng, 2010).

Combined Parent-Child Cognitive Behavioral Therapy (CPC-CBT)

A second CBT-based intervention has integrated individual and group components for parents and their children (Runyon, Deblinger, Ryan, & Thakkar-Kolar, 2004). The intervention includes elements from several treatments, including trauma-focused CBT, AF-CBT, and other methods, and could be especially useful in cases where children report at least some symptoms of PTSD. The focus of treatment is on abuse cases with PTSD symptoms (ages 3 to 17). Treatment involves 16 sessions (16 to 20 weeks) with individual (90 minutes) or group (2 hours). The format includes individual parent and child meetings with clinicians and then joint sessions after these individual sessions. The phases include engagement, skill building, family safety planning, and abuse clarification. Targeted skills are as follows: engagement strategies/motivational interviewing, psychoeducation, positive coping skills in parents and children, family communication skills and positive parenting skills, family safety planning, and abuse clarification process. Anecdotal evidence suggests some initial improvements among families who have participated in this program. Runyon et al. (2009) conducted a pilot study (pre-post data) for children and parents after group sessions. Outcomes included reductions in child PTSD, less physical punishment and parental anger, and fewer child behavior problems. A later controlled study by Runyon et al. (2010) compared the full CPC-CBT program to just parent CBT (without the child). CPC-CBT had greater gains in children's PTSD and positive parenting skills (maintained at three-month follow-up), whereas the parent CBT only had a greater reduction in parental use of physical punishment.

Multisystemic Therapy for Child Abuse and Neglect (MST-CAN)

Additional multicomponent clinical interventions have targeted diverse individual, family, and systemic problems in the home and community. For example, multisystemic therapy (MST) targets problems in the child, parent, family, and social systems (e.g., peer training, child management, family communication) following an individualized family assessment and in accord with a set of treatment principles (e.g., ecologically based, individualized, intensive). An early study found that MST was associated with improved parent-child relationships (parental efforts to control child, child compliance), whereas parent training was more effective in reducing identified social problems (Brunk, Henggeler, & Whelan, 1987).

A more recent trial by Swenson et al. (2010) focused on aggression and violence in school-age children and adolescents. Treatment was six to nine months in duration and was comprehensive, home-based, and tailored to family needs. MST follows nine principles (e.g., family is major agent for changing youth behavior, functional-assessment driven) in its effort to teach diverse skills (e.g., address risk factors across child, parent, parenting, family, and social network; family safety plan; functional analysis of the use of force or physical discipline; treatment for anger management; treatment for trauma/PTSD and substance abuse; family communication training; clarification of abuse). Swenson et al. (2010) found that MST-CAN compared to enhanced outpatient treatment had post-baseline gains (e.g., youth showed greater reductions in internalizing symptoms, total behavior problems, and PTSD symptoms; caregivers showed greater reductions in psychiatric distress and greater increases in social support; parenting outcomes included fewer reductions in appropriate discipline; youth experienced less re-abuse). MST has a long history of successful efficacy trials with behaviorally dysfunctional adolescents (e.g., Brunk et al., 1987).

Parent-Child Interaction Therapy (PCIT)

Parent-child interaction therapy (PCIT) has been adapted for use with physical abuse based on its long history of application to the treatment of behavior problems (Eisenstadt, Eyberg, McNeil, Newcomb, & Funderburk, 1993; Herschell & McNeil, 2005). PCIT addresses issues related to harsh or ineffective parental discipline and heightened behavioral dysfunction in children by providing parents with opportunities to develop more positive relationships with their children and to learn appropriate parenting techniques through ongoing coaching efforts during observed interactions. The focus of PCIT is generally on preschool and young school-age children (ages 2.5 to 7 years). It uses a two-stage approach conducted over 12 to 20 sessions. In phase one, the child-directed interaction (CDI) aims to restructure the parent-child relationship and provide the child with a secure attachment to the caregiver. In phase two, the parent-directed interaction (PDI) aims to increase child behavior management skills. The parent is coached in several behavioral skills (praise, reflection, imitation, description, and enjoyment, or PRIDE). The skills are observed and coached through a one-way mirror during the sessions. Parents are provided with immediate feedback about progress and are given homework to complete. The skills are gradually expanded from structured implementation in treatment sessions to structured sessions in the home to more unstructured situations and then to use in public situations.

Outcome evidence in a study of abused children and their caregivers showed that PCIT was associated with lower recidivism rates than a condition consisting of both PCIT and supplemental family services or a condition involving routine parenting classes conducted in the community (Chaffin et al., 2004). In that trial, Chaffin et al. (2004) found key improvements for PCIT, showing fewer negative parent behaviors. All conditions helped to increase positive parent behaviors. The inclusion of additional services did not improve the efficacy of PCIT. Other evidence shows pre-post benefits of PCIT with maltreated children (see Timmer, Urquiza, Zebell, & McGrath, 2005), such as reduced problem behavior and increased compliance. More recently, Chaffin et al. (2011) found that self-motivation and PCIT combined was even effective in reducing child welfare reports. PCIT has extensive support for efficacy with child behavior problems in young children (see Eyberg, Nelson, & Boggs, 2008), including decreased behavior problems, increased parent skill and decreased parent stress, high satisfaction, and the maintenance of gains. PCIT is noteworthy for its attention to various stages in the treatment process, ranging from assessment and the training of behavioral play skills to the training of discipline skills and use of booster sessions.

While most of the aforementioned treatments are administered in clinic settings (i.e., AF-CBT, CPC-CBT, PCIT), other interventions have been applied in the home on an intensive basis, and directed towards multiple family participants (Corcoran, 2000). Such ecologically based and family-centered services generally have targeted contextual risk factors associated with abuse, specific skills deficits, and/or personal competencies.

For example, intensive family-based reunification services (versus routine reunification services) have been found to improve reunification rates, possibly due to the provision of in vivo services and training in CBT skills (e.g., problem-solving, communication). Evidence on family preservation and support programs, however, did not support their effectiveness in preventing future child maltreatment cases (Chaffin, Bonner, & Hill, 2001; Fraser, Walton, Lewis, Pecora, & Walton, 1996; Walton, Fraser, Lewis, & Pecora, 1993).

It is worth mentioning that other treatments have been developed to address PTSD or related symptoms in children or adolescents exposed to traumatic events, including sexual or physical abuse, family or community violence, loss and grief, and natural disasters, among others. These approaches include child-parent psychotherapy (CPP) for young children exposed to domestic violence and their caregivers (Lieberman & Van Horn, 2008); trauma-focused cognitive behavior therapy (TF-CBT [Cohen, Deblinger, & Mannarino, 2006]), which has reported reductions in behavior problems in traumatized children following exposure to key methods (e.g., trauma narrative, psychoeducation, relaxation, promoting child safety and support); and cognitive behavioral intervention for trauma in schools (CBITS), which has been applied on a group basis in schools and been found to reduce PTSD symptoms in adolescents exposed to violence (Stein et al., 2003).

Interventions that were developed outside of the United States also merit discussion. In 1995, the Children's Mental Health Alliance and the Open Society Institute began a program to address the lack of recognition of the problems of child abuse and neglect. At the time there were no effective laws in place to deal with this issue. The program includes training mental health professionals to deal with child abuse and neglect. The program also fostered the development of multidisciplinary nongovernmental organizations that focus specifically on child abuse. This program raises awareness of the problem, and since it began, nongovernmental organizations have been established in 11 countries (Lewis et al., 2004).

Recent years have shown the emergence of attempted reform measures to deal with child abuse in some of these countries. Japan's Child Abuse Prevention Act, originally enacted in 2000 and subject to several amendments, explicitly defines different forms of abuse, helping to separate parental discipline from excessive abusive behaviors (Hiramaya, 2013). Further revisions provide courts and guidance centers with the means to intervene, allowing courts to call for searches of family homes should parents not respond when summoned to attend a guidance center (Hiramaya, 2013).

However, the act does not address intervention measures, as very few programs offer instruction on re-education of parents and reintroduction of children (Hiramaya, 2013). Abuse continues throughout Japan, due to government inaction and interfamily abuse. The widely held cultural myth that "law should not intrude in the private sphere" (Hiramaya, 2013) unfortunately rings true for Japan, as millions of children remain victims of abusive behavior. Such a custom draws a sharp contrast between the United States, where numerous programs, AF-CBT among them, work to improve family interaction through therapy, and Japan, where the maintenance of cultural norms allows abuse to continue. If Japan hopes to deal with child physical abuse, the change must happen not at the governmental but at the familial level: "Changing the law is one thing. Changing culture and social traditions is quite another" (Magnier, 2002).

Japan's plight exemplifies the struggle to curb abuse on a national level. The Daphne III Project, on the other hand, seeks to confront the issue of child physical abuse on a global scale. Comprising five European countries, Germany, Hungary, Portugal, Sweden, and the Netherlands, the Daphne III Project represents another major step in the right direction. A two-year (2011–2012) project designed to focus on the prevention and treatment of child physical abuse, the end result was the creation of a manual of successful treatment and prevention strategies (Mak & Steketee, 2012). The main findings of the project offer advice on the professional, treatment, institutional, care system, and societal levels; it is an extremely comprehensive guide seeking to regulate an issue filled with local differences and legal complications. Emphasizing the empowerment of the family brought about by specialized professionals, and offering multidisciplinary, varied treatment options for different families while calling for adults from all walks of life to have a deep understanding of abuse in the hopes of identifying and preventing abuse, the Daphne III Project takes great strides towards providing millions of people with a fully formed definition of abuse and hopefully preventing future cases (Mak & Steketee, 2012). Such a project, though still in its infancy, may not yield specific results at this point in time, but simply the creation of a manual containing policies and strategies with ties to American intervention programs like AF-CBT indicates that countries are working together to put an end to child physical abuse.

Such findings provide additional, albeit qualified, support for the continued development of individual, group, and family treatments involving child victims of physical abuse. Additionally, it seems necessary to address caregivers' parenting practices in order to develop a more effective disciplinary repertoire. Also, integrated interventions that can adequately target the broad clinical features of abused children and their parents/families might help to improve positive outcomes. In terms of clinical approaches, most interventions have applied cognitive-behavioral treatment (CBT) and skills training procedures to specific competencies and clinical problems (Kolko, 2002). This general focus is consistent with the four suggested CBT strategies recommended for the treatment of traumatized children and their parents: exposure to the traumatic event, stress management and coping skills training, exploration, and correction of cognitive distortions related to the traumatic event, and interventions with parents (Cohen et al., 2006). There are several potential targets for parents (e.g., negative child perceptions, developmentally appropriate expectations, self-control, affect or stress management, positive discipline, social support) and children (e.g., anger identification and control, relaxation, social skills, peer play activities, misattributions, academic competencies, problem solving).

Providing treatment in the natural environment can be beneficial, but successful treatment also has been conducted in clinic settings where safety and comfort can be provided. Setting type must be determined based on both program and parent input, but can be influenced by the varying needs of the population found in different geographic regions such as rural areas (Paul, Gray, Elhai, Massard, & Stamm, 2006). There also may be times when a family needs different services, such as crisis intervention or concrete or support services (e.g., Homebuilders [Whittaker, Kinney, Tracy, & Booth, 1990]). Because intervention studies have shown mixed evidence for the maintenance of treatment gains, an examination of therapeutic methods that promote greater scope and stability of improvements seems warranted (e.g., "check-ups," service calls [Wesch & Lutzker, 1991; Wolfe et al., 1988]). Much work still needs to be done to promote the development, application, and evaluation of psychosocial interventions designed to modify both the sequelae of an abusive experience and the risk of re-abuse (Chaffin & Schmidt, 2006).

PREVENTION

The available literature on primary prevention highlights a number of alternative programs and activities (Klevens & Whitaker, 2007; Krugman, Lane, & Walsh, 2007). Numerous prevention programs have been directed towards reducing a variety of risk factors for abuse (see Patno, 2011). Klevens and Whitaker conducted a literature review that identified the types of risk factors that were targeted (e.g., individual, family, community) and whether or not the program was evaluated (2007). One-half of the programs were delivered in the home or community, with some programs conducted in hospitals and schools. One-third of the programs targeted three or more risk factors, which were highly diverse (poor early bonding, knowledge of child abuse, lack of child care, harsh discipline, poverty, unemployment). However, only one-fourth of these programs included a rigorous evaluation. On the positive side, programs targeting certain risk factors did report some reduction in abusive behavior (e.g., low education, unwanted pregnancy, poor bonding, expectations, substance abuse, dysphoria, poor parenting, stress, isolation). Some worthy risk factors were generally ignored and deserve further attention in prevention programs, such as social norms regarding physical discipline, poverty, partner violence, and the young age of parents. Each of these factors could be addressed, at least to some extent, in anticipatory guidance of other brief encounters within the primary care setting.

One of the more commonly evaluated approaches involves home visitation to new parents. An early version of this approach involved establishing nurse-family partnerships in which visiting nurses provided educational information, support, some counseling, and referral information over a lengthy time period. Controlled studies showed beneficial maternal and child outcomes, which have been extended to follow-ups of between 4 and 15 years. Positive outcomes included reduced rates of child maltreatment (Olds et al., 2002). Interestingly, use of paraprofessionals was associated with about one-half of the benefits obtained using nurses as home visitors. Indeed, several home visiting programs that rely upon paraprofessionals have been conducted. The effects of these programs have been limited to short-term benefits in self-reported clinical problems or abusive behavior, but no significant improvements in reducing official child abuse reports (Krugman et al., 2007). It also bears mentioning that mixed evidence has sometimes been found using public health nurses (MacMillan et al., 2005).

Parent training programs have also been used to address parental comfort with and competence in parenting skills (Sanders, Cann, & Markie-Dadds, 2003). Such programs often address parenting skills training and parental coping, and may include alternative teaching methods (e.g., seminars) and targets (e.g., stress management). Evidence suggests improvements in attitudes and emotional well-being, but there is only minimal evidence regarding the prevention of child maltreatment. The importance of targeting these types of skills is supported by a recent study in which mothers of three-year-olds were interviewed about disciplinary situations that elicited their strongest reactions, including a situation in which physical punishment occurred (Ateah & Durrant, 2005). The predictors of physical punishment were found to be maternal attitudes towards physical punishment, maternal perception of the seriousness and intent of the child's misbehavior, and maternal anger in response to the child's misbehavior. Such findings highlight the potential benefit of targeting mothers' cognitive and affective repertoires in reducing the decision to use physical punishment.

SUMMARY

This chapter provides a summary of recent research and policies related to child physical abuse and highlights what has been learned about the characteristics of abusers, known risk factors for abuse or victimization, the consequences for or effects on victims, societal influences that influence CPA, and possible intervention and prevention programs. Much of this literature has identified key caregiver and victim characteristics, as well as important consequences on the family. To address these consequences, we have reported on outcome studies that provide empirical support for the utility of specific interventions that address caregiver coercion/abusive behavior, child externalizing and internalizing problems, and family conflict. Of course, continued research is needed that includes diverse cultural groups and work settings, larger and more rigorous clinical trials, and more work in the area of prevention. Developments are needed to enhance the clinical applicability of these interventions, promote community access and training availability, and expand the range of empirical evaluations of their outcomes and cost effectiveness. Such advances may facilitate more widespread implantation of effective assessment and intervention strategies that have the potential to reduce the prevalence and impact of children's exposure to aggressive and possibly abusive behaviors in their homes and neighborhoods across the globe.

ACKNOWLEDGMENT

Preparation of this chapter was supported, in part, by grants from the NIMH (074737) and SAMHSA (SM54319).

REFERENCES

Acton, R. G., & During, S. M. (1992). Preliminary results of aggression management training for aggressive parents. *Journal of Interpersonal Violence, 7,* 410–417.

Annerbäck, E. M., Wingren, G., Svedin, C. G., & Gustafsson, P. A. (2010). Prevalence and characteristics of child physical abuse in Sweden—findings from a population-based youth survey. *Acta Paediatrica, 99*(8), 1229–1236.

Appel, A. E., & Holden, G. W. (1998). The occurrence of spouse and physical child abuse: A review and appraisal. *Journal of Family Psychology, 12,* 578–599.

Ateah, C. A., & Durrant, J. E. (2005). Maternal use of physical punishment in response to child misbehavior: Implications for child abuse prevention. *Child Abuse and Neglect, 29*(2), 169–185.

Azar, S. T., & Wolfe, D. A. (2006). Child physical abuse and neglect. In E. J. Mash & R. A. Barkley (Eds.), *Treatment of childhood disorders* (3rd ed.), (pp. 595–646). New York, NY: Guilford Press.

Barlow, J., Johnston, I., Kendrick, D., Polnay, L., & Stewart-Brown, S. (2006). Individual and group-based parenting programmes for the treatment of physical child abuse and neglect. *Cochrane Database of Systematic Reviews, 3,* CD005463.

Barth, R. P., Blythe, B. J., Schinke, S. P., Stevens, P., & Schilling, R. F. (1983). Self-control training with maltreating parents. *Child Welfare, 62*(4), 313–324.

Belsky, J., & Vondra, J. (1989). Lessons from child abuse: The determinants of parenting. In C. D. Cicchetti & V. Carlson (Eds.), *Child maltreatment: Theory and research on the causes and consequences of child abuse and neglect* (pp. 153–202). New York, NY: Cambridge University Press.

Brown, J., Cohen, P., Johnson, J. G., & Salzinger, S. (1998). A longitudinal analysis of risk factors for child maltreatment: Findings of a 17-year prospective study of officially recorded and self-reported child abuse and neglect. *Child Abuse & Neglect, 22,* 1065–1978.

Brunk, M., Henggeler, S. W., & Whelan, J. P. (1987). Comparison of multisystemic therapy and parent training in the brief treatment of child abuse and neglect. *Journal of Consulting and Clinical Psychology, 55,* 171–178.

Bugental, D. B., Mantyla, S. M., & Lewis, J. (1989). Parental attributions as moderators of affective communication to children at risk for physical abuse. In D. Cicchetti & V. Carlson (Eds.), *Child maltreatment: Theory and research on the causes and consequences of child abuse and neglect* (pp. 254–279). New York, NY: Cambridge University Press.

Bugental, D. B., & Shennum, W. (2002). Gender, power, and violence in the family. *Child Maltreatment, 7*(1), 56–64.

Cadzow, S. P., Armstrong, K. L., & Fraser, J. A. (1999). Stressed parents with infants: Reassessing physical abuse risk factors. *Child Abuse & Neglect, 23*(9), 845–853.

Caliso, J. A., & Milner, J. S. (1992). Childhood history of abuse and child abuse screening. *Child Abuse & Neglect, 16*, 647–659.

Cappa, C., & Khan, S. M. (2001). Understanding caregivers' attitudes towards physical punishment of children: Evidence from 34 low- and middle-income countries. *Child Abuse & Neglect, 35*, 1009–1021.

Central Intelligence Agency. (2012). The World Factbook. Retrieved from https://www.cia.gov/library/publications/download/download-2012/index.html

Chaffin, M., Bonner, B. L., & Hill, R. F. (2001). Family preservation and family support programs: Child maltreatment outcomes across client risk levels and program types. *Child Abuse & Neglect, 25*(10), 1269–1289.

Chaffin, M., Funderburk, B., Bard, D., Valle, L. A., & Gurwitch, R. (2011). A combined motivation and parent-child interaction therapy package reduces child welfare recidivism in a randomized dismantling field trial. *Journal of Consulting and Clinical Psychology, 79*(1), 84–95.

Chaffin, M., & Schmidt, S. (2006). An evidence-based perspective on interventions to stop or prevent child abuse. In J. R. Lutzker (Ed.), *Preventing violence: Research and evidence-based intervention strategies* (pp. 49–68). Washington, DC: American Psychological Association.

Chaffin, M., Silovsky, J. F., Funderburk, B., Valle, L. A., Brestan, E. V., & Balachova, T. (2004). Parent-Child Interaction Therapy with physically abusive parents: Efficacy for reducing future abuse reports. *Journal of Consulting .& Clinical Psychology, 72*(3), 500–510.

Child Welfare Information Gateway. (2008). *What is child abuse and neglect?* (Factsheet April 2008). Washington, DC. Retrieved from www.childwelfare.gov/pubs/factsheets/whatiscan.cfm

Child Welfare Information Gateway. (2011). *Definitions of child abuse and neglect.* Washington, DC.

CHILDLINE 1098. (2013). *Abuse & violence.* Retrieved from http://www.childlineindia.org.in/child-abuse-child-violence-india

Children's Rainbow Center. (2012). *The child abuse prevention law.* Retrieved from http://www.crc-japan.net/english/contents/law/index.html

ChildSafe International. (2007). *Child abuse & dangers for children worldwide.* Retrieved from http://www.childsafe-international.org/PhysicalAbuse.asp

Claussen, A. H. & Crittenden, P. M. (1991). Physical and psychological maltreatment: Relations among types of maltreatment. *Child Abuse and Neglect, 15*, 5–18.

Cohen, J. A., Deblinger, E., & Mannarino, A. P. (Eds.). (2006). *Treating trauma and traumatic grief in children and adolescents.* New York, NY: Guilford Press.

Corcoran, J. (2000). Family interventions with child physical abuse and neglect: A critical review. *Children and Youth Services Review, 22*(7), 563–591.

Culp, R. E., Heide, J. S., & Richardson, M. T. (1987). Maltreated children's developmental scores: Treatment versus nontreatment. *Child Abuse & Neglect, 11*, 29–34.

Culp, R. E., Little, V., Letts, D., & Lawrence, H. (1991). Maltreated children's self-concept: Effects of a comprehensive treatment program. *American Journal of Orthopsychiatry, 61,* 114–121.

Egan, K. J. (1983). Stress management and child management with abusive parents. *Journal of Clinical Child Psychology, 12,* 292–299.

Egeland, B., Yates, T., Appleyard, K., & van Dulmen, M. (2002). The long-term consequences of maltreatment in the early years: A developmental pathway model to antisocial behavior. *Children's Services: Social Policy, Research, & Practice, 5,* 249–260.

Eisenstadt, T. H., Eyberg, S. M., McNeil, C. B., Newcomb, K., & Funderburk, B. (1993). Parent-child interaction therapy with behavior problem children: Relative effectiveness of two stages and overall treatment outcome. *Journal of Clinical Child Psychology, 22*(1), 42–51.

Eyberg, S. M., Nelson, M. M., & Boggs, S. R. (2008). Evidence-based psychosocial treatments for children and adolescents with disruptive behavior. *Journal of Clinical Child and Adolescent Psychology, 37,* 215–237.

Famularo, R., Fenton, T., Augustyn, M., & Zuckerman, B. (1996). Persistence of pediatric post traumatic stress disorder after 2 years. *Child Abuse and Neglect, 20*(12), 1245–1248.

Famularo, R., Fenton, T., Kinscherff, R., Ayoub, C., & Barnum, R. (1994). Maternal and child posttraumatic stress disorder in cases of child maltreatment. *Child Abuse and Neglect, 18*(1), 27–36.

Fantuzzo, J. W., Jurecic, L., Stovall, A., Hightower, A. D., Goins, C., & Schachtel, D. (1988). Effects of adult and peer social initiations on the social behavior of withdrawn, maltreated preschool children. *Journal of Consulting & Clinical Psychology, 56*(1), 34–39.

Fantuzzo, J. W., Stovall, A., Schachtel, D., Goins, C., & Hall, R. (1987). The effects of peer social initiations on the social behavior of withdrawn maltreated preschool children. *Journal of Behavior Therapy and Experimental Psychiatry, 18,* 357–363.

Fantuzzo, J. W., Sutton-Smith, B., Atkins, M., Meyers, R., Stevenson, H., Coolahan, K. (1996). Community-based resilient peer treatment of withdrawn maltreated preschool children. *Journal of Consulting and Clinical Psychology, 64*(6), 1377–1386.

Fennell, D. C., & Fishel, A. H. (1998). Parent education: An evaluation of STEP on abusive parents' perceptions and abuse potential. *Journal of Child & Adolescent Psychiatric Nursing, 11*(3), 107–120.

FindTheData.org. (2012). How much money was spent on child abuse prevention and treatment grants federal government program? Retrieved from http://federal-government-ratings.findthedata.org/q/342/1919/How-much-money-was-spent-on-Child-Abuse-Prevention-and-Treatment-Grants-federal-government-program

Finkelhor, D., Ormrod, R., Turner, H., & Hamby, S. L. (2005). The victimization of children and youth: A comprehensive national survey. *Child Maltreatment, 10,* 5–25.

Flores, E., Cicchetti, D., & Rogosch, F. A. (2005). Predictors of resilience in maltreated and nonmaltreated Latino children. *Developmental Psychology, 41*(2), 338–351.

Fogarty, C. T., Fredman, L., Heeren, T. C., & Liebschutz, J. (2008). Synergistic effects of child abuse and intimate partner violence on depressive symptoms in women. *Preventive Medicine, 46*(5), 463–469.

Ford, J. D., Racusin, R., Daviss, W. B., Ellis, C., Thomas, J., & Rogers, K. (1999). Trauma exposure among children with oppositional defiant disorder and attention deficit-hyperactivity disorder. *Journal of Consulting & Clinical Psychology, 67,* 786–789.

Fraser, M. W., Walton, E., Lewis, R. E., Pecora, P. J., & Walton, W. K. (1996). An experiment in family reunification: Correlates of outcomes at one-year follow-up. *Children and Youth Services Review, 18*(4–5), 335–361.

Gelles, R. J., & Straus, M. A. (1987). Is violence toward children increasing? A comparison of 1975 and 1985 National Survey rates. *Journal of Interpersonal Violence, 2,* 212–222.

Gilbert, R., Widom, C. S., Browne, K., Fergusson, D., Webb, E., & Janson, S. (2009). Child maltreatment 1: Burden and consequences of child maltreatment in high-income countries. *Lancet, 373*(9657), 68–81.

Grogan-Kaylor, A. (2005). Relationship of corporal punishment and antisocial behavior by neighborhood. *Archives of Pediatrics & Adolescent Medicine, 159,* 938–942.

Hawkins, A. O., Danielson, C. K., de Arellano, M. A., Hanson, R. F., Ruggiero, K. J., & Smith, D. W. (2010). Ethnic/racial differences in the prevalence of injurious spanking and other child physical abuse in a national survey of adolescents. *Child Maltreatment, 15*(3), 242–249. doi:10.1177/1077559510367938

Henry, B. M., Ueda, R., Shinjo, M., & Yoshikawa, C. (2003). Health education for nurses in Japan to combat child abuse. *Nursing & Health Sciences, 5*(3), 199–206.

Herrenkohl, R. C., Herrenkohl, E. C., & Egolf, B. P. (1983). Circumstances surrounding the occurrence of child maltreatment. *Journal of Consulting and Clinical Psychology, 51,* 424–431.

Herschell, A. D., & McNeil, C. B. (2005). Theoretical and empirical underpinnings of Parent-Child Interaction Therapy with child physical abuse populations. *Education and Treatment of Children, 28*(2), 142–162.

Hiramaya, M. (2013). Child protection in Asia. In J. Liu, B. Hebenton, & S. Jou (Eds.), *Handbook of Asian Criminology* (pp. 359–366). New York, NY: Springer-Verlag.

Kayama, M., Sagami, A., Watanabe, Y., Senoo, E., & Ohara, M. (2004). Child abuse prevention in Japan: An approach to screening and intervention with mothers. *Public Health Nursing, 21*(6), 513–518.

Kelly, M. L., Grace, N., & Elliot, S. N. (1990). Acceptability of positive and punitive discipline methods: Comparisons among abusive, potentially abusive, and
nonabusive parents. *Child Abuse & Neglect, 14,* 219–226.

Kitamura, T., Kijima, N., Iwata, N., Senda, Y., Takahashi, K., & Hayashi, I. (1999).
Frequencies of child abuse in Japan: Hidden but prevalent crime. *International
Journal of Offender Therapy and Comparative Criminology, 43*(1), 21–33.

Klevens, J., & Whitaker, D. J. (2007). Primary prevention of child physical abuse and
neglect: Gaps and promising directions. *Child Maltreatment, 12*(4), 364–377.

Kolko, D. J. (1996). Individual cognitive-behavioral treatment and family therapy
for physically abused children and their offending parents: A comparison of
clinical outcomes. *Child Maltreatment, 1,* 322–342.

Kolko, D. J. (2002). Child physical abuse. In J. E. B. Myers, L. Berliner, J. Briere,
C. T. Hendrix, C. Jenny & T. Reid (Eds.), *APSAC handbook of child maltreatment* (2nd ed.) (pp. 21–54). Thousand Oaks, CA: Sage.

Kolko, D. J., Baumann, B. L., Herschell, A. D., Hart, J. A., Holden, E. A., &
Wisniewski, S. R. (2012). Implementation of AF-CBT by community prac-
titioners serving child welfare and mental health: A randomized trial. *Child
Maltreatment, 17*(1), 30–44. doi:10.1177/1077559511427346

Kolko, D. J., Brown, E. J., & Berliner, L. (2002). Children's perceptions of their
abusive experience: Measurement and preliminary findings. *Child Maltreatment, 7*(1), 42–55.

Kolko, D. J., Campo, J. V., Kelleher, K., & Cheng, Y. (2010). Improving access
to care and clinical outcome for pediatric behavioral problems: A randomized trial of a nurse-administered intervention in primary care. *Journal of
Developmental & Behavioral Pediatrics, 31*(5), 393–404. doi:10.1097/
DBP.0b013e3181dff307

Kolko, D. J., Campo, J. V., Kilbourne, A. M., & Kelleher, K. (2012). Doctor-office
collaborative care for pediatric behavioral problems. *Archives of Pediatrics &
Adolescent Medicine, 166*(3), 224–231. doi:10.1001/archpediatrics.2011.201

Kolko, D. J., Iselin, A. M., & Gully, K. J. (2011). Evaluation of the sustainability and clinical outcome of Alternatives for Families: Cognitive-Behavioral
Therapy (AF-CBT) in a child protection center. *Child Abuse & Neglect, 35*(2),
105–116. doi:10.1016/j.chiabu.2010.09.004

Kolko, D. J., & Kolko, R. P. (2010). Psychological impact and treatment of child
physical abuse. In C. Jenny (Ed.), *Child abuse and neglect: Diagnosis, treatment and evidence* (pp. 476–489). New York, NY: Elsevier, Inc.

Krugman, S. D., Lane, W. G., & Walsh, C. M. (2007). Update on child abuse prevention. *Current Opinion in Pediatrics, 19,* 711–718.

Leventhal, J. M., Martin, K. D., & Gaither, J. R. (2012). Using US data to estimate the incidence of serious physical abuse in children. *Pediatrics, 129*(3),
458–464.

Lewis, O., Sergen, J., Chaffin, M., Friedrich, W. N., Cunningham, N., & Cantor, P.
(2004). Progress report on the development of abuse prevention, identification,

and treatment systems in Eastern Europe. *Child Abuse & Neglect, 28*(1), 93–111.

Lieberman, A. F., & Van Horn, P. (2008). *Psychotherapy with infants and young children: Repairing the effects of stress and trauma on early attachment.* New York, NY: Guilford Press.

Lung, C. T., & Daro, D. (1996). Current trends in child abuse reporting and fatalities: The results of the 1995 annual fifty state survey. Chicago, IL: National Committee to Prevent Child Abuse.

Macmillan, H. L., Tanaka, M., Duku, E., Vaillancourt, T., & Boyle, M. H. (1997). Child physical and sexual abuse in a community sample of young adults: Results from the Ontario Child Health Study. *Journal of the American Medical Association, 278*(2), 131–135.

MacMillan, H. L., Thomas, B. H., Jamieson, E., Walsh, C. A., Boyle, M. H., & Shannon, H. S. (2005). Effectiveness of home visitation by public-health nurses in prevention of the recurrence of child physical abuse and neglect: A randomised controlled trial. *Lancet, 365,* 1786–1793.

Magnier, M. (2002). Battery behind the Shoji screen, *The Los Angeles Times.* Retrieved from http://articles.latimes.com

Mak, J., & Steketee, M. (2012). *Prevent and combat child abuse and neglect.* Retrieved from http://www.verwey-jonker.nl/doc/jeugd/International-Prevent-and-Combat-Child-Abuse-and-Neglect7254.pdf

Mammen, O. K., Pilkonis, P. A., Kolko, D. J., & Groff, A. (2007). Anger and anger attacks as precipitants of aggression: What we can learn from child physical abuse. In T. A. Cavell & K. T. Malcolm (eds.), *Anger, aggression and interventions for interpersonal violence* (pp. 283–311). Mahwah, NJ: Lawrence Erlbaum.

Milner, J. S. (1998). Individual and family characteristics associated with intrafamilial child physical and sexual abuse. In P. K. Trickett & C. J. Schellenbach (Eds.), *Violence against children in the family and the community* (pp. 141–170). Washington, DC: American Psychological Association.

Mollerstrom, W. W., Patchner, M. A., & Milner, J. S. (1992). Family functioning and child abuse potential. *Journal of Clinical Psychology, 48,* 445–454.

Mulvaney, M. K., & Mebert, C. J. (2007). Parental corporal punishment predicts behavior problems in early childhood. *Journal of Family Psychology, 21*(3), 389–397.

National Institutes of Health. (2012, March 22). Estimates of funding for various research, condition, and disease categories. Retrieved from http://report.nih.gov/rcdc/categories/

National Society for the Prevention of Cruelty to Children. (2010). *The definitions and signs of child abuse.* London, UK: NSPCC.

National Society for the Prevention of Cruelty to Children. (2011). *Constitution and governance of the NSPCC.* Retrieved from http://www.nspcc.org.uk/what

-we-do/about-the-nspcc/how-nspcc-is-organised/constitution/constitution
_wda72246.html

Nuris, P. S., Lovell, M., & Edgar, M. (1988). Self-appraisals of abusive parents: A contextual approach to study and treatment. *Journal of Interpersonal Violence, 3,* 458–467.

Oates, R. K., & Bross, D. C. (1995). What have we learned about treating child physical abuse? A literature review of the last decade. *Child Abuse & Neglect, 19,* 463–473.

Olds, D. L., Robinson, J., O'Brien, R., Luckey, D. W., Pettitt, L. M., & Henderson, C. R., Jr. (2002). Home visiting by paraprofessionals and by nurses: A randomized controlled trial. *Pediatrics, 110,* 486–496.

Patno, K. (2011). The prevention of child abuse and neglect. In C. Jenny (Ed.), *Child abuse and neglect: Diagnosis, treatment, and evidence* (pp. 605–609). St. Louis, MO: Elsevier Saunders.

Paul, L. A., Gray, M. J., Elhai, J. D., Massard, P. M., & Stamm, B. H. (2006). Promotion of evidence-based practices for child traumatic stress in rural populations: Identification of barriers and promising solutions. *Trauma Violence and Abuse, 7*(4), 260–273.

Pianta, R., Egeland, B., & Erickson, M. F. (1989). The antecedents of maltreatment: Results of the mother-child interaction research project. In D. Cicchetti & V. Carlson (Eds.), *Child maltreatment: Theory and research on the causes and consequences of child abuse and neglect* (pp. 203–253). New York, NY: Cambridge University Press.

Ponce, A. N., Williams, M. K., & Allen, G. J. (2004). Experience of maltreatment as a child and acceptance of violence in adult intimate relationships: Mediating effects of distortions in cognitive schemas. *Violence and Victims, 19*(1), 97–108.

Runyon, M. K., Deblinger, E., Ryan, E. E., & Thakkar-Kolar, R. (2004). An overview of child physical abuse: Developing an integrated parent-child cognitive-behavioral treatment approach. *Trauma Violence & Abuse, 5*(1), 65–85.

Runyon, M. K., Deblinger, E., & Schroeder, C. M. (2009). Pilot evaluation of outcomes of combined parent-child cognitive-behavioral group therapy for families at risk for child physical abuse. *Cognitive and Behavioral Practice, 16,* 101–118.

Runyon, M. K., Deblinger, E., & Steer, R. A. (2010). Group cognitive behavioral treatment for parents and children at risk for physical abuse: An initial study. *Child & Family Behavior Therapy, 32,* 196–218.

Sanders, M. R., Cann, W., & Markie-Dadds, C. (2003). The Triple-P Positive Parenting Programme: A universal population-level approach to the prevention of child abuse. *Child Abuse Review, 12,* 155–171.

Sankey, C. C., Elmer, E., Halechko, A. D., & Schulberg, P. (1985). The development of abused and high-risk infants in different treatment modalities: Residential versus in-home care. *Child Abuse and Neglect, 9,* 237–243.

Shackman, J. E., Shackman, A. J., & Pollak, S. D. (2007). Physical abuse amplifies attention to threat and increases anxiety in children. *Emotion, 7*(4), 838–852.

Simons, R. L., Whitbeck, L. B., Conger, R. D., & Wu, C. (1991). Intergenerational transmission of harsh parenting. *Developmental Psychology, 27,* 159–171.

Stein, B. D., Jaycox, L. H., Kataoka, S. H., Wong, M., Tu, W., & Elliott, M. N. (2003). A mental health intervention for schoolchildren exposed to violence: A randomized controlled trial. *Journal of the American Medical Association, 290*(5), 603–611.

Steiner, H. (1997). Practice parameters for the assessment and treatment of children and adolescents with conduct disorder. *Journal of the American Academy of Child & Adolescent Psychiatry, 36,* 122S–139S.

Stith, S. M., Liu, T., Davies, L. C., Boykin, E. L., Alder, M. C., & Harris, J. M. (2009). Risk factors in child maltreatment: A meta-analytic review of the literature. *Aggression and Violent Behavior, 14*(1), 13–29. doi:10.1016/j.avb.2006.03.006

Straus, M. A. (1994). *Beating the devil out of them: Corporal punishment in American families.* Lexington, MA: Lexington Books.

Straus, M. A., Gelles, R. J., & Steinmetz, S. K. (1980). *Behind closed doors.* New York, NY: Doubleday.

Sullivan, P. M., & Knutson, J. F. (1998). The association between child maltreatment and disabilities in a hospital-based epidemiological study. *Child Abuse and Neglect, 22*(4), 271–288.

Swenson, C. C., & Brown, E. J. (1999). Cognitive behavioral group treatment for physically abused children. *Cognitive & Behavioral Practice, 6*(3), 212–220.

Swenson, C. C., Schaeffer, C. M., Henggeler, S. W., Faldowski, R., & Mayhew, A. M. (2010). Multisystemic Therapy for child abuse and neglect: A randomized effectiveness trial. *Journal of Family Psychology, 24*(4), 497–507.

Timmer, S. G., Urquiza, A. J., Zebell, N. M., & McGrath, J. M. (2005). Parent-Child Interaction Therapy: Application to maltreating parent-child dyads. *Child Abuse & Neglect, 29*(7), 825–842.

Trickett, P. K., Aber, J. L., Carlson, V., & Cicchetti, D. (1991). Relationship of socioeconomic status to the etiology and developmental sequelae of physical child abuse. *Developmental Psychology, 27,* 148–158.

UNICEF. (2005, 1 September). Convention on the Rights of the Child. GE.05-43805 (E) 140905. from http://www.unicef.org/protection/files/CRCGC6_EN.pdf

U.S. Department of Health and Human Services, Administration for Children and Families, Administration on Children, Youth and Families; & Children's Bureau. (2011). *Child Maltreatment 2010.*

Walton, E., Fraser, M. W., Lewis, R. E., & Pecora, P. J. (1993). In-home family-focused reunification: An experimental study. *Child Welfare, 72*(5), 473–487.

Webster-Stratton, C. (1985). Comparison of abusive and nonabusive families with conduct-disordered children. *American Journal of Orthopsychiatry, 55,* 59–69.

Wesch, D., & Lutzker, J. R. (1991). A comprehensive 5-year evaluation of Project 12-Ways: An ecobehavioral program for treating and preventing child abuse and neglect. *Journal of Family Violence, 6,* 17–35.

Whipple, E. E., & Webster-Stratton, C. (1991). The role of parental stress in physically abusive families. *Child Abuse & Neglect, 15,* 279–291.

Whipple, E. E., & Wilson, S. R. (1996). Evaluation of a parent education and support program for families at risk of physical child abuse. *Families in Society, 77*(4), 227–239.

Whiteman, M., Fanshel, D., & Grundy, J. F. (1987). Cognitive-behavioral interventions aimed at anger of parents at risk of child abuse. *Social Work, 32*(6), 469–474.

Whittaker, J., Kinney, J., Tracy, E. M., & Booth, C. (1990). *Reaching high-risk families: Intensive family preservation in human services.* New York, NY: Aldine de Guyter.

Wolfe, D. A., Edwards, B., Manion, I., & Koverola, C. (1988). Early intervention for parents at risk of child abuse and neglect: A preliminary investigation. *Journal of Consulting & Clinical Psychology, 56*(1), 40–47.

World Health Organization. (2010). Child Maltreatment. *Media centre.* Retrieved from http://www.who.int/mediacentre/factsheets/fs150/en/index.html

Youngblade, L. M., & Belsky, J. (1990). Social and emotional consequences of child maltreatment. In R. T. Ammerman & M. Hersen (Eds.), *Children at risk: An evaluation of factors contributing to child abuse and neglect* (pp. 109–140). New York, NY: Plenum.

Zolotor, A. J., & Puzia, M. E. (2010). Bans against corporal punishment: A systematic review of the laws, changes in attitudes and behaviours. *Child Abuse Review, 19*(4), 229–247.

6

What Do We Know about Child Neglect? A Global Perspective

Rajeev Seth and Shanti Raman

DEFINITION OF NEGLECT

Child neglect can be simply defined as a deficit in meeting a child's basic needs. Neglect is classified as one of the four main types of mal-treatment by the World Health Organization's *World Report on Violence and Health* (Butchart, Harvey, Mian, & Fürniss, 2006). Basic needs include adequate food, clothing, health care, supervision, protection, education, nurturance, emotional support, and a safe home. An adequate definition of neglect must also take into account the needs of children, which vary with their age, development, physical and mental health, and cultural background. However, there are no clear cross-cultural standards for adequate child rearing practices, or indeed "good enough parenting." Society generally believes there are necessary behaviors a caregiver must provide a child in order for the child to develop nor-mally, but these behaviors can vary significantly. For example, Asian parents might expect to feed their children up to and beyond five years of age, whereas Western parents might expect their infants to be feeding themselves at 18 months; in many poor and traditional societies children as young as five years may take on caring for younger siblings. In the face of pluralistic notions of what constitutes adequate care, defining children's needs and determining what constitutes neglect have been problematic. It therefore remains an under-recognized form of child maltreatment (Glaser, 2002).

There is no universally accepted, all-encompassing definition of the concept of "neglect," and identifying the presenting features of neglect is difficult for both practitioners and researchers (Appleton, 2012). The World Health Organization has defined neglect as inattention or omission by the caregiver to provide for the child's health, education, emotional development, nutrition, shelter, and safe living conditions in the context of resources reasonably available to the family or caretakers, such that it causes, or has a high probability of causing, harm to the child's health or physical, mental, spiritual, moral, or social development (WHO, 1999). Neglect in this definition includes the failure to properly supervise and protect children from harm. The advantages of the above definition lie in the fact that it moves us beyond the narrow focus on parents and makes us consider other contributors to child neglect. It encourages a broader response, different intervention strategies, and a more constructive and less blaming approach towards parents (Dubowitz, 2009). Moreover, it fits with our broad interest in children's health, development, and safety. However, as a concept, "supervisory neglect" certainly does not easily cross national or cultural boundaries. According to the American Academy of Pediatrics, "supervisory neglect occurs whenever a caregiver's supervisory decisions or behaviors place a child in his or her care at significant ongoing risk for physical, emotional, or psychological harm" (Hymel, 2006). Many caregivers in developing countries may themselves be children. Injuries may occur while a child is being supervised, and at the same time many poorly supervised children do not get injured. Straus and Kantor (2005) propose the following definition for researchers: "Neglectful behaviour is behaviour by a caregiver that constitutes a failure to act in ways that are presumed by the culture of a society to be necessary to meet the developmental needs of a child and which are the responsibility of a caregiver to provide." It may be quite acceptable for families living in many traditional or poor societies for children, especially females, to take on not only caring for, but also supervising and disciplining, their younger siblings, whereas in many Western societies there are legal statutes determining when a child may be left unsupervised.

MAGNITUDE OF THE PROBLEM

Child neglect is the most frequent form of child maltreatment worldwide, both in developing and developed countries. From the U.S. Department of Health and Human Services' National Child Abuse and Neglect Data System, we know that "neglect" accounts for 78 percent of substantiated or indicated maltreatment (U.S. Department of Health and Human Services, 2011). Even in the United Kingdom, neglect is the most common category of abuse among children who are the subject of a child protection plan (Appleton, 2012). A recent meta-analysis of relevant global child protection research found overall estimated prevalence for physical neglect was 163 out of 1,000, and 184 out of 1,000 for emotional neglect, with no apparent gender differences (Stoltenborgh, Bakermans-Kranenburg, & IJzendoorn, 2013). There was a paucity of studies from low-resource countries, and the authors concluded that although child neglect was a considerable global problem, it was a neglected type of maltreatment in scientific research. Research shows that neglect often coexists with other forms of abuse and adversity (Claussen & Cicchetti, 1991; Daniel, 2005). Neglect rarely comes to light as a result of a specific incident (Hildyard & Wolfe, 2002), but often relies on practitioners making a judgment about the adequacy of ongoing care for a particular child and within the context of a given family. Slee outlines how in the Northern Territory of Australia, failure to send children to school is classified as neglect by the Department of Health and Families (Slee, 2012). In her informative paper, she contends that failure to provide children with culturally appropriate learning opportunities that encourage maximum participation and a lack of insistence by authorities on attendance are forms of systemic neglect.

The International Society for Prevention of Child Abuse and Neglect (ISPCAN) has recently published its official *World Perspectives on Child Abuse* (Dubowitz, 2012). This document offers glimpses of "child neglect" in many countries, as well as an opportunity to track trends and news on the latest progress of interventions in this field. The ISPCAN Working Group on National Child Maltreatment collected data from the following countries: Australia, Belgium, Canada, England, Italy, Lebanon, New Zealand, Philippines, and the United States. It also included information on child neglect from Hong Kong, Turkey, and several countries from Arab regions. Overall, it provides a general snapshot of child maltreatment country profiles, and a survey of laws, policies, and programs in 69 countries. While it is difficult to know the accuracy of what was reported and even to compare these data, as different countries have different definitions of neglect, it is very clear that neglect has high prevalence and is a significant problem worldwide.

In developing countries with adverse socioeconomic conditions and a large population base, child neglect is a serious, widely prevalent public health problem. Poverty, illiteracy, and poor access to health and family planning services result in provision of very little care to children during the early formative years. Even services that are freely available are poorly utilized. The urban underprivileged migrating population (a very sizable number) and rural communities are particularly affected. In large cities, there are serious problems of street children (abandoned and often homeless) and child laborers employed in menial work. Children in difficult circumstances, such as children affected by disasters, those in conflict zones, refugees, and those affected by HIV/AIDS, are a particular cause of concern. By contrast, in developed countries, children in "difficult circumstances" and prone to being neglected include children of substance-using parents, children of parents with a mental health disorder, and children living in high-risk neighborhoods such as the urban poor.

In India, where the biggest child population lives, for example, there are about 440 million children; 40 percent of them are vulnerable or experiencing difficult circumstances. The situation of newborns and those in infancy and early childhood is particularly critical, and morbidity and mortality rates for those groups continue to remain very high. Maternal malnutrition, unsafe deliveries, and neglect of early development and education are major issues that need to be appropriately addressed. Child rearing practices reflect social norms, and very often adverse traditions may be passed from one generation to the next, especially in illiterate and poorly informed communities.

The extent to which a child's needs are met exists on a continuum from optimal to grossly inadequate (Dubowitz, 2009). A crude categorization of situations as "neglect" or "no neglect" often is simplistic. For example, it is difficult to determine at what point inadequate sanitation is associated with harmful outcomes.

COST

The financial costs for victims and society are substantial, although there is no clear breakdown of what the burden of neglect is per se. A recent CDC study found the total lifetime estimated financial costs associated with just one year of confirmed cases of child maltreatment (physical abuse, sexual abuse, psychological abuse, and neglect) is approximately $124 billion in the United States (Fang, Brown, Florence, & Mercy, 2012). In fact, the costs of child abuse and neglect rival other major public health problems such as type 2 diabetes. A recent study from Germany based on the best available international estimates found that the lifetime follow-up costs of child maltreatment (physical and sexual abuse as well as physical and emotional neglect) were about €11 billion (euros) based on estimates from similar studies in Australia and €30 billion based on studies from Canada, or €135 and €364 billion respectively, per capita, for the German population (Habetha, Bleich, Weidenhammer, & Fegert, 2012). We can extrapolate from these figures that the costs to society of child neglect, which are certainly more than just the financial costs, may be monumental. It is impossible to measure the lost potential of neglected children to contribute to society over a lifetime, let alone the emotional costs to a single child growing up in neglect. Given the substantial economic burden of child maltreatment, the benefits of prevention will likely outweigh the costs of effective programs for treatment, particularly in developing countries.

TYPES OF CHILD NEGLECT AND ASSOCIATED MORBIDITY/MORTALITY

Neglect is a serious form of child maltreatment (NSPCC, 2007). Depending on the laws and child protective policies in respective regions, leaving a young child unsupervised may be considered neglect, especially if doing so places the child in danger (NICHD, 2006). In clinical practice, often more than one type of neglect exists, and if not managed early, will inevitably lead to substantial and long-term effects on a child's physical, mental, psychosocial, and cognitive development (Dubowitz, 2009; Dubowitz & Bennett, 2009). Longitudinal research has found linkages between child neglect (as well as abuse and other adverse childhood experiences) and adult health decades later, such as increased risk of ischemic heart disease and liver diseases and other chronic diseases (Dong, Dube, Felitti, Giles, & Anda, 2003; Dong et al., 2004; Felitti et al., 1998). The following illustrations describe the various forms and subgroups of child neglect.

Physical Neglect

This refers to the failure to provide the basic physical needs of a child, such as maintaining proper hygiene, cleanliness, clothing, food, shelter, etc. Inadequate food can lead to failure to thrive (Krugman & Dubowitz, 2003). In low and middle income countries, undernutrition is the most prevalent type of nutritional neglect. The best available evidence suggests that 50 percent of child deaths are attributed to malnutrition (Rice, Sacco, Hyder, & Black, 2000). In Pakistan, nearly 40 percent of children below five years of age suffer from undernutrition; nearly 50 percent are stunted. Physical neglect may include failure to seek timely and appropriate medical care for physical injury. Abandonment, expulsion, lack of supervision, and custody issues are also considered as forms of physical neglect (Mehnaz, 2013).

Medical Neglect

Medical neglect occurs when caregivers do not meet children's basic health care needs. This can include nonadherence (or noncompliance), delay or failure in obtaining health care, drug-exposed newborns, and inadequate dental care (Jenny & Committee on Child Abuse and Neglect, 2007). In the United States, medical neglect accounts for 2 to 3 percent of all substantiated cases of child maltreatment, although this is likely to be a gross underestimate. An effective response by a health professional to medical neglect requires a comprehensive assessment of the child's needs, the parents' resources, the parents' efforts to provide for the needs of the child, as well as options for ensuring optimal health of the child (Jenny & Committee on Child Abuse and Neglect, 2007). Although under-recognized, this phenomenon is potentially a major problem in developing countries, where cultural beliefs or reliance on religious or faith healers may contribute to the medical neglect of a child, sometimes with devastating consequences (Ertem, Bingoler, Ertem, Uysal, & Gozdasoglu, 2002; International NGO Council on Violence against Children, 2012).

Emotional Neglect

The failure to provide love, affection, and emotional bonding to a child equates to emotional neglect. Lack of positive attention, ignoring or isolating the child, rejecting him or her, not comforting the child when he or she is upset, and absence of positive reinforcement and physical affection results in emotional neglect and/or abuse. Neglected children are more likely to exhibit mental, emotional, and behavioral problems (Dubowitz, 2009; Dubowitz, Papas, Black, & Starr, 2002). In one of the largest studies of its kind from low-resource environments, the survey of child abuse in India with a sample size of 12,447, found the prevalence of emotional abuse/neglect was 50 percent. In 83 percent of the cases, parents were the abusers (Kacker, Varadan, & Kumar, 2007). We would suggest that emotional neglect is essentially the failure to provide a developmentally appropriate, supportive environment, including the availability of a primary attachment figure, so that children can develop stable emotional and social competencies commensurate with their full potential in the context of their culture and society.

Educational/Developmental Neglect

This is the failure to provide education or early stimulation for proper development. Education is a fundamental right of every child, as enshrined in the United Nations Convention on the Rights of the Child (UNCRC) (Goldhagen, 2003). A large number of children in low and middle income countries are still denied this right to education. The UNCRC does not absolve either the family or community or society at large of responsibility, but firmly puts the onus on the state. Governments are the ultimate duty bearer. In low and middle income countries, the state *should* ensure that all vulnerable children have access to school, basic health care, and nutrition, besides social welfare and juvenile justice systems (Srivastava, 2011). These child protection systems can contribute to breaking down the cycle of intergenerational poverty and exploitation in these settings. Research from developed countries reveals that neglected children perform worse academically than non-neglected children, especially when neglect co-occurs with other forms of maltreatment (Kendall-Tackett & Eckenrode, 1996). Children who face neglect have more school absences and lower grades and retention.

"New" Forms of Child Neglect

"New" forms of neglect have been described in the Western world. They include exposure to intimate partner violence, exposure to tobacco smoke, absence of car safety restraint, access to guns, and lack of health insurance (Dubowitz, 2009; Webster & Starnes, 2000). These emerging forms of neglect may be arguably unintentional on the part of a child's caretakers, often simply due to ignorance, but clearly an act of omission. The neglect may appear minor, but may have serious effects on the child's health and well-being.

WHAT ARE THE CAUSES OF CHILD NEGLECT?

The causes of child neglect are complex and often interrelated, and can be conceptualized as operating at three levels: intrapersonal, interpersonal/

family, and social/ecological (Turney & Tanner, 2005). Studies have shown that parental mental health problems, substance use, domestic violence, poverty, and family unemployment increase the likelihood of neglect (NSPCC, 2007). Neglectful families often experience a variety and/or a combination of adverse factors. At the intrapersonal level, studies have focused on the individual characteristics of parents and the discussion has primarily focused on mothers, reflecting traditional notions of women as primary caregivers. Studies report that mothers who neglect their children often present as depressed, helpless/fatalistic, lacking in emotional maturity, and with little faith in the competence and responsiveness of others. Particular attributes of these mothers include a young age (teenager), poor ability to plan, difficulty with managing money, lack of knowledge of children's needs, having a large number of children, high levels of stress, and poor socioeconomic circumstances (Turney & Tanner, 2005). At the interpersonal/family level, lone mother-headed households with transient males and family violence have been shown to be factors. There is also some literature supporting the intergenerational transmission of neglect and abuse (Harmer, Sanderson, & Mertin, 1999; Sylvestre & Mérette, 2010), although more robust research is needed to posit a clear link.

Poverty and Child Neglect

At the macro-ecological level, the association between poverty and neglect has frequently been made. Even among wealthy countries the links between material poverty and child well-being are in place, with the United Kingdom and the United States among the poorest performers (Spencer, 2008). Lack of basic needs, inadequate housing, homelessness, inadequate supervision, increased parental stress, substance abuse, and domestic violence can be major factors contributing to poverty exacerbating risks for child neglect. Other risk factors, such as living in a single-parent family or low parent education levels, especially when combined with poverty, can markedly increase children's chances of adverse outcomes (Schlee, Mullis, & Shriner, 2009). Effects of poverty on children's health and development depend on its timing, duration, and intensity. Risks are greatest for children who experience poverty when they are in early childhood, as the "architecture" of a child's brain—the foundation for future learning—is being critically formed (Seguin et al., 2005; Spencer, 2005).

While there is ample evidence suggesting that poverty increases the likelihood of neglect, poverty does *not* predetermine neglect (McSherry, 2004).

There is still a debate about which comes first, poverty or neglect. One argument is that child neglect occurs in the context of a neglectful society that allows child poverty to exist; in effect, societal poverty harms children. There is also concern about societal failure to build and maintain an infrastructure that values children and promotes positive parenting (Swift, 1995). Another perspective is that it is not poverty but parental characteristics that result in those parents and families living in poverty and lead to a consequence of neglect. Ecological studies of neighborhood effects have not been unidirectional. In fact, neighborhood effects are weaker than they appear to be in aggregate studies of official child maltreatment reports, and variation in child abuse potential within neighborhoods is greater than between neighborhoods (Coulton, Korbin, & Su, 1999). The danger with concluding that it is individual parent characteristics or family characteristics at the center of antecedents of child neglect is that this may be used to excuse social policy deficits. There is good evidence from the United States suggesting that child maltreatment can lead to increased risk for financial and employment-related difficulties in adulthood, suggesting a potential mechanism in the intergenerational transmission of neglect and abuse (Zielinski, 2009).

Acknowledging the role of poverty and social disadvantage in child neglect raises the big question of how to assess and address child neglect in low-resource settings. Most of the discussion about child neglect occurs in Western countries, yet the debilitating effects of poverty on children are experienced in a grand scale in developing countries. For example, India alone houses more than one-third of the world's poor and a third of its population fall below the international poverty line of U.S. $1.25 per day (India New Global Poverty Estimates, 2010). Child neglect may be the most difficult area of maltreatment to define internationally, as there is less agreement within societies about what constitutes neglect. According to Runyan and Eckenrode, neglect may be distinguished from poverty in that *culpable* neglect is thought to occur only when there are resources available to the family or caretakers not offered to the child (Runyan & Eckenrode, 2004). In her explorations of cross-cultural considerations in child maltreatment, Korbin argues that societal conditions such as poverty, inadequate housing, poor maternal and child health care, and lack of nutritional resources either contribute powerfully to child maltreatment or are considered maltreatment in and of themselves. These situations are beyond individual parental control, and societies and nation-states are culpable in this maltreatment (Korbin, 1991). Most impoverished families do not neglect their children, and do the best they can within their limited means. Interestingly, in Kenya, abandonment and neglect were the most commonly cited aspects of child maltreatment that adults acknowledged, and over one-fifth of children surveyed in that study reported being neglected (ANPPCAN, 2000). Mulinge, in his essay on children's rights in Africa, suggests that poverty is the leading factor preventing most African countries from protecting the rights of the child (Mulinge, 2010). Severe poverty in many developing countries is responsible for eroding the capacity of millions of children from participating in society and for inhibiting their potential. Nearly half of the children living in developing countries live in poverty; this poverty deprives children of adequate or nutritious meals; predisposes them to abandonment, violence, abuse, discrimination, and stigmatization; and impedes access to education, health care, safe drinking water, decent sanitation facilities, and decent shelter (UNICEF, 2004). On the flip side, as the longitudinal study on 12,000 children living in poverty shows, overall the economic situation for all of them is improving and, importantly, children living in poor families show remarkable resilience (Young Lives, 2012). Clearly understanding the sociocultural context of poverty and child neglect is crucial, and large-scale societal violations against children, which must form part of the discussion on neglect, can be tackled only by advocacy for societal change.

SPECIFIC SUBGROUPS AT RISK OF NEGLECT

The Girl Child

Globally, one person in eight is a girl or young woman, and most live in developing countries; arguably the category of the "girl child" is most at risk of abuse and neglect. The poorest, least developed countries tend to have the largest share of young people in their populations, and it is the girls and young women who face the greatest disadvantages (Levine, Lloyd, Greene, & Grown, 2008). Girls and young women are generally less educated, less healthy, and less free than their male counterparts. Despite all the evidence suggesting that female education and female empowerment are the keys to a society's well-being (Emmanuela, Krycia, Rafael, & Christopher, 2010; World Bank, 2011), we know that the status of girls, not just in the poorest settings but in the largest populations of India and China, is abysmal. There has been a significant international spotlight on harmful traditional practices such as female genital mutilation/cutting and honor killing, which affect girls and young women (International NGO Council

Ruma:[1] Girl-child on the Streets

Ruma's family are illegal immigrants from Bangladesh who have joined a rag-pickers colony in New Delhi, India, where thousands of rag-picker families are clustered. Now 13 years of age, Ruma has a father, mother, three sisters, and two brothers, all of whom are engaged in rag-picking or domestic work. The parents wanted Ruma to do domestic work, but Ruma wanted to go to school, study, and play with her friends. Due to her attitude, her parents beat her constantly; sometimes she was starved or thrown out of her home. Since she had no place to go, she often slept on the street near her home. An unending downward spiral of verbal and sexual abuse continued to unfold, drowning Ruma in self-pity, frustration, and depression. Homeless and lonely, Ruma slept where she could, falling victim to sexual abuse repeatedly. Eventually, Ruma found work as a housemaid in the neighborhood homes, where she was exploited sexually again by males in the households. Ruma was also sent with an escort on a five-day trip to Nepal to get involved with sex work, but she escaped from that situation and visited our drop-in center (DIC) in the city. The DIC offered her nonformal education, medical assistance, food, and other services. What Ruma needed most was a place to live, but the shelter home accommodates only boys. After several weeks of inquiry, an organization was able to find Ruma a shelter home for girls. Everyone thought that this would be a happy end to the story, but no. Ruma stayed at the shelter home for a couple of weeks, but then ran away. She is back on the streets, destiny unknown.

Case Formulation

Child issues	Parent/Family issues	Health and developmental concerns
One of 6 living children Girl child Lack of education Homeless: street child Verbal and sexual abuse Child trafficking Child laborer	Marginalized in society Illegal immigrants Extreme poverty, rag-pickers Unresponsive, neglectful parenting Poor living conditions Housing instability Family violence	Health and immunization status unknown Nutritional neglect Sexual assault and consequences High risk: pregnancy, HIV/AIDS, sexually transmitted infections Risk of substance abuse Risk of ongoing exploitation

Note
[1] All names have been changed.

on Violence against Children, 2012). There is also some acknowledgement, although nowhere nearly enough, of the shocking statistics of missing girls in many countries around the world, chiefly in India and China, due to infanticide, feticide, or "gendercide," as it is now understood (International NGO Council on Violence against Children, 2012; Sahni et al., 2008). What needs to be addressed is that girls and young women, particularly in low-resource settings, are systematically neglected from before birth all the way through their life cycle. Girls may lack formal recognition (e.g., birth registration), legal protection, and social networks; they are disproportionately burdened both at home with household chores and outside the home doing domestic labor, and are less likely to be in secondary education or in the formal paid workforce (Levine et al., 2008).

Disabled Children

Several international studies have established that children with disabilities are at greater risk of child maltreatment (Govindshenoy & Spencer, 2007; Hibbard, Desch, et al., 2007; Spencer et al., 2005; Sullivan & Knutson, 1998). The systematic review by Govindshenoy & Spencer in 2007, however, suggested that the evidence base for an association of disability with abuse and neglect was actually weak. They postulated that psychological/emotional problems and learning difficulties appear to be associated with maltreatment possibly due to a shared etiological pathway (Govindshenoy & Spencer, 2007). Sullivan and Knutson's 1998 study of a hospital-based sample of children in the United States with a range of disabilities found that disabled children were 3.8 times more likely to be neglected than non-disabled children (Sullivan & Knutson, 1998). Sullivan and Knutson repeated their study using a population-based sample and found that children with disabilities were 3.4 times more likely to be maltreated than those without (Sullivan & Knutson, 2000). Their study also found that most disabled children who were maltreated endured multiple forms of maltreatment, neglect being the most common. For children with disabilities, the usual risk factors for maltreatment may be intensified. Their impairments may make participation in family and community activities difficult; they are more likely to be living outside birth families, which can mean they are more vulnerable to abuse. Parents/caregivers of a child with disabilities may be stressed by ongoing health needs, difficulties in finding suitable childcare, financial burdens, and social isolation, along with difficulties relating to depression and marital discord. The most recent systematic review has found that children with disabilities are 3.6 times more likely to

Jay: Child with a Learning Disability

Jay is a healthy and energetic seven-year-old boy from a middle-class family background in a developing country. He had no prenatal, natal or postnatal developmental problems. In school, his reading ability was below his classmates and his writing illegible; he lacked attention and was hyperactive. He repeatedly failed his exams despite putting in his best efforts. The teacher blamed the boy and his parents (as both parents work). The parents explained that Jay is intelligent and good in oral recitation, understanding, and memory. The headmistress threatened Jay's mother that he would be expelled from school if his grades did not improve. The mother developed anxiety, depression, and other mental health problems. Jay was made to work day and night; however, his grades failed to improve. Jay developed a school phobia, suffered from poor self-esteem, and was sad, restless, inattentive, and more confused.

The parents sought appropriate professional help. Jay was subjected to psychometric tests. The intelligence tests revealed a full-scale IQ score of 103. Jay's behavioral checklist health score was poor, with significant impairment in attention, poor self-esteem, and school phobia. Jay was enrolled in remedial education to help him cope with the regular school system. Yearly reassessment revealed that his performance improved from his remedial education; even his self-esteem improved. However, the attitude of mainstream schoolteachers did not show any improvement. The teachers did not follow the recommendations from the detailed assessment by the psychologist and special educators. Jay was not given extra time during exams; his spelling errors were highlighted and marks deducted. He was not provided with any school support and was gradually not able to cope with his increased workload and learning disability. Jay was subjected to silent but harsh abuse. Jay's accomplishments in vocal skills, debates, music, drama, and sports were not appreciated. Finally, Jay had to drop out of school.

Case Formulation

Child issues	Parent/Family issues	Health and developmental concerns
Learning disorder (dyslexia) Lack of school support Emotional abuse Unresponsive teachers	Both parents working Resource-poor country Maternal depression Parental stress Delay in seeking and getting appropriate professional help	Behavioral problem Poor self-esteem Lack of individual educational support School drop-out Lack of vocational skills— at risk of future mental health concerns

be victims of violence than are their peers who are not disabled (Jones et al., 2012). Stalker and McArthur's excellent scoping review suggests that there is an interaction of age, gender, and/or sociocultural factors, with impairment giving rise to different patterns of maltreatment as opposed to those found among nondisabled children, although the reasons for this require further exploration (Stalker & McArthur, 2012). Their review also found that therapeutic services and criminal justice systems often fail to take account of disabled children's heightened needs, that little is known about what happens to disabled children who have been maltreated, and that few studies have sought disabled children's own accounts of maltreatment. Children with disabilities may comprise up to about 10 percent of school children and as such their needs are even more likely to be ignored in developing countries. Education practices in developing countries lack an understanding about the science of neurological development and how children learn. Inadequacies in the school system fail to meet children's educational needs; this leads to neglect, beyond parental control.

Marginalized Populations, Culturally Diverse or Minority Populations

The literature on culturally diverse (or "minority") groups and child maltreatment is contradictory and inadequate (Raman & Hodes, 2012). Data from the U.S. Department of Health and Human Services has consistently recorded overrepresentation of African American children and underrepresentation of Asian Pacific Island children and white children (Fontes, 2005). Elevated rates of child maltreatment in "immigrant" families, particularly refugee families, have also been reported from European countries (Euser, van IJzendoorn, Prinzie, & Bakermans-Kranenburg, 2010) and the United Kingdom (NSPCC, 2007), and among indigenous children in Australia (Berlyn & Bromfield, 2010). However, this does not necessarily show that ethnic minority families neglect or maltreat their children more than other families; it merely indicates that minority ethnic children may be more likely to be registered for child protection concerns. Poverty, unemployment, poor and overcrowded housing, and reliance on social housing are common problems for many black and minority populations in the West, common factors that also put children at an increased risk of neglect (NSPCC, 2007).

Responding to the needs of culturally diverse or minority children is even more of a challenge in developing countries. A particular subgroup at heightened risk of all forms of maltreatment including neglect is street children, many of whom come from marginalized ethnic or tribal groups.

Kiara: Urban Indigenous Child

Kiara is a 20-month-old female, part Aboriginal background, brought in for a medical assessment due to being taken into care recently along with her five siblings. There is a well-documented, long history of maltreatment and neglect involving all children in the family. A previous sibling died in the bath at 18 months of age (due to lack of adult supervision), and other siblings have significant medical, developmental, and behavioral problems. The biological mother is 34 years old, of Aboriginal background, has a known history of drug and alcohol abuse including opiates, is hepatitis C positive, and has mental health problems and significant family violence. The mother presented at 33 weeks' gestation in premature labor, having had no prenatal care. Birth was by emergency caesarean section; the birth weight was 2100 grams. The baby needed minor respiratory support including CPAP briefly, then was discharged to the district hospital for care. Kiara had two presentations to emergency departments this year, one involving a fall in the bathroom with a laceration to head/scalp requiring surgery, and the second following a fall into a hot bath, resulting in extensive scalds. She had no other health encounters, including immunization. On examination, Kiara was a silent toddler within normal growth parameters who exhibited frozen watchfulness. There were extensive early childhood caries, evidence of impetigo, and second-degree burns on her lower limbs.

Case Formulation

Child issues	Parent/Family issues	Health and developmental concerns
One of 6 living children Children born close together Poor prenatal/perinatal care Ex-premature, low birth weight Inadequate healthcare	Marginalized in society (Aboriginal) Poor, single mother Parental drug use and mental health problems Unresponsive, neglectful parenting Poor living conditions Housing instability Family violence Absent father figure	Immunization status unknown Delayed development globally Significant language delay Attachment disorder Dental caries Skin: infected lesions, burn/scald lesions

Studies of street children have found that they suffer from various types of maltreatment, including medical neglect (Mathur, Rathore, & Mathur, 2009; Navipour & Mohebbi, 2004; Njord, Merrill, Njord, Pachano, & Hackett, 2008; Senanayake, Ranasinghe, & Balasuriya, 1998). Indeed the very existence of large numbers of homeless and street children suggests criminal and culpable neglect by the state. Another major subgroup at risk of all forms of neglect is the population engaged in child labor, and as with other similar indicators, the major burden is in South Asia (Gulzar, Vertejee, & Pirani, 2009; Hadi, 2000).

PRINCIPLES OF ASSESSING NEGLECT

The *General Principles for the Assessment of Children in Need and Their Families* document introduced by the U.K. Department of Health provides really good guidance for the multidisciplinary assessment of at-risk children and their families (Department of Health, 2009). Principles embedded within this framework are that:

- Assessments should be child-centered and rooted in child development
- Professionals should recognize and work with diversity
- Assessment practice means working, whenever possible, with children and families and building on the family strengths as well as identifying difficulties; the quality of the human environment is linked to the development of the child
- A range of professionals are the assessors and providers of services to children in need; therefore assessments should be multidisciplinary
- Assessment is a continuing process; interventions and services should be provided alongside the assessment
- Effective assessment practice is dependent on the combination of evidence-based practice grounded in knowledge with finely balanced professional judgment

While this framework does provide an ambitious guide to assessment, Horwath cautions that "frameworks" are really only aides-memoires, or organizing principles for effective practice. She suggests that there are likely to be several blocks to the effective implementation of the assessment framework, particularly as the impact of neglect on a child is not often apparent immediately (Horwath, 2002). Maintaining a strong focus on the child is imperative, as the child is often forgotten in the frenzy of the assessment process!

Much of the international research done on children in alternative or foster care has also provided some guidance to the assessment process. A high proportion of the children in foster care have been neglected, so the guidelines developed for health assessments of this group of children have taken heed of the health and developmental consequences of neglect. The Child Welfare League of America, the American Academy of Pediatrics, and the American Academy of Child and Adolescent Psychiatry have all published guidelines stressing the importance of *comprehensive* health and developmental assessments and appropriate referral to early intervention services for children in out-of-home or foster care (Child Welfare League of America, 1988; Committee on Early Childhood, 2002; Leslie et al., 2005). Similarly, standards and guidelines exist in Australia (National Framework Implementation Working Group, 2010; RACP, 2006) and in the United Kingdom (U.K. Department of Health, 2009).

Most of these guidelines developed in Western countries have an expectation that health assessments will be comprehensive and multidisciplinary, that they will respond to developmental and psychosocial concerns, and that they will provide adequate referrals for ongoing intervention or other relevant assessments. In essence, these assessments take time. They also require skilled clinicians with a range of skills, including expertise in child development, pediatric physical and psychosocial assessments, family functioning and attachment, cross-cultural interactions, advocacy, and being able to work within a strengths-based paradigm. While the need for a multidisciplinary approach seems obvious, the NSPCC cautions against an assumption that information shared is information understood, and offers a warning about case-responsibility being diluted in the context of multiagency working, impacting both referrals and response (Broadhurst et al., 2010). How these guidelines can be translated effectively for use in low-resource settings, without the luxury of time or access to adequately trained health or support workers, is a major concern. At the very least, professionals working in this field in low-resource settings need to keep the child in focus and be sensitive to the sociocultural and family constraints—and, making using of their considerable experience, be the strongest advocates they can be for the child.

ADDRESSING NEGLECT

The approaches to addressing neglect can be divided into the following broad categories.

Without Involvement of Child Protective Services (CPS)

Concerns about neglect should be conveyed to the family kindly but forthrightly (Dubowitz, 2009). One should avoid blaming parents, and remain empathetic and interested in order to help the family. All contributory factors, which are amenable to correction, should be prioritized. Parents' problems should be addressed, and where appropriate, referral and treatment can help. We should establish specific objectives (adequate control of asthma) and measurable outcomes (e.g., no nocturnal cough), and engage the family in developing a specific plan. A written contract, with one copy for the parents and one for the patient chart, can be useful. We should build on strengths and encourage positive family experiences. Encourage informal supports from family and friends, and consider community resources and support through family religious affiliations. Consider provision of child needs, such as direct nutrition or health care intervention.

Involvement of Child Protective Services (CPS)

This approach should be considered when the above nonintrusive methods have failed and serious harm is expected to the child (Dubowitz, 2009). The focus should be on supporting the families to do better, rather than investigation of what went wrong. Parents should be approached constructively, without blaming them, in a conciliatory attempt. Sometimes parenting programs can help; follow-up, review of interventions, support, and monitoring are all needed.

Additional Strategies in Resource-Poor/Developing Countries

Unlike developed countries, child protection systems are not well developed in many resource-poor countries. The problems of socially marginalized and economically backward groups are immense, particularly among children in urban slums, street children, child laborers, children of construction workers, and exploited and trafficked children. Committed groups of multidisciplinary child health professionals and local agencies should work together and monitor government efforts in promotion and protection of various aspects of the systemic neglect of child rights. What works is if child advocates and leaders from resource-poor settings form meaningful partnerships with their peers in rich countries. As the Turkish example showed, multidisciplinary child protection assessment teams were successfully established as a result of collaborating with culturally competent instructors from the United States, focusing on improving recognition and management of child abuse and neglect (Agirtan et al., 2009).

"Child labor" is a serious violation of fundamental rights of children. It deprives children of their childhood, their potential, and their dignity, and that is harmful to their physical and mental development. It is essentially a socioeconomic problem, inextricably linked to poverty and illiteracy. There is a consensus emerging that when a child is not in school, the child would perforce be part of the labor pool. In linking child labor to education, the tasks of eliminating child labor and universalizing education have become synonymous. There is an essential need in developing countries to create a comprehensive plan to withdraw children from work and mainstream them into schools, in order to satisfy their basic right to education (Seth, 2013a).

Child protection services should also reach rural areas. A comprehensive approach to child protection in these areas should include the established local form of self-government. These local government officials

---

Pintu: Street Child, Successfully Integrated and Supported

Pintu, an 18-year-old boy from a village in Bihar, India, lived with his parents, three brothers, an uncle, and a grandmother. Like any other child, Pintu wanted to be cared for and loved; he had a deep desire to study. His poor, illiterate father pushed him to work for hours in the fields looking after cattle. If he showed any reluctance, he was abused and beaten. He ended up getting into gambling. His father caught him and an ugly altercation ensued. Before he knew what had happened, Pintu was pushed out of his home when he was only 10. With no money or food, he ran for a long time. He reached the nearest railway station and jumped onto the first train he saw. After what seemed an eternity, the train reached Mumbai. A train companion took Pintu to one of his relatives. Scared and worried, Pintu sensed something fishy in the kindness showered on him. Sure enough, his instincts proved right: he discovered he was to be bonded into slavery. Pintu remembers that he ran again for more than an hour and reached the railway station. This time, he took another train, to the Old Delhi railway station. Luckily, he was spotted by a peer educator of a nongovernmental organization, PCI, the next morning. He was taken to the PCI drop-in center, counseled, and then moved to the shelter home.

The Shelter Home at Mewat, Haryana, is a safe haven providing boys with shelter, nutrition, clothing, health care, psychological support, and access to formal and informal education in a supportive rural community. Located on five acres of sylvan land, it can house 40 boys for up to 18 years. Like a family, the older boys look after the younger ones and all take part in daily chores. The home provides space for the boys to enjoy outdoor games and physical activities. Pintu was enrolled in a local government school and has recently graduated from high school, passing his examinations well. He is

(Continued)

now enrolled at a local university. Pintu is thankful for the support he received. Very few street children are fortunate enough to be able to live their dreams.

Case Formulation

Child issues	Parent/Family issues	Health and developmental concerns
One of 4 living children Deprived of love and care Neglect of education Street child Intellectually bright Resilient	Poor and illiterate parents Abusive father Unresponsive, neglectful parenting Poor living conditions Family violence	Health and immunization status unknown Nutritional neglect Physical, emotional, and mental abuse Educational deprivation Risk of substance abuse

should be given responsibility to ensure that basic education, nutrition, health care, and sanitation are available for the proper development of every child in their village. The local government should be duty-bound to ensure that every child is in school and protected from agrarian and allied rural occupations as a part of family or individual child labor (Seth, 2013b).

PREVENTING CHILD NEGLECT

There is no doubt that primary prevention of child neglect is the most preferable approach both in developed and developing countries. Multidisciplinary professional strategic approaches can support parents and families in promoting normal child development, health, and safety. In Western countries, sustained home visiting for vulnerable families has been shown to prevent child maltreatment, although it is a resource-intensive intervention and not all home-visiting programs are comparable (Council on Community Pediatrics, 2009; Donelan-McCall, Eckenrode, & Olds, 2009). The global systematic review of reviews on child maltreatment prevention programs found that home visiting, parent education, and multicomponent interventions showed promise in preventing actual maltreatment. However, outcome evaluations of child maltreatment prevention interventions are exceedingly rare in low-resource settings, making up less than 1 percent of the evidence base (Miktona & Butcharta, 2009). A recent Australian review found that the most cost-effective home-visiting programs use professional home visitors in a multidisciplinary team; they target high-risk populations and include more than just home visiting (Dalziel & Segal, 2012). While effective child maltreatment prevention efforts exist, not all programs provide the same effectiveness, or target the same maltreatment issues. Clinicians may be in a key position to offer support to families in their own practice settings, as well as to direct families to the appropriate resources available (Scribano, 2010). From an individual clinician's perspective, detailed psychosocial history and screening questionnaires can detect high-risk family problems such as depression, substance abuse, intimate partner violence, large family size, and poverty (Dubowitz et al., 2011). Anticipatory guidance to prevent neglect and ensure child safety is essential. Efforts should also be made to identify family strengths and community support mechanisms. Parents and caregivers should be made aware of children's rights. Ideally they can be effective advocates for their children and demand appropriate interventions and services from the appropriate avenues.

Specific Policy, Practice, and Intervention Strategies to Address Neglect in Poor Families

Recognizing that poverty plays a substantial role in child neglect, some child welfare systems are experimenting with strategies to address risks associated with poverty. Neglect of young children in low-income families to develop to their full cognitive and emotional potential is a major obstacle to their economic well-being. Early child development (ECD), therefore, should become a key priority component of an economic strategy (Alderman, 2011). ECD, during the period from 0–6 years, is emerging as the most cost-effective form of human capital investment compared with subsequent interventions (Engle et al., 2007). A series of papers in the *Lancet* have assessed the lost development potential due to missed opportunities for early child health and stimulation (Grantham-McGregor et al., 2007; Walker et al., 2007). The early developmental shortfalls contribute substantially to the intergenerational transmission of poverty through reduced employability, productivity, and overall well-being later in life. Policies and interventions, including center-based and home-based interventions and conditional cash transfer to poor families with young children, are likely to improve cognitive and overall developmental outcome. ECD is therefore promoted as a rights-based intervention to offset early malnutrition; focused quality preschool programs can also be a strategy to reduce the intergenerational transmission of poverty.

ADVOCACY

All child rights and protection professionals working in the area of clinical, research, public health, or policy encounter situations each day where positive advocacy for children and their families is required. Child neglect is a major societal and a public health problem. Problems at various levels can contribute to neglect. Therefore, advocacy is also needed at various levels. Advocacy is an integral part of all service sectors engaged with the care and support of children. There is also an emerging need to do research, and to investigate more systemically how to use advocacy most effectively (Bross & Krugman, 2009). The following range of activities may play a part in effective advocacy to combat child neglect.

Using the UNCRC as a Tool in Advocacy

While there is a compelling moral imperative to ensure that children's needs are met adequately, to be an effective advocate for children, one needs to be familiar with the language of the UNCRC (Goldhagen, 2003). Meeting children's needs is a human rights concern, articulated in the United Nations Convention on the Rights of the Child (Doek, 2009).While there is perhaps justifiable cynicism about the CRC being just another global policy statement without "teeth," there are several examples from low-resource countries that attest to the power of using such a tool in advocacy for children. A wonderful example is the African Child Policy Forum (ACPF), which established a CRC-based methodology to monitor African nation-states and their progress against the CRC (Bequele, 2010; Lee & Svevo-Cianci, 2009). They created an innovative "Child-Friendliness Index" to specifically measure child-related services/outcomes, resources, and legal policy framework. The ACPF was able to identify several African countries that were leaders in their region in child protection. The authors concluded that three things matter for policy and advocacy for children: politics that put children at the center of public policy; laws that protect children; and budgets that provide for children's basic needs and full development (Bequele, 2010).

Professional Identity and Membership

Governments and statutory bodies listen to groups of individuals assembled in accredited societies such as the American Academy of Pediatrics (U.S.), Royal College of Paediatrics & Child Health (U.K.), and child maltreatment prevention–focused organizations such as the International Society for prevention of Child Abuse and Neglect (an international body). These organizations can be extremely effective in evidence-based advocacy for children; indeed, pediatric societies and bodies have had documented success in many child protection campaigns (Raman, Woolfenden, Williams, & Zwi, 2007; Waterston & Mann, 2005). International and regional bodies can also make explicit through their conference statements what is needed for children. An example is the outcome document entitled the *Delhi Declaration,* which emerged from the ninth Asia Pacific conference of Child Abuse and Neglect in 2011. The conference focused on regional issues for children, and the declaration emphasizes that neglect includes denial or deficiency of provisions of services such as health care and education.

Local Legislation and Legal Advocacy

Given the magnitude of the problem of child neglect, there is an urgent need to lobby governments, elected representatives, and policy makers, and to oversee proper implementation of government legislation and programs, in order to achieve positive impact on overall child health and development. Legislative advocacy has been an important avenue for improvements in children's health and well-being, and health and welfare professionals can be trained to effectively advocate for legislative change (Berman, 1998). The landmark Right to Education Act in India, for example, has had ongoing scrutiny from health and welfare advocates, and government and nongovernment agencies (Bhargava, 2010).

Individual, Family, and Anticipatory Guidance for Individual Parents

Partnerships with parents are a crucial form of advocacy in which health and welfare workers and parents together monitor the growth and development, problems, and appropriate response to identified concerns (Bross & Krugman, 2009). While it is challenging to work with "neglectful" parents, implementing culturally sensitive positive parenting skills programs is a step in the right direction. Home visitation by health workers, or by lay workers focusing on parenting, has been found to be effective in building early childhood potential, especially if appropriately targeted (Caldera et al., 2007; Donelan-McCall et al., 2009). At the individual parent level, the use of targeted interventions directed at improving parental sensitivity to a child's cues during infancy, and later parent-child interactions such as cognitive behavioral parenting programs, anticipatory guidance, and other psychotherapeutic interventions show promise (Hibbard, Barlow, MacMillan, et al., 2012).

Public Education and Working with Media

Child neglect intervention programs should target the whole community. Education of the masses by employing all means of communication, including electronic and print media, advocacy, and awareness-raising sessions by trained professionals, is a crucial plank of advocacy. For example, the Chicago-based National Center for the Prevention of Child Abuse supported broad-based public education campaigns that moved from encouraging the public to report child abuse to prevention through home visitation and attempting to implement "Children's Trust Funds" as a source of needed prevention funding (Bross & Krugman, 2009). The media can both clarify and confuse the understanding of crucial issues involving children; therefore timely and carefully crafted interviews and editorials are an important form of child advocacy (Krugman, 1996).

CONCLUSIONS

We have demonstrated the global burden of the problem of child neglect. There are compelling reasons for believing that a public health approach to child protection is the only way of ensuring that all children are protected within a population, including children at high risk (Barlow & Calam, 2011). This is particularly true for low and middle income countries. There are creative and courageous child welfare leaders, legislators, media advocacy campaigners, parents, and "coalitions of the willing" everywhere, developing innovative policy system reform and practice strategies that promise to lead the way toward improving child welfare in accordance with the UNCRC. We need to partner with them effectively "in the best interests of the child."

REFERENCES

Agirtan, C. A., Akar, T., Akbas, S., Akdur, R., Aydin, C., Aytar, G., . . . Contributing Multidisciplinary Teams. (2009). Establishment of interdisciplinary child protection teams in Turkey 2002–2006: Identifying the strongest link can make a difference! *Child Abuse & Neglect, 33*(4), 247–255.

Alderman, H. (2011). *No small matter: The impact of poverty, shocks and human capital investment in early childhood development.* Washington, DC: World Bank.

ANPPCAN. (2000). *Study on awareness and views regarding child abuse and child rights in selected communities in Kenya.* Nairobi: African Network for the Prevention and Protection against Child Abuse and Neglect.

Appleton, J. V. (2012). Perspectives of neglect. *Child Abuse Review, 21,* 77–80.

Barlow, J., & Calam, R. (2011). A public health approach to safeguarding in the 21st century. *Child Abuse Review, 20*(4), 238–255. doi:10.1002/car.1194

Bequele, A. (2010). Monitoring the commitment and child-friendliness of governments: A new approach from Africa. *Child Abuse & Neglect, 34*(1), 34–44.

Berlyn, C., & Bromfield, L. (2010). Child protection and Aboriginal and Torres Strait Islander children. Canberra: National Child Protection Clearinghouse, Australian Institute of Family Studies. Retrieved from http://www.aifs.gov.au/nch/pubs/sheets/rs10/rs10.pdf

Berman, S. (1998). Training pediatricians to become child advocates. *Pediatrics, 102*(3), 632–635.

Bhargava, P. M. (2010, July 26). RTE Act: Some rights and some wrongs. *The Hindu.*

Broadhurst, K., White, S., Fish, S., Munro, E., Fletcher, K., & Lincoln, H. (2010). *Ten pitfalls and how to avoid them: What research tells us.* London, UK: National Society for the Prevention of Cruelty to Children.

Bross, D. C., & Krugman, R. D. (2009). Child maltreatment law and policy as a foundation for child advocacy. *Pediatric Clinics of North America, 56*(2), 429–439.

Butchart, A., Harvey, A. P., Mian, M., & Fürniss, T. (2006). *Preventing child maltreatment: A guide to taking action and generating evidence.* Geneva: World Health Organization and International Society for Prevention of Child Abuse.

Caldera, D., Burrell, L., Rodriguez, K., Crowne, S. S., Rohde, C., & Duggan, A. (2007). Impact of a statewide home visiting program on parenting and on child health and development. *Child Abuse & Neglect, 31*(8), 829–852.

Child Welfare League of America. (1988). *Standards for health care services for children in out-of-home care.* Washington, DC: Child Welfare League of America.

Claussen, A., & Cicchetti, P. (1991). Physical and psychological maltreatment: Relations among types of maltreatment. *Child Abuse & Neglect 15,* 5–18.

Committee on Early Childhood, Adoption, and Dependent Care. (2002). Health care of young children in foster care. *Pediatrics, 109*(3), 536–541. doi:10.1542/peds.109.3.536

Coulton, C. J., Korbin, J. E., & Su, M. (1999). Neighborhoods and child maltreatment: A multi-level study. *Child Abuse & Neglect, 23*(11), 1019–1040.

Council on Community Pediatrics. (2009). The role of preschool home-visiting programs in improving children's developmental and health outcomes. *Pediatrics, 123*(2), 598–603. doi:10.1542/peds.2008-3607

Dalziel, K., & Segal, L. (2012). Home visiting programmes for the prevention of child maltreatment: Cost-effectiveness of 33 programmes. *Archives of Disease in Childhood, 97,* 787–798.

Daniel, B. (2005). Introduction to Issues for Health and Social Care in Neglect. In J. Taylor & B. Daniel (Eds.), *Child neglect: Practice issues for health and social care* (pp. 11–25). London, UK: Jessica Kingsley Publishers.

Delhi declaration: Outcome document of 9th Asia Pacific Conference on Child Abuse and Neglect, (APCCAN 2011) New Delhi, India. (2011). Paper presented at the 9th Asia Pacific Conference on Child Abuse and Neglect, New Delhi, India.

Department of Health. (2000). Assessing children in need and their families: Practice guidance. London, UK: Stationery Office.

Doek, J. E. (2009). The CRC 20 years: An overview of some of the major achievements and remaining challenges. *Child Abuse & Neglect, 33*(11), 771–782.

Donelan-McCall, N., Eckenrode, J., & Olds, D. L. (2009). Home visiting for the prevention of child maltreatment: Lessons learned during the past 20 years. *Pediatric Clinics of North America 56*(2), 389–403.

Dong, M., Anda, R. F., Dube, S. R., Giles, W. H., & Felitti, V. J. (2003). The relationship of exposure to other forms of abuse, neglect, and household dysfunction during childhood. *Child Abuse & Neglect, 27,* 625–639.

Dong, M., Anda, R. F., Felitti, V. J., Dube, S. R., Williamson, D. F., Thomson, T. J., et al. (2004). The interrelatedness of multiple forms of childhood abuse, neglect, and household dysfunction. *Childhood Abuse & Neglect, 28,* 771–784.

Dubowitz, H. (2009). Tackling child neglect: A role for pediatricians. *Pediatr Clin N Am, 56,* 363–378. doi:10.1016/j.pcl.2009.01.003

Dubowitz, H. (Ed.). (2012). *World perspectives on child abuse* (10th ed.). Chicago, IL: International Society for Prevention of Child Abuse & Neglect.

Dubowitz, H., & Bennett, S. (2009). Physical abuse and neglect of children. *The Lancet, 369*(9576), 1891–1899.

Dubowitz, H., Kim, J., Black, M. M., Weisbart, C., Semiatin, J., & Magder, L. S. (2011). Identifying children at high risk for a child maltreatment report. *Child Abuse & Neglect, 35*(2), 96–104.

Dubowitz, H., Papas, M. A., Black, M. M., & Starr, R. H. (2002). Child neglect: Outcomes in high-risk urban preschoolers. *Pediatrics, 109*(6), 1100–1107.

Emmanuela, G., Krycia, C., Rafael, L., & Christopher, J. L. M. (2010). Increased educational attainment and its effect on child mortality in 175 countries between 1970 and 2009: A systematic analysis. *The Lancet, 376*(9745), 959–974.

Engle, P. L., Black, M. M., Behrman, J. R., Cabral de Mello, M., Gertler, P. J., Kapiriri, L., . . . Young, M. E. (2007). Strategies to avoid the loss of developmental potential in more than 200 million children in the developing world. *The Lancet, 369*(9557), 229–242.

Ertem, I. O., Bingoler, B. E., Ertem, M., Uysal, Z., & Gozdasoglu, S. (2002). Medical neglect of a child: Challenges for pediatricians in developing countries. *Child Abuse & Neglect, 26,* 751–761.

Euser, E. M., van IJzendoorn, M. H., Prinzie, P., & Bakermans-Kranenburg, M. J. (2010). Elevated child maltreatment rates in immigrant families and the role of socioeconomic differences. *Child Maltreatment, 16*(1): 63–73. doi:10.1177/1077559510385842

Fang, X., Brown, D. S., Florence, C. S., & Mercy, J. A. (2012). The economic burden of child maltreatment in the United States and implications for prevention. *Child Abuse & Neglect, 36,* 156–165. doi:10.1016/j.chiabu.2011.10.006

Felitti, V. J., Anda, R. F., Nordenberg, D., Williamson, D. F., Spitz, A. M., Edwards, V., . . . Marks, J. S. (1998). Relationship of childhood abuse and household dysfunction to many of the leading causes of death in adults: The adverse childhood experiences (ACE) study. *American Journal of Preventive Medicine, 14*(4), 245–258.

Fontes, L. A. (2005). *Child abuse and culture: Working with diverse families.* New York, NY: The Guildford Press.

Glaser, D. (2002). Emotional abuse and neglect (psychological maltreatment): A conceptual framework. *Child Abuse & Neglect, 26*(6–7), 697–714.

Goldhagen, J. (2003). Children's rights and the United Nations Convention on the Rights of the Child. *Pediatrics, 112*(3), 742–745.

Govindshenoy, M., & Spencer, N. (2007). Abuse of the disabled child: A systematic review of population-based studies. *Child: Care, Health and Development, 33*(5), 552–558. doi:10.1111/j.1365-2214.2006.00693.x

Grantham-McGregor, S., Cheung, Y. B., Cueto, S., Glewwe, P., Richter, L., & Strupp, B. (2007). Developmental potential in the first 5 years for children in developing countries. *The Lancet, 369*(9555), 60–70. doi:http://dx.doi.org/10.1016/S0140-6736(07)60032-4

Gulzar, S. A., Vertejee, S., & Pirani, L. (2009). Child labour: A public health issue. *JPMA: Journal of the Pakistan Medical Association, 59*(11), 778–781.

Habetha, S., Bleich, S., Weidenhammer, J., & Fegert, J. (2012). A prevalence-based approach to societal costs occurring in consequence of child abuse and neglect. *Child and Adolescent Psychiatry and Mental Health, 6*(1), 35.

Hadi, A. (2000). Child abuse among working children in rural Bangladesh: Prevalence and determinants. *Public Health, 114*(5), 380–384.

Harmer, A. L. M., Sanderson, J., & Mertin, P. (1999). Influence of negative childhood experiences on psychological functioning, social support, and parenting for mothers recovering from addiction. *Child Abuse & Neglect, 23*(5), 421–433. doi:10.1016/S0145-2134(99)00020-4

Hibbard, R., Barlow, J., MacMillan, H., & the Committee on Child Abuse and Neglect and American Academy of Child and Adolescent Psychiatry, Child Maltreatment and Violence Committee. (2012). Psychological maltreatment. *Pediatrics, 130,* 372–378. doi:10.1542/peds.2012-1552

Hibbard, R. A., Desch, L. W., the Committee on Child Abuse and Neglect, & the Council on Children with Disabilities. (2007). Maltreatment of children with disabilities. *Pediatrics, 119*(5), 1018–1025. doi:10.1542/peds.2007-0565

Hildyard, K. L., & Wolfe, D. A. (2002). Child neglect: Developmental issues and outcomes. *Child Abuse & Neglect, 26*(6–7), 679–695.

Horwath, J. (2002). Maintaining a focus on the child? *Child Abuse Review, 11,* 195–213. doi:10.1002/car.742

Hymel, K., and Committee on Child Abuse and Neglect. (2006). When is lack of supervision neglect? *American Academy of Pediatrics, 118*(3), 1296–1298.

India New Global Poverty Estimates. (2010). Retrieved from http://en.wikipedia .org/wiki/Poverty_in_India

International NGO Council on Violence against Children. (2012). *Violating children's rights: Harmful practices based on tradition, culture, religion or superstition.* New York, NY: International NGO Council on Violence against Children.

Jenny, C., & the Committee on Child Abuse and Neglect. (2007). Recognizing and responding to medical neglect. *Pediatrics, 120*(6), 1385–1389. doi:10.1542/ peds.2007-2903

Jones, L., Bellis, M. A., Wood, S., Hughes, K., McCoy, E., Eckley, L., . . . Officer, A. (2012). Prevalence and risk of violence against children with disabilities: A systematic review and meta-analysis of observational studies. *The Lancet, 380,* 899–907.

Kacker, L., Varadan, S., & Kumar, P. (2007). *Study on Child Abuse: India 2007.* New Delhi, IN: Ministry of Women and Child Development, Government of India.

Kendall-Tackett, K. A., & Eckenrode, J. (1996). The effects of neglect on academic achievement and disciplinary problems: A developmental perspective. *Child Abuse & Neglect, 20*(3), 161–169. doi:http://dx.doi.org/10.1016/ S0145-2134(95)00139-5

Korbin, J. E. (1991). Cross-cultural perspectives and research directions for the 21st century. *Child Abuse & Neglect, 15*(Sup1), 67–77.

Krugman, R. D. (1996). The media and public awareness of child abuse and neglect: It's time for a change. *Child Abuse & Neglect 20*(4), 259–260.

Krugman, S. D., & Dubowitz, H. (2003). Failure to thrive. *American Family Physician, 68,* 879–884.

Lee, Y., & Svevo-Cianci, K. A. (2009). Twenty years of the Convention on the Rights of the Child: Achievements and challenges for child protection. *Child Abuse & Neglect, 33*(11), 767–770.

Leslie, L. K., Gordon, J. N., Lambros, K., Premji, K., Peoples, J., & Gist, K. (2005). Addressing the developmental and mental health needs of young children in foster care. *Journal of Developmental & Behavioral Pediatrics, 26*(2), 140–151.

Levine, R., Lloyd, C., Greene, M., & Grown, C. (2008). *Girls count: A global investment and action agenda.* Washington, DC: Center for Global Development.

Mathur, M., Rathore, P., & Mathur, M. (2009). Incidence, type and intensity of abuse in street children in India. *Child Abuse & Neglect, 33*(12), 907–913.

McSherry, D. (2004). Which came first, the chicken or the egg? Examining the relationship between child neglect and poverty. *British Journal of Social Work, 34*(5), 727–733.

Mehnaz, A. (2013). Child neglect: Wider dimensions. In R. N. Srivastava, R. Seth, & J. v. Niekerk (Eds.), *Child abuse and neglect in Asia Pacific countries: Challenges and opportunities* (pp. 101–109). New Delhi: Jaypee Brothers Medical Publishers.

Miktona, C., & Butcharta, A. (2009). Child maltreatment prevention: A systematic review of reviews. *Bulletin of the World Health Organization, 87,* 353–361.

Mulinge, M. M. (2010). Persistent socioeconomic and political dilemmas to the implementation of the 1989 United Nations Convention on the Rights of the Child in sub-Saharan Africa. *Child Abuse & Neglect, 34*(1), 10–17.

National Framework Implementation Working Group. (2010). *National standards for out of home care. Consultation paper.* Canberra: Commonwealth of Australia.

Navipour, R., & Mohebbi, M. R. (2004). Street children and runaway adolescents in Iran. *Indian Pediatrics, 41*(12), 1283–1284.

NICHD. (2006). *Descriptions of NICHD career development projects related to child abuse, child maltreatment, and child violence.* Washington, DC: NICHD.

Njord, L., Merrill, R. M., Njord, R., Pachano, J. D. R., & Hackett, A. (2008). Characterizing health behaviors and infectious disease prevalence among Filipino street children. *International Journal of Adolescent Medicine and Health, 20*(3), 367–374.

NSPCC. (2007). *Child neglect. NSPCC research briefing.* London, UK: NSPCC.

Pillai, A., Andrews, T., & Patel, V. (2009). Violence, psychological distress and the risk of suicidal behaviour in young people in India. *International Journal of Epidemiology, 38*(2), 459–469.

RACP. (2006). Health of children in "out-of-home" care: Paediatric policy. Sydney: The Royal Australasian College of Physicians.

Raman, S., & Hodes, D. (2012). Cultural issues in child maltreatment. *Journal of Paediatrics and Child Health, 48,* 30–37. doi:10.1111/j.1440-1754.2011.02184.x

Raman, S., Woolfenden, S., Williams, K., & Zwi, K. (2007). Human rights and child health. *Journal of Paediatrics and Child Health, 43*(9), 581–586. doi:10.1111/j.1440-1754.2007.01147.x

Rice, A. L., Sacco, L., Hyder, A., & Black, R. E. (2000). Malnutrition as an underlying cause of childhood deaths associated with infectious diseases in developing countries. *Bulletin of the World Health Organization 78,* 1207–1221.

Runyan, D. K., & Eckenrode, J. (2004). International perspectives on the epidemiology of child neglect and abuse. *Annales Nestle, 62*(1), 1–12.

Sahni, M., Verma, N., Narula, D., Varghese, R. M., Sreenivas, V., & Puliyel, J. M. (2008). Missing girls in India: Infanticide, feticide and made-to-order pregnancies? Insights from hospital-based sex-ratio-at-birth over the last century. *PLoS ONE, 3*(5), e2224.

Schlee, B. M., Mullis, A. K., & Shriner, M. (2009). Parents' social and resource capital: Predictors of academic achievement during early childhood. *Children and Youth Services Review, 31*(2), 227–234. doi:http://dx.doi.org/10.1016/j .childyouth.2008.07.014

Scribano, P. V. (2010). Prevention strategies in child maltreatment. *Current Opinion in Pediatrics, 22*(5), 616–620.

Seguin, L., Xu, Q., Gauvin, L., Zunzunegui, M.-V., Potvin, L., & Frohlich, K. L. (2005). Understanding the dimensions of socioeconomic status that influence toddlers' health: Unique impact of lack of money for basic needs in Quebec's birth cohort. *J Epidemiol Community Health, 59*(1), 42–48.

Senanayake, M. P., Ranasinghe, A., & Balasuriya, C. (1998). Street children: A preliminary study. *Ceylon Medical Journal, 43*(4), 191–193.

Seth, R. (2013a). Child labour. In R. N. Srivastava, R. Seth, & J. v. Niekerk (Eds.), *Child abuse and neglect in Asia Pacific countries: Challenges and opportunities,* 79–85. New Delhi: Jaypee Brothers Medical Publishers.

Seth, R. (2013b). Child protection: Assigning responsibilities? In R. N. Srivastava, R. Seth, & J. v. Niekerk (Eds.), *Child abuse and neglect in Asia Pacific countries: Challenges and* opportunities, 129–134. New Delhi: Jaypee Brothers Medical Publishers.

Slee, J. (2012). Addressing systemic neglect of young indigenous children's rights to attend school in the Northern Territory, Australia. *Child Abuse Review, 21*(2), 99–113. doi:10.1002/car.1166

Spencer, N., Devereux, E., Wallace, A., Sundrum, R., Shenoy, M., Bacchus, C., & Logan, S. (2005). Disabling conditions and registration for child abuse and neglect: A population-based study. *Pediatrics, 116*(3), 609–613. doi:10.1542/peds.2004-1882

Spencer, N. J. (2005). Disentangling the effects of different components of socioeconomic status on health in early childhood. *J Epidemiol Community Health, 59*(1), 2. doi:10.1136/jech.2004.027789

Spencer, N. J. (2008). Child poverty in perspective: The UNICEF report on child well-being in rich countries. *Arch Dis Child,* adc.2007.120048. doi:10.1136/adc.2007.120048

Srivastava, R. N. (2011). Child abuse and neglect: Asia Pacific Conference and the Delhi Declaration. *Indian Pediatrics, 49,* 11–12.

Stalker, K., & McArthur, K. (2012). Child abuse, child protection and disabled children: A review of recent research. *Child Abuse Review, 21*(1), 24–40. doi:10.1002/car.1154

Stoltenborgh, M., Bakermans-Kranenburg, M. J., & IJzendoorn, M. H. (2013). The neglect of child neglect: A meta-analytic review of the prevalence of neglect. *Social Psychiatry and Psychiatric Epidemiology, 48*(3), 345–355. doi:10.1007/s00127-012-0549-y

Straus, M. A., & Kantor, G. K. (2005) Definition and measurement of negectful behavior: Some principles and guidelines. *Child Abuse & Neglect, 29*(1), 19–29.

Sullivan, P. M., & Knutson, J. F. (1998). The association between child maltreatment and disabilities in a hospital-based epidemiological study. *Child Abuse and Neglect, 22,* 271–288.

Sullivan, P. M., & Knutson, J. F. (2000). Maltreatment and disabilities: A population-based epidemiological study. *Child Abuse & Neglect, 24*(10), 1257–1273. doi:http://dx.doi.org/10.1016/S0145-2134(00)00190-3

Swift, K. J. (1995). An outrage to common decency: Historical perspectives on child neglect. *Child Welfare, 74*(1), 71–91.

Sylvestre, A., & Mérette, C. (2010). Language delay in severely neglected children: A cumulative or specific effect of risk factors? *Child Abuse & Neglect, 34*(6), 414–428.

Turney, D., & Tanner, K. (2005). Understanding and working with neglect. *Research and Practice: Every Child Matters Research Briefings, 10,* 1–8.

U.K. Department of Health. (2009). Promoting the health and wellbeing of looked after children: Revised statutory guidance. London, UK: Department of Health.

UNICEF. (2004). The State of the World's Children 2005: Childhood under threat. New York, NY: UNICEF.

U.S. Department of Health and Human Services, Administration for Children and Families, Administration on Children, Youth and Families, & Children's Bureau. (2011). *Child Maltreatment 2010.*

Walker, S. P., Wachs, T. D., Meeks Gardner, J., Lozoff, B., Wasserman, G. A., Pollitt, E., & Carter, J. A. (2007). Child development: Risk factors for adverse outcomes in developing countries. *The Lancet, 369*(9556), 145–157. doi:http://dx.doi.org/10.1016/S0140-6736(07)60076-2

Waterston, T., & Mann, N. (2005). Children's rights. *Arch Dis Child, 90*(2), 171–173. doi:10.1136/adc.2004.064899

Webster, D. W., & Starnes, M. (2000). Reexamining the association between child access prevention gun laws and unintentional shooting deaths of children. *Pediatrics, 106*(6), 1466–1469.

WHO. (1999). Child maltreatment. Retrieved from http://www.who.int/topics/child_abuse/en/

World Bank. (2011). World Development Report 2012: Gender equality and development. Washington, DC: World Bank.

Young Lives. (2012). Changing Lives in a changing world: Young Lives children growing up. Oxford, UK: Young Lives, Department of International Development.

Zielinski, D. S. (2009). Child maltreatment and adult socioeconomic well-being. *Child Abuse & Neglect, 33*(10), 666–678.

7

The Effects of Childhood Maltreatment and of Exposure to Early Toxic Stress

Kathleen Kendall-Tackett

Child maltreatment is, unfortunately, a common experience for children in industrialized nations and around the world, and researchers have been documenting the effects of maltreatment for more than three decades. More recent research has indicated that exposure to abuse and neglect constitutes "early toxic stress," and has long-term implications for both physical and mental health (Shonkoff, Boyce, & McEwen, 2009).

THE IMPACT OF ADVERSE CHILDHOOD EXPERIENCES

An increasing number of studies have specifically addressed common conditions that increase the rate of premature mortality, such as cardiovascular disease, metabolic syndrome, and diabetes (Kendall-Tackett, 2007a). But adult survivors of childhood maltreatment comprise a large percentage of patients with conditions, such as depression, post-traumatic stress disorder, chronic pain syndromes, and sexually transmitted infections.

The first major study to find a link between abuse and physical health in adults was the Adverse Childhood Experiences (ACE) study. Felitti and colleagues (Felitti et al., 1998) studied more than 17,000 adult patients from the Kaiser Permanente Health Maintenance Organization in San Diego, California. The events that they defined as adverse childhood experiences included psychological abuse; physical abuse; sexual abuse; emotional abuse; and parental substance abuse, mental illness, partner violence, and criminal behavior. They found that patients who experienced four or more types of adverse childhood events were at significantly increased risk for such diverse conditions as ischemic heart disease, cancer, stroke, chronic bronchitis, emphysema, diabetes, skeletal fractures, and hepatitis.

The ACE study results underscored the need to study abuse in the overall context of other types of abuse, maltreatment, and adversity. Dong and colleagues analyzed data from 8,629 adult members of an HMO, and found that ACEs were highly likely to co-occur (Dong et al., 2004). Two-thirds of their participants reported at least one ACE, and 81 to 98 percent of those who had experienced one had experienced more than one. Most had experienced from two to four other types.

Other researchers have found similar results with large data sets. For example, using data from the National Comorbidity Survey, researchers found that a history of childhood abuse increased the risk of cardiovascular disease for women by ninefold. There was not a similar relationship for men, and depression did not explain this relationship (Batten, Aslan, Maciejewski, & Mazure, 2004). The National Comorbidity Survey is a nationally representative study of prevalence, risk factors, and social consequences of psychiatric disorders in the United States with a large sample of 5,877 adults.

A meta-analysis of 24 studies (N = 48,801) found that physical and sexual child abuse increased the risk of adult-onset neurological and musculoskeletal conditions (including migraines, arthritis, and broken bones), respiratory problems, cardiovascular disease and stroke, gastrointestinal conditions, and metabolic disorders, including diabetes and obesity (Wegman & Stetler, 2009).

Physical and sexual abuse in childhood or adolescence increased the risk of type 2 diabetes in adult women using data from the Nurses' Health Study II (Rich-Edwards et al., 2010). Both physical and sexual abuse increased the risk, in a dose-response way: the more severe the abuse, the more severe the symptoms. The highest hazards ratio was for repeated forced sex. Girls who had experienced repeated forced sex had 69 percent higher risks of diabetes than girls who were not sexually abused. There was also an additive effect, with those who experienced both types of abuse at higher risk than those who experienced only one type. Adult BMI (body mass index) explained some of the relationship between abuse and diabetes, but the physically and sexually abused girls had higher BMIs than nonabused girls. Further, the trajectories between abused and nonabused girls had grown wider by adulthood, meaning that the BMIs of the abused girls increased at a faster rate than those of nonabused girls. These findings were particularly true for the girls exposed to repeated forced sex in childhood or adolescence.

Talbot and colleagues (Talbot et al., 2009) also found that severe childhood sexual abuse was associated with higher cumulative medical illness burden, worse physical functioning, and greater bodily pain in a study of 163 male and female psychiatric patients. In terms of illness burden, child sexual abuse was comparable to adding eight years of chronological age. In terms of activities of daily living and bodily pain, sexual abuse was comparable to adding 20 years of chronological age. The authors concluded that early detection of patients' abuse histories could lead to interventions that prevent or decelerate the progression of morbidity in this group.

Chronic pain syndromes are also more likely in men and women who have experienced childhood abuse. A study of 6,593 high school students in mainland China found that physical and sexual abuse was associated with higher levels of a number of physical symptoms including stomach pain, nightmares, poor appetite, shortness of breath, chest pain, dizziness, irregular menstruation, and suicidal ideation (Wong et al., 2009). These symptoms often appear in childhood and continue on in adults. Severe abuse led to more severe symptoms.

PATHWAYS BY WHICH ABUSE CAN CAUSE SEQUELAE

As the above-cited studies indicate, child maltreatment increases the likelihood of a number of different chronic health conditions for adults, and the roots of these conditions often start during childhood. The intriguing question is why this occurs. These health effects highlight the various ways that childhood maltreatment impacts developing children, and how these changes manifest in physical and mental health sequelae in adults. Child maltreatment impacts children and adults in five domains of functioning: physiological, behavioral, cognitive, social, and emotional. These are pathways by which childhood abuse can produce sequelae in adults. Each of these five pathways is briefly described below and together they provide a more complete picture of the impact of childhood abuse.

Physiological Pathways

Children's brains and neurological systems mature at the most rapid rate during the first five years of life but continue to mature throughout childhood, and are, therefore, especially vulnerable to the impact of traumatic events due to their effects on young brain development (DeBellis, 2011; Heim & Nemeroff, 2009). For example, Sherin and Nemeroff (2011) note:

> There is a burgeoning literature documenting that early adverse experience, including prenatal stress and stress throughout childhood, has profound and long-lasting effects on the development of neuro-biological systems, thereby "programming" subsequent stress reactivity and vulnerability to develop PTSD. (p. 273)

Similarly, Teicher (2002) noted that early abuse and neglect may result in permanent changes to the developing brain:

> Stress can set off a ripple of hormonal changes that permanently wire a child's brain to cope with a malevolent world. Through this chain of events, violence and abuse pass from generation to generation as well as from one society to the next. Our stark conclusion is that we see the need to do much more to ensure that child abuse does not happen in the first place, because once these key brain alterations occur, there may be no going back. (p. 75)

One way to understand the effects of toxic stress is to understand the components of the normal stress response and how that can be overwhelmed by abuse and neglect. The earlier and more severe the abuse, the more pervasive the effects appear to be (Shonkoff et al., 2009).

The Stress Response

The stress response is designed to preserve the life of the organism, and begins when a person perceives a potential threat (DeBellis, 2011; Kendall-Tackett, 2010; Lovallo, 1997). The response begins with the response of the sympathetic nervous system, which responds to perceived threat by releasing catecholamines (norepinephrine, epinephrine, and dopamine). This is the fight-or-flight response, and it occurs instantly after threat exposure (DeBellis, 2011). Norepinephrine accounts for classic symptoms of PTSD including hyperarousal, heightened startle, and increased coding of fear memories (Sherin & Nemeroff, 2011). The physiologic response is the same for physical or psychological threat.

The hypothalamic-pituitary-adrenal (HPA) axis is also central to the stress response. The HPA axis produces a cascade of hormonal responses, starting with the hypothalamus, which secretes corticotrophin-releasing hormone (CRH). CRH causes the pituitary gland to release the stress hormone adrenocorticotrophic hormone (ACTH). ACTH signals the cortex of the adrenal glands to secrete the stress hormone cortisol (Heim & Nemeroff, 2009; Lovallo, 1997).

The final component of the stress response is the immune system, which responds to threat by increasing inflammation (Corwin & Pajer, 2008; Kendall-Tackett, 2007b). Like other aspects of the stress response, the inflammatory response is meant to preserve the life of the organism. It has two main functions: fight infection and heal wounds. In anticipation of a possible threat, the body is prepared to mend itself. The difficulty is when the inflammatory response is chronically elevated, as researchers have recently found in samples of abuse survivors.

Researchers in the field of psychoneuroimmunology generally assess inflammation by measuring plasma levels of proinflammatory cytokines, which are messenger molecules of the immune system (Kendall-Tackett, 2010; Miller, Cohen, & Ritchey, 2002). The proinflammatory cytokines that are most often measured in depression and trauma research are interleukin-1β (IL-1β), interleukin-6 (IL-6), and tumor necrosis factor-α (TNF-α). Researchers sometimes include other measures of inflammation in their studies. These include interferon-γ (IFN-γ), soluble-intercellular adhesion molecule (sICAM), fibrinogen, or C-reactive protein (CRP). Inflammation is specifically harmful because it increases the risk of depression, heart disease, metabolic syndrome, and diabetes (Kendall-Tackett, 2007a, 2010).

Childhood maltreatment was shown to affect clinically relevant levels of C-reactive protein, a general measure of inflammation, when measured 20 years after the abuse (Danese, Pariante, Caspi, Taylor, & Poulton, 2007). The more severe the abuse, the higher the level of inflammation. The participants (N = 1,037) were part of the Dunedin Multidisciplinary Health and Development Study, a longitudinal, birth-cohort study from Dunedin, New Zealand. White blood cell count and fibrinogen were also elevated in those who experienced childhood physical or sexual abuse. Fibrinogen is of concern because it increases the "stickiness" of blood and increases clotting, which can increase the risk of both heart attack and stroke.

At the 32-year follow-up of the same cohort, the participants were assessed for the impact of childhood adversity on three age-related disease markers: major depression, high inflammation, and a cluster of metabolic risk factors that included overweight, high blood pressure, high LDL and low HDL cholesterol (Danese et al., 2009). "Childhood adversity" was defined as low socioeconomic status (SES), child maltreatment, and social isolation. Children exposed to childhood adversities had elevated risk of depression, high inflammation levels, and high rates of the metabolic risk factors.

Effects of Childhood Maltreatment on Sleep

Childhood maltreatment can also impact sleep, and that can affect both physical and mental health in children and adults. Sleep difficulties are remarkably common in abuse survivors. For example, in a French sample, 33 percent of teens who had been raped indicated that they "slept badly" compared with 16 percent of the nonassaulted comparison group (Choquet, Darves-Bornoz, Ledoux, Manfredi, & Hassler, 1997). In an adult community sample from Germany, Austria, and Switzerland, 68 percent of sexual abuse survivors reported having sleep difficulties, with 45 percent having repetitive nightmares (Teegan, 1999).

Hulme (2000) found that sleep problems among female sexual abuse survivors were common in a primary-care sample. Fifty-two percent of sexual abuse survivors reported that they could not sleep at night (compared with 24 percent of the nonabused group), and 36 percent reported nightmares (compared with 13 percent). Intrusive symptoms were also common, with 53 percent of sexual abuse survivors reporting sudden thoughts or images of past events (compared with 18 percent of the nonabused group).

Sleep problems and nightmares often begin in childhood and can have lasting effects on the health and well-being of abuse survivors. Sleep difficulties are related to an upregulation of the stress response. In a lab study, 20 healthy participants were in a within-subjects crossover-design study comparing a good night's sleep with a night of total sleep deprivation (Franzen et al., 2011). The day after each night, participants were exposed to a lab-induced stressor. Sleep deprivation made people more vulnerable to stress and increased their systolic blood pressure. The authors speculated that sleep loss may increase cardiovascular risk by dysregulating stress physiology.

Childhood family environment moderated the relationship between daily stress and sleep in a seven-day study of 87 undergraduates (Hanson & Chen, 2010). As predicted, participants with more difficult family environments reported poorer sleep and had an increased cortisol response on days where they experienced more stress. The students slept longer and had lower levels of cortisol if they described their parents as "warm."

Chronically disturbed sleep can elevate cortisol and glucose levels, and increases both insulin and insulin resistance (McEwen, 2003). Sleep deprivation also provokes an inflammatory response. Long-term sleep deprivation can seriously impair mental and physical health and increases the risk of depression and PTSD, and cardiovascular disease, metabolic syndrome, and diabetes (Suarez & Goforth, 2010).

In summary, abuse and neglect can lead to sequelae in both children and adults because it alters the physiological response to stress in some dysfunctional ways. Maltreatment can also lead to poor sleep, which can also cause physical and mental health sequelae—both immediately and long term. Unfortunately, maltreatment does not simply alter the child's physiology. It also increases the likelihood of participation in harmful behaviors.

Behavioral Pathways

Childhood abuse also increases the likelihood of several harmful behaviors. Below is a brief description of studies on the effects of child maltreatment on substance abuse, smoking, suicide, and high-risk sexual activity.

Substance Abuse

Abuse survivors are at increased risk for abusing alcohol and drugs, and a number of studies have found that a high percentage of substance abusers have a history of childhood maltreatment. The findings are remarkably consistent across study type and population. For example, a study from Australia compared 967 opioid-dependent patients of an outpatient treatment program with a matched group of 346 non-opioid-dependent controls (Conroy, Degenhardt, Mattick, & Nelson, 2009). Fifty-six percent of the opioid-dependent females reported penetrative child sexual abuse compared to 28 percent of the females in the control group. For physical abuse, approximately 58 percent of the opioid-dependent males and females reported physical abuse, compared to 36 to 42 percent of the control group (males and females respectively). Men were more likely to report physical and emotional abuse; women were more likely to report sexual abuse. There was no difference in rates of neglect between the opioid-dependent and control groups.

Unfortunately, substance abuse can also increase the risk of revictimization. A prospective study of 276 college women examined the impact of childhood victimization on revictimization risk (Messman-Moore, Ward, & Brown, 2009). During the eight-month follow-up, 9 percent of the sample was raped. In 88 percent of the cases, substance abuse was involved. The authors concluded that college women with PTSD symptoms are at greater risk of rape if they abuse substances in order to reduce their distress and self-medicate. They may also consume alcohol to reduce tension, and to improve (in their perception, at least) social and sexual interactions.

Smoking

Smoking is also more likely among teens and adults with a history of abuse. In a sample from the ACE study of 9,215 middle-aged adults, smoking was related to each type of childhood adversity (Anda et al., 1999). Those who had experienced five or more adverse childhood experiences were five times more likely to have started smoking before age 15, twice as likely to still be smoking, and almost three times more likely to be heavy smokers. Indeed, a person with a history of four or more types of adverse childhood experiences was 390 percent more likely to have chronic obstructive pulmonary disease (COPD) than was a person with a history of none of these types of adverse experiences. The only exception was one finding with regard to sexual abuse: sexual abuse that happened before age 14 and predated the age of smoking was associated with a fourfold increase in smoking initiation (Anda et al., 1999).

Suicide

In data from the National Comorbidity Survey, men and women with a history of child sexual abuse had increased risk of suicide (Molnar, Berkman, & Buka, 2001). The odds of suicide attempts for women were two to four times higher than the nonabused group, and 4 to 11 times higher for men. The people at highest risk were those who experienced child rape. For women, 27 percent of those who experienced child rape reported suicide attempts, as did 31 percent of the men who reported child rape. This was compared to 3 percent of the total sample.

A study from New Zealand of 1,000 young adults also found that childhood abuse increased risks of suicidal ideation, suicide attempts between the ages of 16 to 25 (Fergusson, Boden, & Horwood, 2008). Severity of sexual abuse also made a difference. Those who had experienced attempted or completed penetration had 2.4 times the rates of mental disorders compared to those not exposed to sexual abuse.

High-Risk Sexual Behavior

Risky sexual behavior is the most highly documented form of harmful behavior in abuse survivors. This finding holds true for males and females, and is consistent across the range of ages, ethnic groups, income levels, and sexual orientations. The overwhelming majority of studies involve sexual abuse survivors. However, physical abuse and neglect also increase risk.

Childhood or adolescent sexual abuse was related to sexual-risk behavior in a population study of 2,810 Swedish adults (Steel & Herlitz, 2005). In this sample, history of sexual abuse was associated with younger age at first intercourse, younger age at first diagnosis of sexually transmitted disease (chlamydia, HPV, gonorrhea, and herpes), higher rates of unintended pregnancies, greater likelihood of participation in group sex, greater likelihood of exchanging sex for money or other necessities, more frequent substance abuse in the past 48 hours, and higher likelihood of adult sexual and physical assault. Legal abortions were also higher in the sexually abused versus nonabused groups.

Childhood sexual abuse was also related to increased rates of abortion in adolescence or early adulthood in a sample of 1,265 young adults in New Zealand (Boden, Fergusson, & Horwood, 2009). Severity of sexual abuse was significantly related to the number of abortions: those exposed to severe child sexual abuse had twice as many as their nonabused counterparts, or those who experienced milder forms of sexual abuse (i.e., without penetration). The authors concluded that their findings indicated a causal chain in which child sexual abuse leads to increased rates of pregnancy, which leads to increased rates of abortion.

In a sample of 30 African American women, higher post-traumatic stress symptoms were associated with more sexual partners, greater frequency of vaginal sex without a condom, and having sex while intoxicated (Munroe, Kibler, Ma, Dollar, & Coleman, 2010). PTSD symptoms were negatively correlated with perceived sexual control, but were not correlated with sexual compulsivity or sensation seeking.

In summary, people with a history of childhood abuse are more likely to participate in a wide range of harmful behaviors. High-risk sexual behavior and substance abuse are the behaviors with the largest body of research support. But abuse and neglect have been shown to increase smoking and suicide as well. Interventions designed to curb harmful behaviors will not be effective unless they also address the beliefs that underlie the harmful behaviors. These are also known as the cognitive pathways.

Cognitive Pathways

Childhood abuse can influence what abused children and adults think about themselves and other people. The beliefs can have a substantial impact on abuse survivors. Cognitions influence the abuse survivors' risk of depression, PTSD, substance abuse, high-risk sexual behavior, revictimization, and the quality of their social relationships. Yet these cognitions are rarely addressed. Below are some of the cognitions that are common in abuse survivors.

Shame

Shame is one of the most commonly occurring beliefs that follows a history of childhood abuse, and it is one of the most harmful. Shame is the key emotional component of a coordinated psychobiological response to perceived social evaluation or rejection (Dickerson, Gruenewald, & Kemeny, 2004), and involves an upregulation of all three components of the stress response (Kendall-Tackett, 2013). It is a painful emotion that usually results following conduct or circumstances damaging to self-respect. It involves feelings of self-contempt, and leaves people feeling exposed, vulnerable, and "defective" (Persons, Kershaw, Sikkema, & Hansen, 2010).

Children who are subjected to "severe or humiliating abuse are at high risk of feeling bad about themselves at the very core of their being" (34), where shame becomes a part of their "permanent landscape" (Whiffen & MacIntosh, 2005). An individual who experiences shame expects others to be rejecting and scornful about their supposed defects. Thus, as adults, shame may be elicited as a response to both real and imagined mistreatment by others. The internalization of shame can lead survivors to withdraw from others in order to protect themselves from further humiliation or, alternatively, to attach to others to conceal their shame. Thus, shame may link the intrapersonal world to the interpersonal one, and it may isolate the survivor from the very relationships that could be used to manage distress and to create a more positive sense of self.

Self-Efficacy

Self-efficacy refers to a person's confidence in his or her ability to manage the vicissitudes of life. It is grounded in attachment theory, where the quality of children's primary attachment provides the "safe base" from which they gain mastery of the world (Ryan, Solberg, & Brown, 1996; Weinfield, Sroufe, Egeland, & Carlson, 1999). Children with secure attachments learn that they can get their needs met through their own efforts. In contrast, when children are abused or neglected, and their attachments are insecure, they grow up believing that their efforts are ineffective and they must rely on others who may or may not meet their needs (Weinfield et al., 1999). In the Physical Health and Disability Study, a survey of older adults

(N = 1,460), the researchers found that childhood abuse was related to lower self-efficacy and the number of current medical problems (Sachs-Ericsson, Cromer, Hernandez, & Kendall-Tackett, 2009). Self-efficacy explained, in part, the abuse-health relationship.

Hostility

Hostility is another cognition that is common among abuse survivors. It includes interpersonal mistrust, suspiciousness, cynicism about human nature, and a tendency to interpret the actions of others as aggressive (Kubzansky & Kawachi, 2000; Lewis et al., 2009; Smith, 1992). It is a reasonable response, given the abuse survivors' experience of the world. However, it can lead to a number of consequences for both health and interpersonal relationships. Trait hostility increases physiological arousal because of the way hostile people interpret the world; they are more likely to perceive even neutral events in a negative way, responding strongly because they perceive interpersonal threat (Kiecolt-Glaser & Newton, 2001).

In a study of undergraduates, students who reported family dysfunction had a negative or malevolent view of themselves and the world. Child abuse of all types was related to symptom distress, whereas parental alcoholism was not (Harter & Vanecek, 2000). A study of 294 newly abstinent cocaine/opiate-dependent patients (Roy, 2001) found a significant correlation between hostility and childhood maltreatment. Maltreatment included physical, sexual, and emotional abuse, as well as physical and emotional neglect.

Hostile persons can undermine relationships through their mistrustful thoughts and antagonistic actions, and are more likely to have negative social relations with others (Smith & Ruiz, 2002). Hostile people are more likely to be socially isolated, to be insecure about their current relationships, and to perceive that others are making negative judgments about them.

Betrayal Trauma

A construct related to hostility is betrayal trauma. Betrayal trauma refers to traumas in which people are betrayed or violated in some way by individuals or institutions that they depend upon for survival (Freyd, Klest, & Allard, 2005). It suggests that conscious appraisals of betrayal may be inhibited at the time of the trauma and as long as the victim is dependent on the perpetrator. Betrayal trauma may not threaten death or injury, but it can be damaging to well-being, relationships, self-concept, and beliefs about others and the world. These experiences represent a mismatch between what *should be* and what *is*. Traumas with high levels of betrayal are more likely to result in depression, anxiety, and other symptoms compared to traumas with high physical threat but not betrayal (e.g., car accidents) (Freyd et al., 2005).

In summary, what we believe about ourselves or others has a significant impact on our health and our resiliency to stress. Not surprisingly, our beliefs also can impact the quality of relationships. Unfortunately, these too can be influenced by childhood abuse.

Social Pathways

Social bonds are essential to our health and well-being. Eisenberger (2011) argues that over the course of our evolutionary history, avoiding social rejection and staying socially connected increased our chances of survival. Being part of a group provided resources, protection, and safety. Recent neuroscience research has found that our bodies process threats to our relationships as threats to our survival (Jenson-Campbell & MacDonald, 2011).

Rejection or negative social evaluation is associated with increases in stress hormones, increased cardiovascular response, and greater proinflammatory cytokines. Social losses, emotional pain, grief, or loneliness shares the same neural pathways as physical pain (Eisenberger, 2011; Panksepp, 2011). Social losses during childhood are especially noxious and can predispose people to chronically elevated psychic pain, which predisposes them to depression for the rest of their lives.

Quality of Current Primary Intimate Relationship

Unfortunately, childhood abuse can disrupt relationships abuse survivors have as adults. In an Australian study, sexual abuse survivors were more likely to be involved with alcoholic partners and to report dissatisfaction with their current relationships. But sexual abuse had no significant impact on perceived level of social support, having someone to confide in, or currently being in a current relationship (Fleming, Mullen, Sibthorpe, & Bammer, 1999).

In another study, abuse survivors were more likely to report that their partners were low on care and high on control (Mullen, Martin, Anderson, Romans, & Herbison, 1994). They were also more likely to report that their partners did not provide emotional support. However, the abuse survivors in this study reported that they did receive emotional support from peers. Abuse survivors were as likely as the control group to confide in friends, siblings, or their own children as the nonabused group.

Abuse can also impact stability of adult partnerships. In a longitudinal study from Avon, in the United Kingdom (N = 8,292) (Roberts, O'Connor, Dunn, Golding, & the ALSPAC Study Team, 2004), women who had been sexually abused were more likely than nonabused women to be single parents, cohabitating in their current relationships or stepparents, and less satisfied with their current partners. Similarly, a study of 1,196 men and women (676 abused/neglected, and 520 controls) found that male and female abuse survivors reported higher rates of cohabitation, walking out on partnerships, and divorce than was true for the controls. Abused or neglected females were less likely than female controls to have positive perceptions of their current romantic partners or to be sexually faithful (Colman & Widom, 2004). Abuse survivors were more likely to report that they were not currently involved in a relationship, and all types of maltreatment increased the risk for divorce, with the highest likelihood among the sexually abused males.

Socioeconomic Status

Another way childhood abuse can influence survivors is in their lifetime socioeconomic status. Adult survivors of childhood abuse can be affected in both their level of lifetime income and their educational attainment. For example, in a study of gay and bisexual men, men who were sexually abused were more likely to have a lower lifetime income and to have completed less education than their nonabused counterparts (Jinich et al., 1998). In a sample from primary care, sexually abused women were more likely to use public aid and to have lower educational and occupational status than women without a history of sexual abuse (Hulme, 2000).

Mullen and colleagues also found that sexual abuse survivors had a lower income than a matched comparison group (Mullen et al., 1994). The abuse survivors who experienced the most serious abuse had the lowest lifetime income. Their jobs were also significantly more likely to include unskilled labor despite education levels that were comparable to the nonabused group. Along these same lines, a recent study of 172 men and women from Victoria, Australia, found that 64 percent of CSA survivors were unemployed at the time of the study, and 61 percent had completed high school or had fewer years of education (O'Leary, Coohey, & Easton, 2010).

Homelessness

Homelessness can also be a consequence of past abuse, and it may begin during the teen years. A qualitative study of 28 homeless youths found that family environment and abuse experiences were related to their homelessness (Ferguson, 2009). The teens identified a number of issues related to their homelessness, including instability at home, abandonment, and caregiver substance abuse. The parents provided little structure for the teens as the parents themselves were struggling with mental illness, substance abuse, or homelessness. Many of the teens had experienced repeated incidents of abandonment by multiple caregivers, and reported verbal, emotional, physical, and sexual abuse.

In another qualitative study, 302 homeless young people (ages 12 to 20) were asked about their reasons for leaving home (Mallet & Rosenthal, 2009). Out of the total, 103 indicated that they left home because of a parents or stepparent's physical violence. Females were more likely to be targeted by mothers, while males were more likely to be targeted by stepmothers. Most of the stories indicated that maternal violence was a common rather than a one-time occurrence. The majority did not attempt to return home again.

Revictimization

In a particularly cruel twist of fate, abused children are at increased risk of being revictimized throughout their lives. And revictimization is shockingly common among abuse survivors. For example, in a community sample of child sexual abuse survivors, 41 percent reported that they had experienced sexual revictimization in relationships, at work, or in therapy (Teegan, 1999). Grauerholz's review indicated that anywhere from 32 to 82 percent of people who are sexually victimized as children are sexually revictimized as adults (Grauerholz, 2000). Most previous research has focused on the link between childhood sexual abuse and sexual revictimization. But recent studies have found that child physical abuse and neglect can also increase risk of physical or sexual revictimization.

Revictimization can begin during childhood. Two prospective studies of preschoolers revealed that child maltreatment in early life predicted peer victimization in elementary school. These children's home experiences included harsh discipline, marital conflict, stress, abuse, and maternal hostility (Schwartz, Dodge, Pettit, & Bates, 2000). Children from abusive homes who were able to make friends, however, were less likely to be victimized by peers. In the second study, early maltreatment also predicted both bullying and peer victimization in a study of 169 maltreated and 98 nonmaltreated boys and girls. All types of maltreatment put children at risk for peer victimization and bullying. These findings were true for both boys and girls (Shields & Cicchetti, 2001).

Revictimization can also occur in college students. Messman-Moore and Brown (2004) studied the child abuse and adult rape histories of 925 college women. Logistic regression indicated that a history of child sexual abuse almost doubled the risk for adult rape. The rates of adult rape varied widely depending on if they had experienced zero, one, two, or three types of abuse: 14 percent of women who experienced zero types of child abuse were raped, 21 percent of women who experienced one type, 36 percent of women who experienced two types, and 43 percent of women who experienced all three types.

One possible reason why abuse survivors are at higher risk could be their history of psychiatric disorders. In a survey of representative samples of 2,030 youth (ages 2 to 17) and their parents, Cuevas and colleagues found that psychiatric diagnoses increased risk of victimization (Cuevas, Finkelhor, Ormrod, & Turner, 2009). Using logistic regression, the researchers found that psychiatric diagnoses increased the risk for several types of victimization, including poly-victimization, conventional crime victimization, maltreatment, and peer or sibling victimization, but did not increase the risk of sexual abuse.

Post-traumatic stress disorder from earlier abuse may also increase the risk of revictimization. Messman-Moore, Brown, and Koelsch (2005) examined the role of post-traumatic stress symptoms and self-dysfunction as both consequences and predictors of sexual revictimization. Self-dysfunction refers to maladaptive efforts to regulate affect, disturbances in intimate and sexual relationships, and disrupted sense of self, all of which lead to increased risk of revictimization. Disturbed relatedness refers to self-concept, sexual identity, and distortion of basic beliefs about trust, safety, and control in significant relationships. The authors noted that self-dysfunction may turn out to be more important to revictimization in that it affects social functioning and interpersonal behavior.

In summary, without intervention, childhood abuse also has a pervasive negative effect on social relationships. Unfortunately, this breakdown of social ties increases risk of revictimization, homelessness, and lower lifetime income. Psychiatric disorders, such as depression and PTSD, can lead to further deterioration of social relationships, but are also harmful to abuse survivors in and of themselves.

Emotional Pathways

The most common sequelae of past abuse are emotional sequelae: depression and post-traumatic stress disorder. These are both emotional outcomes, but are mechanisms by which abuse can lead to difficulties with relationships, harmful behaviors, and physical health problems.

Depression

Depression is a common sequela of past abuse. For example, adolescents who had been raped in a nationally representative sample of French teens were significantly more likely to report that they "felt depressed" and "felt unhappy" than were their counterparts who had not been raped (Choquet et al., 1997). Similarly, in another sample of teens and young adults, those with a history of child maltreatment were three times more likely to be depressed or suicidal (Brown, Cohen, Johnson, & Smailes, 1999). In the Commonwealth Fund Adolescent Health Survey, physically and sexually abused girls were five times more likely to report depressive symptoms than nonabused girls (Diaz, Simatov, & Rickert, 2000).

Felitti (1991) found that 83 percent of sexually abused patients were depressed compared with 32 percent of the nonabused group. The majority of the depressed patients had never been treated. In another primary care sample, 65 percent of the women with a history of child sexual abuse were depressed compared with 35 percent of the nonabused group (Hulme, 2000). In a study of chronic pain in primary-care patients, women with a history of child or domestic abuse were significantly more likely to be depressed than a matched group of nonabused women (Kendall-Tackett, Marshall, & Ness, 2003).

In a sample of 357 first-time mothers, women who had been sexually abused as children were significantly more likely to be depressed during their pregnancies and to have been both physically and verbally abused before and during pregnancy (Benedict, Paine, Paine, Brandt, & Stallings, 1999). They were also more likely to report negative life events. In a community sample of women, every woman whose sexual abuse involved penetration was depressed (Cheasty, Clare, & Collins, 1998). The lifetime prevalence of major depression was 86 percent in sexual abuse survivors with PTSD, and 29 percent of these women were currently depressed (Bremner et al., 1997). Another study of 201 undergraduates found that survivors of childhood sexual abuse were more likely to ruminate on sadness, which increased their vulnerability to depression, than their nonabused counterparts (Conway, Mendelson, Giannopoulos, Csank, & Holm, 2004).

A sample of 172 sexual abuse survivors in their thirties and forties from Victoria, Australia, examined such symptoms as guilt, sadness, grief, helplessness, emotional numbness, depression, anxiety, panic attacks, fears and phobias, dissociation, and a sense of vulnerability (O'Leary et al., 2010). The authors found that the more severe the abuse, the higher the number of mental health symptoms. There was no increase for a younger age of onset. Participants who told someone at the time of the abuse had more symptoms. The authors speculated that this may reflect an inadequate response from the people to whom they disclosed. Only 11 percent of participants discussed their abuse with someone within a year after the abuse. These participants reported fewer symptoms.

Post-Traumatic Stress Disorder

Post-traumatic stress disorder (PTSD) is another common, but not universal, response to childhood maltreatment and adversity (Heim & Nemeroff, 2009). For example, a sample of 157 children ages 8 to 17 found that physical abuse, sexual abuse, and witnessing domestic violence were each significantly associated with PTSD (Luthra et al., 2009). Other trauma exposures were not related to PTSD. These included witnessing or being the victim of a crime, and exposure to accidents, fire, or disaster.

A study of 20 sexually abused children in Turkey found that 35 percent met the criteria for PTSD at their first assessment, 10 percent for general anxiety disorder, and 10 percent for major depression (Ozbaran et al., 2009). There were no significant associations between the diagnoses and demographic characteristics and type or duration of abuse. Two years later and following treatment, the children no longer met criteria for PTSD, generalized anxiety disorder, or major depression, but they still showed a significant number of behavior problems, such as attentional problems, aggressiveness, social withdrawal, and somatization.

In a randomized representative study of youth ages 10 to 16, sexual assault that occurred between the two interviews was significantly related to both depression and PTSD symptoms (Boney-McCoy & Finkelhor, 1996). Because of the prospective nature of the design, the authors felt a causal link could be made between victimization and the subsequent development of depression and PTSD. In a study of 100 consecutive referrals to an inner-city child and adolescent psychiatry clinic, 59 reported trauma exposure (Silva et al., 2000). Of the 59 children, 22 met full criteria for PTSD, 32 percent had some symptoms, and 46 percent had no symptoms. Witnessing domestic violence and being physically abused predicted PTSD. Higher IQ appeared to protect children and adolescents from PTSD.

A study of 221 female veterans who were receiving primary care found that childhood emotional abuse was associated with increased bodily pain and somatic symptoms, greater odds of using pain medication in the past six months, and more visits to healthcare providers (Lang et al., 2006). Sexual abuse was significantly associated with the number of visits to primary care, but with *less* utilization. PTSD mediated the relationship between childhood abuse and adult health outcomes.

A study of medical students from Sri Lanka also showed increased PTSD among those students who witnessed or experienced parental violence (Haj-Yahia, Tishby, & deZoysa, 2009). The more severe their experiences, the more severe their PTSD symptoms. Higher levels of PTSD were also associated with the students' perceptions that their families were rejecting or dysfunctional. In contrast, the more support the participants experienced in their families, the lower their levels of PTSD.

A study of 40 sexual abuse survivors found that 95 percent had post-traumatic stress symptoms that were clinically significant (Shakespeare-Finch & De Dassel, 2009). This study also examined post-traumatic growth. Post-traumatic growth is one step beyond successful coping; it is the actual perception of benefits from the traumatic event. Some of these benefits included increased appreciation of life and positive spiritual changes. Participants in this study also indicated that they had experienced post-traumatic growth at rates comparable to other trauma samples.

A study of 467 female college undergraduates examined the impact of childhood physical and sexual abuse, peritraumatic dissociation, and adult victimization (Hetzel & McCanne, 2005). The research indicated that the young women who had experienced both childhood physical and sexual abuse, or sexual abuse only, had higher rates of PTSD than those who experienced physical abuse only or no abuse. The women in the child abuse groups were more likely to be sexually victimized as adults than women in the nonabused group. Across all groups, peritraumatic dissociation rates were associated with both higher levels of PTSD and adult sexual or physical revictimization.

In summary, numerous previous studies have found increased rates of depression and PTSD in abuse survivors. Of the two, depression is more common. However, survivors can also show post-traumatic stress symptoms without meeting full criteria for PTSD, and these symptoms can also affect their functioning and well-being.

CONCLUSIONS

The above-cited studies indicate that childhood maltreatment has a pervasive negative impact across multiple life domains. Abuse survivors can be affected physiologically, especially if the abuse happened in early life. Their behaviors can be affected, and harmful behaviors are more likely to be the result of dysfunctional beliefs about themselves or others. What abuse survivors think about themselves and others can also influence the quality of their current relationships, their rates of revictimization, and how they negotiate their way through the wider world. Because they are more likely to be impaired in general functioning, they are also at increased risk for both lower lifetime income and for homelessness than their nonmaltreated counterparts. Exacerbating these difficulties are the emotional effects of abuse, including depression and PTSD.

As bleak as this picture is, however, there is still room for hope. Not everyone who experiences childhood maltreatment succumbs to these various problems, and may in fact navigate the shoals of life well. In addition, since we now understand the various ways that men and women *can* be influenced by past abuse, we are in a much better position to offer effective interventions that address all the ways by which child maltreatment could lead to harm. Finally, these studies underscore the need for early intervention. Children can and do heal from trauma. But this is more likely to happen if professionals respond promptly and appropriately when confronted with cases of child maltreatment.

REFERENCES

Anda, R. F., Croft, J. B., Felitti, V. J., Nordenberg, D., Giles, W. H., Williamson, D. F., & Giovino, G. (1999). Adverse childhood experiences and smoking during adolescence and adulthood. *Journal of the American Medical Association, 282,* 1652–1658.

Batten, S. V., Aslan, M., Maciejewski, P. K., & Mazure, C. M. (2004). Childhood maltreatment as a risk factor for adult cardiovascular disease and depression. *Journal of Clinical Psychiatry, 65,* 249–254.

Benedict, M. I., Paine, L. L., Paine, L. A., Brandt, D., & Stallings, R. (1999). The associations of childhood sexual abuse with depressive symptoms during pregnancy, and selected pregnancy outcomes. *Child Abuse & Neglect, 23,* 659–670.

Boden, J. M., Fergusson, D. M., & Horwood, L. J. (2009). Experience of sexual abuse in childhood and abortion in adolescence and early adulthood. *Child Abuse & Neglect, 33,* 870–876.

Boney-McCoy, S., & Finkelhor, D. (1996). Is youth victimization related to trauma symptoms and depression after controlling for prior symptoms and family relationships? A longitudinal, prospective study. *Journal of Consulting & Clinical Psychology, 64,* 1406–1461.

Bremner, J. D., Randall, P., Vermetten, E., Staib, L., Bronen, R. A., Mazure, C. M., . . . Charney, D. S. (1997). Magnetic resonance imaging-based measurements of hippocampal volume in posttraumatic stress disorder related to childhood physical and sexual abuse: A preliminary report. *Biological Psychiatry, 41,* 23–32.

Brown, J., Cohen, P., Johnson, J. G., & Smailes, E. M. (1999). Childhood abuse and neglect: Specificity of effects on adolescent and young adult depression and suicidality. *Journal of the American Academy of Child and Adolescent Psychiatry, 38,* 1490–1496.

Cheasty, M., Clare, A. W., & Collins, C. (1998). Relation between sexual abuse in childhood and adult depression: Case-control study. *British Medical Journal, 316,* 198–201.

Choquet, M., Darves-Bornoz, J.-M., Ledoux, S., Manfredi, R., & Hassler, C. (1997). Self-reported health and behavioral problems among adolescent victims of rape in France: Results of a cross-sectional survey. *Child Abuse and Neglect, 21,* 823–832.

Colman, R. A., & Widom, C. S. (2004). Childhood abuse and neglect and adult intimate relationships: A prospective study. *Child Abuse & Neglect, 28,* 1133–1151.

Conroy, E., Degenhardt, L., Mattick, R. P., & Nelson, E. C. (2009). Child maltreatment as a risk factor for opioid dependence: Comparison of family characteristics and type and severity of child maltreatment with a matched control group. *Child Abuse & Neglect, 33,* 343–352.

Conway, M., Mendelson, M., Giannopoulos, C., Csank, P. A. R., & Holm, S. L. (2004). Childhood and adult sexual abuse, rumination on sadness, and dysphoria. *Child Abuse & Neglect, 28,* 393–410.

Corwin, E. J., & Pajer, K. (2008). The psychoneuroimmunology of postpartum depression. *Journal of Women's Health, 17*(9), 1529–1534.

Cuevas, C. A., Finkelhor, D., Ormrod, R., & Turner, H. (2009). Psychiatric diagnosis as a risk marker for victimization in a national sample of children. *Journal of Interpersonal Violence, 24*(4), 636–652.

Danese, A., Moffitt, T. E., Harrington, H., Milne, B. J., Polanczyk, G., Pariante, C. M., . . . Caspi, A. (2009). Adverse childhood experiences and adult risk factors for age-related disease: Depression, inflammation, and clustering of metabolic risk markers. *Arch Pediatr Adolesc Med, 163*(12), 1135–1143. doi:163/12/1135 [pii]10.1001/archpediatrics.2009.214

Danese, A., Pariante, C. M., Caspi, A., Taylor, A., & Poulton, R. (2007). Childhood maltreatment predicts adult inflammation in a life-course study. *Proceedings of the National Academy of Sciences USA, 104*(4), 1319–1324. doi:0610362104 [pii]10.1073/pnas.0610362104

DeBellis, M. D. (2011). Neurodevelopmental biology associated with childhood sexual abuse. *Journal of Child Sexual Abuse, 20,* 548–587.

Diaz, A., Simatov, E., & Rickert, V. I. (2000). The independent and combined effects of physical and sexual abuse on health: Results from a national survey. *Journal of Pediatric & Adolescent Gynecology, 13,* 89.

Dickerson, S. S., Gruenewald, T. L., & Kemeny, M. E. (2004). When the social self is threatened: Shame, physiology, and health. *Journal of Personality, 72*(6), 1191–1216.

Dong, M., Anda, R. F., Felitti, V. J., Dube, S. R., Williamson, D. F., Thomson, T. J., et al. (2004). The interrelatedness of multiple forms of childhood abuse, neglect, and household dysfunction. *Childhood Abuse & Neglect, 28,* 771–784.

Eisenberger, N. I. (2011). The neural basis of social pain: Findings and implications. In G. MacDonald & L. A. Jensen-Campbell (Eds.), *Social pain: Neuropsychological and health implications of loss and exclusions* (pp. 53–78). Washington, DC: American Psychological Association.

Felitti, V. J. (1991). Long-term medical consequences of incest, rape, and molestation. *Southern Medical Journal, 84,* 328–331.

Felitti, V. J., Anda, R. F., Nordenberg, D., Williamson, D. F., Spitz, A. M., Edwards, V., . . . Marks, J. S. (1998). Relationship of childhood abuse and household dysfunction to many of the leading causes of death in adults: The Adverse Childhood Experiences (ACE) Study. *American Journal of Preventative Medicine, 14*(4), 245–258. doi:S0749379798000178 [pii]

Ferguson, K. M. (2009). Exploring family environment characteristics and multiple abuse experiences among homeless youth. *Journal of Interpersonal Violence, 24*(11), 1875–1891.

Fergusson, D. M., Boden, J. M., & Horwood, L. J. (2008). Exposure to childhood sexual and physical abuse and adjustment in early adulthood. *Child Abuse & Neglect, 32,* 607–619.

Fleming, J., Mullen, P. E., Sibthorpe, B., & Bammer, G. (1999). The long-term impact of childhood sexual abuse in Australian women. *Child Abuse & Neglect, 23,* 145–159.

Franzen, P. L., Gianaros, P. J., Marsland, A. L., Hall, M. H., Siegle, G. J., Dahl, R. E., & Buysse, D. J. (2011). Cardiovascular reactivity to acute psychological stress following sleep deprivation. *Psychosomatic Medicine, 73,* 679–682.

Freyd, J. J., Klest, B., & Allard, C. B. (2005). Betrayal trauma: Relationship to physical health, psychological distress, and a written disclosure intervention. *Journal of Trauma & Dissociation, 6*(3), 83–104.

Grauerholz, L. (2000). An ecological approach to understanding sexual revictimization: Linking personal, interpersonal, and sociocultural factors and processes. *Child Maltreatment, 5,* 5–17.

Haj-Yahia, M., Tishby, O., & deZoysa, P. (2009). Posttraumatic stress disorder among Sri Lankan university students as a consequence of their exposure to family violence. *Journal of Interpersonal Violence, 24*(12), 2018–2038.

Hanson, M. D., & Chen, E. (2010). Daily stress, cortisol, and sleep: The moderating role of childhood psychosocial environments. *Health Psychology, 29*(4), 394–402.

Harter, S. L., & Vanecek, R. J. (2000). Cognitive assumptions and long-term distress in survivors of childhood abuse, parental alcoholism, and dysfunctional family environments. *Cognitive Therapy and Research, 24,* 445–472.

Heim, C., & Nemeroff, C. B. (2009). Neurobiology of posttraumatic stress disorder. *CNS Spectrums, 14*(1 Suppl 1), 13–24.

Hetzel, M. D., & McCanne, T. R. (2005). The roles of peritraumatic dissociation, child physical abuse, and child sexual abuse in the development of posttraumatic stress disorder and adult victimization. *Child Abuse & Neglect, 29,* 915–930.

Hulme, P. A. (2000). Symptomatology and health care utilization of women primary care patients who experienced childhood sexual abuse. *Child Abuse and Neglect, 24,* 1471–1484.

Jenson-Campbell, L. A., & MacDonald, G. (2011). Introduction: Experiencing the ache of social injuries—An integrative approach to understanding social pain. In G. MacDonald & L. A. Jensen-Campbell (Eds.), *Social pain: Neuropsychological and health implications of loss and exclusion* (pp. 3–8). Washington, DC: American Psychological Association.

Jinich, S., Paul, J. P., Stall, R., Acree, M., Kegeles, S., Hoff, C., & Coates, T. J. (1998). Childhood sexual abuse and HIV risk-taking behavior among gay and bisexual men. *AIDS & Behavior, 2*(1), 41–51.

Kendall-Tackett, K. A. (2007a). Cardiovascular disease and metabolic syndrome as sequelae of violence against women: A psychoneuroimmunology approach. *Trauma, Violence and Abuse, 8,* 117–126.

Kendall-Tackett, K. A. (2007b). A new paradigm for depression in new mothers: The central role of inflammation and how breastfeeding and anti-inflammatory treatments protect maternal mental health. *International Breastfeeding Journal, 2*(6). Retrieved from http://www.internationalbreastfeedingjournal.com/content/2/1/6)

Kendall-Tackett, K. A. (2013). *Treating the lifetime health effects of childhood victimization* (2nd ed.). Kingston, NJ: Civic Research Institute.

Kendall-Tackett, K. A. (Ed.). (2010). *The psychoneuroimmunology of chronic disease.* Washington, DC: American Psychological Association.

Kendall-Tackett, K. A., Marshall, R., & Ness, K. E. (2003). Chronic pain syndromes and violence against women. *Women and Therapy, 26,* 45–56.

Kiecolt-Glaser, J. K., & Newton, T. L. (2001). Marriage and health: His and hers. *Psychological Bulletin, 127,* 472–503.

Kubzansky, L. D., & Kawachi, I. (2000). Going to the heart of the matter: Do negative emotions cause coronary heart disease? *Journal of Psychosomatic Research, 48,* 323–337.

Lang, A. J., Laffaye, C., Satz, L. E., McQuaid, J. R., Malcarne, V. L., Dreselhaus, T. R., & Stein, M. B. (2006). Relationships among childhood maltreatment, PTSD, and health in female veterans with a history of child maltreatment. *Child Abuse & Neglect, 30,* 1281–1292.

Lewis, T. T., Everson-Rose, S. A., Karavolos, K., Janssen, I., Wesley, D., & Powell, L. H. (2009). Hostility is associated with visceral, but not subcutaneous, fat in middle-aged African American and white women. *Psychosomatic Medicine, 71,* 733–740.

Lovallo, W. R. (1997). *Stress and health: Biological and psychological interactions.* Newbury Park, CA: Sage.

Luthra, R., Abramowitz, R., Greenberg, R., Schoor, A., Newcorn, J., Schmeidler, J., . . . Chemtob, C. M. (2009). Relationship between type of trauma exposure and posttraumatic stress disorder among urban children and adolescents. *Journal of Interpersonal Violence, 24*(11), 1919–1927.

Mallet, S., & Rosenthal, D. (2009). Physically violent mothers are a reason for young people's leaving home. *Journal of Interpersonal Violence, 24*(7), 1165–1174.

McEwen, B. S. (2003). Mood disorders and allostatic load. *Biological Psychiatry, 54,* 200–207.

Messman-Moore, T. L., & Brown, A. L. (2004). Child maltreatment and perceived family environment as risk factors for adult rape: Is child sexual abuse the most salient experience? *Child Abuse & Neglect, 28,* 1019–1034.

Messman-Moore, T. L., Brown, A. L., & Koelsch, L. E. (2005). Posttraumatic symptoms and self-dysfunction as consequences and predictors of sexual revictimization. *Journal of Traumatic Stress, 18*(3), 1–9.

Messman-Moore, T. L., Ward, R. M., & Brown, A. L. (2009). Substance use and PTSD symptoms impact the likelihood of rape and revictimization in college women. *Journal of Interpersonal Violence, 24*(3), 499–521.

Miller, G. E., Cohen, S., & Ritchey, A. K. (2002). Chronic psychological stress and the regulation of pro-inflammatory cytokines: A glucocorticoid-resistance model. *Health Psychology, 21,* 531–541.

Molnar, B. E., Berkman, L. F., & Buka, S. L. (2001). Psychopathology, childhood sexual abuse and other childhood adversities: Relative links to subsequent suicidal behaviour in the U.S. *Psychological Medicine, 31,* 965–977.

Mullen, P. E., Martin, J. L., Anderson, J. C., Romans, S. E., & Herbison, G. P. (1994). The effect of child sexual abuse on social, interpersonal, and sexual function in adult life. *British Journal of Psychiatry, 165,* 35–47.

Munroe, C. D., Kibler, J. L., Ma, M., Dollar, K. M., & Coleman, M. (2010). The relationship between posttraumatic stress symptoms and sexual risk: Examining potential mechanisms. *Psychological Trauma, 2*(1), 49–53.

O'Leary, P., Coohey, C., & Easton, S. D. (2010). The effect of severe child sexual abuse and disclosure on mental health during adulthood. *Journal of Child Sexual Abuse, 19,* 275–289.

Ozbaran, B., Erermis, S., Bukusoglu, N., Bildik, T., Tamar, M., Ercan, E. S., . . . Cetin, S. K. (2009). Social and emotional outcomes of child sexual abuse: A clinical sample in Turkey. *Journal of Interpersonal Violence, 24*(9), 1478–1493.

Panksepp, J. (2011). The neurobiology of social loss in animals: Some keys to the puzzle of psychic pain in humans. In G. MacDonald & L. A. Jensen-Campbell (Eds.), *Social pain: Neuropsychological and health implications of loss and exclusion* (pp. 11–51). Washington, D.C.: American Psychological Association.

Persons, E., Kershaw, T., Sikkema, K. J., & Hansen, N. B. (2010). The impact of shame on health-related quality of life among HIV-positive adults with a history of childhood sexual abuse. *AIDS Patient Care & STDs, 24*(9), 571–580.

Rich-Edwards, J. W., Spiegelman, D., Lividoti Hibert, E. N., Jun, H.-J., Todd, T. J., Kawachi, I., & Wright, R. J. (2010). Abuse in childhood and adolescence as a predictor of type 2 diabetes in adult women. *American Journal of Preventive Medicine, 39*(6), 529–536.

Roberts, R., O'Connor, T., Dunn, J., Golding, J., & the ALSPAC Study Team. (2004). The effects of child sexual abuse in later family life: Mental health, parenting and adjustment of offspring. *Child Abuse & Neglect, 28,* 525–545.

Roy, A. (2001). Childhood trauma and hostility as an adult: Relevance to suicidal behavior. *Psychiatry Research, 102,* 97–101.

Ryan, N. E., Solberg, V. S., & Brown, S. D. (1996). Family dysfunction, parental attachment, and career search self-efficacy among community college students. *Journal of Counseling Psychology, 43,* 84–89.

Sachs-Ericsson, N., Cromer, K., Hernandez, A., & Kendall-Tackett, K. A. (2009). Childhood abuse, health and pain-related problems: The role of psychiatric disorders and current life stress. *Journal of Trauma & Dissociation, 10,* 170–188.

Schwartz, D., Dodge, K. A., Pettit, G. S., & Bates, J. E. (2000). Friendship as a moderating factor in the pathway between early harsh home environment and later victimization in the peer group. *Developmental Psychology, 36,* 646–662.

Shakespeare-Finch, J., & De Dassel, T. (2009). Exploring posttraumatic outcomes as a function of childhood sexual abuse. *Journal of Child Sexual Abuse, 18,* 623–640.

Sherin, J. E., & Nemeroff, C. B. (2011). Post-traumatic stress disorder: The neurobiological implications of psychological trauma. *Dialogues in Clinical Neuroscience, 13*(3), 263–278.

Shields, A., & Cicchetti, D. (2001). Parental maltreatment and emotion dysregulation as risk factors in the pathway between early harsh home environment and later victimization. *Journal of Clinical Child Psychology, 30,* 349–363.

Shonkoff, J. P., Boyce, W. T., & McEwen, B. S. (2009). Neuroscience, molecular biology, and the childhood roots of health disparities: Building a new framework for health promotion and disease prevention. *JAMA, 301*(21), 2252–2259. doi:301/21/2252 [pii]10.1001/jama.2009.754

Silva, R. R., Alpert, M., Munoz, D. M., Singh, S., Matzner, F., & Dummit, S. (2000). Stress and vulnerability to posttraumatic stress disorder in children and adolescents. *American Journal of Psychiatry, 157,* 1229–1235.

Smith, T. W. (1992). Hostility and health: Current status of a psychosomatic hypothesis. *Health Psychology, 11,* 139–150.

Smith, T. W., & Ruiz, J. M. (2002). Psychosocial influences on the development and course of coronary heart disease: Current status and implications for research and practice. *Journal of Consulting and Clinical Psychology, 70,* 548–568.

Steel, J. L., & Herlitz, C. A. (2005). The association between childhood and adolescent sexual abuse and proxies for sexual risk behavior: A random sample of the general population of Sweden. *Child Abuse & Neglect, 29*(10), 1141–1153.

Suarez, E. C., & Goforth, H. (2010). Sleep and inflammation: A potential link to chronic diseases. In K. A. Kendall-Tackett (Ed.), *The psychoneuroimmunology of chronic disease* (pp. 53–75). Washington, DC: American Psychological Association.

Talbot, N. L., Chapman, B., Conwell, Y., McCollumn, K., Franus, N., Cotescu, S., & Duberstein, P. R. (2009). Childhood sexual abuse is associated with physical illness burden and functioning in psychiatric patients 50 years of age or older. *Psychosomatic Medicine, 71,* 417–422.

Teegan, F. (1999). Childhood sexual abuse and long-term sequelae. In A. Maercker, M. Schutzwohl, & Z. Solomon (Eds.), *Posttraumatic stress disorder: A lifespan developmental perspective* (pp. 97–112). Seattle, WA: Hogrefe & Huber.

Teicher, M. H. (2002, March). Scars that won't heal: The neurobiology of child abuse. *Scientific American,* 68–75.

Wegman, H. L., & Stetler, C. (2009). A meta-analytic review of the effects of childhood abuse on medical outcomes in adulthood. *Psychosomatic Medicine, 71,* 805–812.

Weinfield, N. S., Sroufe, L. A., Egeland, B., & Carlson, E. A. (1999). The nature of individual differences in infant-caregiver attachment. In J. Cassidy & P. R. Shaver (Eds.), *The handbook of attachment: Theory, research, and clinical applications* (pp. 68–88). New York, NY: Guilford Press.

Whiffen, V. E., & MacIntosh, H. B. (2005). Mediators of the link between childhood sexual abuse and emotional distress: A critical review. *Trauma, Violence, & Abuse, 6*(1), 24–39.

Wong, W.C.W., Leung, P.W.S., Tang, C.S.K., Chen, W-Q., Lee, A., Ling, D. C. (2009). To unfold a hidden epidemic: Prevalence of child maltreatment and its health implications among high school students in Guangzhou, China. *Child Abuse & Neglect, 33*(7), 441–450.

8

Legal Responses to Child Maltreatment

Henry J. Plum

INTRODUCTION

Children have always presented a unique challenge to the legal system regardless of country, culture, religious beliefs, or rules of their particular society. The reasons are both subtle and obvious. A child's age and capacity to communicate as well as its need for protection and assistance place the child in a unique situation, unlike the adult who is presumed to possess the capacity to articulate and advocate his or her needs, rights, and wants. Unlike the adult, the child, because of his or her perceived incapacities and inabilities, is often powerless to select or communicate outcomes despite being victimized and subject to maltreatment at the hands of a caretaker. The standard for determining "best interests" is left to the adults in the legal system; they cobble together a solution that hopefully provides not only protection for the child from maltreatment, both present and future, but also provides treatment, stability, and the opportunity for development of the child to reach his or her potential as an adult.

There have been multiple attempts to create a legal system that is both protective of the child and yet also provides those elements that are necessary for a child to grow. One of the key changes to creating a successful system is creating a paradigm shift from the benevolent perspective of the child's best interests to a child-rights approach. This shift changes the perception and some of the traditional approaches and assumptions that are made about children. For example, if a child has a right to be heard in legal proceedings, then a legal system must adapt to a child-centered approach through creating mechanisms for this to occur. The mechanism might allow for the child to speak, either personally, through a representative, or through the statements made by the child but preserved in such a manner that the child's voice and position are not ignored. The document that embodies this approach is the United Nations Convention on the Rights of the Child (henceforth referred to as CRC).

IMPACT OF INTERNATIONAL CONVENTIONS

The UN Convention on the Rights of the Child was approved on November 20, 1989, by the United Nations General Assembly. It is the most widely adopted international human rights treaty in history. This convention sets forth a universally agreed set of standards and obligations that place children at center stage in the legal systems that exist in our society (Zeldin, 2007). The convention spells out basic human rights for all children, including the right to survival and to develop to the fullest, as well as protection from abuse and exploitation. These new rights for children under international law did not previously exist (Kilkelly, 2001). The convention protects these rights by establishing standards in health care, education, and legal and civil services. The standards serve as a marker against which progress can be assessed for countries that have ratified the CRC and are obligated to apply the principles of the rights of children throughout their respective legal systems.

Issues surrounding maltreatment of children are both complex and far-reaching. Often the cause of the maltreatment is only the first determination that must be made. Other determinations, such as who caused the maltreatment, the relationship of the maltreater to the child, and the outcome of such maltreatment are determined by more than one legal system. Since these issues also involve both criminal and civil responsibility, the questions of how maltreatment is detected and identified, whether the caretaker of such maltreatment should be punished or rehabilitated, and whether the child needs long- or short-term treatment are all issues that need to be decided and are unique to child maltreatment cases.

OVERVIEW OF ISSUES

This chapter will examine various legal approaches that are available or present in many jurisdictions. This examination will provide an overview rather than a detailed analysis of each legal system existing in each country. Effective access to legal interventions on behalf of maltreated children requires the professional to become familiar with the specific legal systems and mechanisms that exist in the specific country in which the maltreated child is located. Within existing legal systems there are both similarities but also significant differences. In selecting from the various methods for legal intervention, one must consider the outcomes that are likely to occur from accessing or pursuing a particular legal system. Recognizing that more than one legal system is present in most countries and that these systems are not mutually exclusive is important. Thus a child might be taken into custody and removed from the parent-maltreater in an "in care and protection proceeding" (Care and Protection of Children Act, 2007) through the juvenile court jurisdiction. Whereas the maltreater might be removed from the home of the child as a result of criminal proceedings being initiated in the criminal court system, orders prohibiting contact between the maltreater and the child might be entered by a civil court through a protection order. Thus more than one legal system can and is frequently accessed simultaneously to obtain a good outcome for the child. This chapter will summarize the types of legal systems that exist and the anticipated outcome of each legal system.

HISTORICAL SUMMARY

The concept that children have rights did not emerge until the twentieth century, when children were referenced in various children and family codes. Prior to that time, children were viewed as quasi-property and economic assets. The case of Mary Ellen Wilson in the United States in 1874 was one of the first examples of a legal intervention on behalf of a child. However, the laws were not developed for intervening on behalf of an abused child. Mary Ellen was the victim of deliberate cruelties and deprivations inflicted upon her by her adoptive parents (Markel, 2009). The court allowed private citizens to bring legal action to save Mary Ellen. This case is significant in that it recognizes that there are degrees of child maltreatment that society will not tolerate and that the state may remove a child from a caregiver (Vieth, 2006, p. 85).

The expansion of international laws affecting children occurred after World War II. In the United States the philosophy of *parens patriae* gave way to a rights-based approach in the early 1960s with two landmark U.S. Supreme Court cases in which the Court struck down the unlimited *parens patriae* authority of the court (Vieth, 2006, p. 88). In its landmark decision of *In Re Gault,* the U.S. Supreme Court declared that "neither the Fourteenth

Amendment nor the Bill of Rights is for adults alone" (*In Re Gault,* 1967). These decisions caused a paradigm shift to occur in which the Supreme Court articulated its recognition that children are individuals with rights that must be acknowledged by the courts.

The children's rights movement really took hold in the latter part of the twentieth century. The major global and regional legal instruments of the twentieth and twenty-first centuries on an international level continue to be part of an evolving process. Some of the documents developed include the Declaration of Rights of the Child (1959), the United Nations Convention on the Rights of the Child (1989), the African Charter on the Rights and Welfare of the Child (1990), the Hague Convention on Jurisdiction or the Protection of Children (1996) (adopted October 19, 1996, but entered into force January 1, 2002) and the Optional Protocols to the Convention of the Rights of the Child on Sex Trafficking of Children (2000) (Zeldin, 2007). Although these international instruments are significant, it is important to clarify that their passage, ratification, acceptance, or adoption by international bodies does not necessarily guarantee that these instruments are incorporated into each individual country's legislation. As of April 2013, 195 nations have ratified, accepted, or adopted the CRC. However, 64 countries have registered such acceptance subject to specific reservations (Status of Treaties: Chapter IV, Section 11: United Nations Treaty Collection). *Ratification* defines the international act whereby a state indicates its consent to be bound to a treaty, whereas a *reservation* is a declaration made by a state by which it purports to exclude or alter the legal effect of certain provisions of the treaty in their application to that state. Thus nearly one-third of the countries ratifying the CRC have either excluded or altered its legal effect (Overview: Glossary: United Nations Treaty Collection).

Each country is a sovereign nation and that sovereignty confers the capacity of that country to create its own rules or laws within its border for its citizenry. Documents that usually reflect both the authority as well as the limitations of the government within each country are reflected in the individual country's constitution or a similarly identified document. However, there are some countries that do not have a document that sets out fundamental rights; in those jurisdictions, the constitution is composed of statutes, case law, and convention. Often, the constitution of a particular country has additional documents that provide clarification as to the rights of its citizenry. For example, the U.S. Constitution must be read along with its amendments. Similarly, the constitution of each country will clarify the significance of entering into international agreements and the binding or nonbinding effect of those international agreements on its citizenry. Thus one must become familiar with the particular laws of a country to determine whether an international agreement is binding and to what degree it becomes law.

International law is consent-based governance. This means that a state member of the international community is not obliged to abide by international law unless it has expressly consented to a particular course of conduct (Slomanson, 2011). This is an issue of *state sovereignty* (Slomanson, 2011). For example, the Greek Constitution under article 28 indicates that the signing of a convention has the force of law from the date of ratification and publication. It takes precedence over conflicting domestic legislation (Papademetriou, 2007). However, in other countries, signing on to a convention does not have the same binding effect. For example, Canadian constitutional law does not generally permit the federal government to legislate matters that fall under provincial jurisdiction even for the purpose of implementing an international agreement. Thus Canada enters reservations to international agreements if implementation of the international agreement would require provincial cooperation (Clarke, 2007).

Similarly, Germany ratified the CRC, and it became effective in April 1992. However, Germany made it clear that the CRC is not considered a self-executing law. When Germany ratified the CRC, it did so with the following clarification: "The Federal Republic of Germany . . . *declares that domestically the CRC does not apply directly*" (Convention on the Rights of the Child, BGBL, 1992). Other countries, such as Saudi Arabia and Iran, reserve the right not to apply articles of the CRC that are incompatible with Islamic laws. As of April 2013, 64 countries have ratified the CRC, but they have done so subject to reservations (Status of Treaties: Chapter IV, Section 11: United Nations Treaty Collection). This underscores the need to identify and understand individual country laws and procedures, given that there is no uniform set of applicable laws despite international conventions such as the CRC.

Understanding an individual country's legal approach to child maltreatment requires a two-step process. Within the first step is a general description of the types of legal systems that exist within the spectrum of most countries. This description provides a compilation of general principles that apply in these systems, recognizing that each country's particular legal system will differ for multiple reasons, including cultural, economic, religious, historical, political, and philosophical. The second step includes a discussion of how these various systems, although different, could be accessed to achieve a good outcome for the child.

TYPES OF LEGAL SYSTEMS AND COURTS

The various legal systems include criminal, juvenile, family, civil, religious, and cultural courts. Although these describe general legal systems and decision-making systems, it is noteworthy that in some countries the function of the decision maker may be similar but the name is different. For example, some jurisdictions function as a juvenile court but are called family courts, whereas a family court may be referred to as a civil court in another jurisdiction. In addition, not all legal systems have a judiciary or magistrate; some will have administrative boards or individuals making decisions without a hearing process. Thus each system must be assessed for its unique characteristics. In addition, some legal systems are adversarial in that they are two-sided, pitting the prosecution against the accused. This adversarial system is generally adopted in common law countries where the legal systems have their origin in English common law (Hale, 2004). In contrast, the other legal system is the inquisitorial system, which has a judge or a group of judges who work together and whose task is to investigate the case. In evaluating which court or court system should be accessed, the legal system that is followed is country-specific. Thus the professional will need to identify which system is present in the country in question.

In order to effectively access a legal system, it is more important to understand the underlying principles and approaches to child maltreatment of a given legal system along with the possible outcomes of the particular legal system than it is to focus on the particular nomenclature of the court or whether it is adversarial or inquisitorial.

CRIMINAL LAW SYSTEM

Most, if not all, countries have a legal system or mechanism for levying punishment to an adult for violating laws. The crimes are frequently classified into categories such as crimes against persons, which might include murder, battery, sexual assault, or rape, in contrast to crimes against property, such as theft, robbery, or burglary. These categories of crimes have been expanded to include crimes against the government and administration (Canada, R.S.C., c.46, s.14-33, 1985), crimes against public order (Canada, R.S.C., c.46, s.46, 1985), and even crimes against children (Philippine Rep. Act No. 7610, 1992). The crimes against children include crimes of maltreatment such as child abuse (Philippine Rep. Act No. 7610, 1992), child neglect (Philippine Rep. Act No. 7610, 1992), and child sexual abuse. However, this categorization of crimes is not uniform and each country's criminal code will have its specific method for categorizing crimes as well as identifying the punishment prescribed for each crime.

It is essential for the child abuse professional to understand the philosophical focus and outcome of the criminal system in that it will assist in 1) deciding whether to access this criminal system, 2) identifying the particular procedural requirements in the criminal system that may impact a child abuse victim, and 3) anticipating the potential outcomes that are available through the criminal system.

The primary emphasis of the criminal system is judging the guilt of the accused. Any rights that exist, any procedural requirements followed, and any outcomes or sentences available to the court if guilt is adjudicated have as their primary focus the accused/offender and not the victim. Although the underlying principles do vary within criminal systems, most do include theories of retribution, deterrence, and punishment (Waller & Williams, 1993, pp. 13–17), along with others such as protection of society, rehabilitation, and a more recent trend towards restorative justice. Other criminal systems have additional principles based on culture or religion that are not necessarily shared in a majority of other nations' criminal systems. One such concept is the principle of "*Qisas,*" an Islamic term meaning "Equal Retaliation," and follows the principle "*of an eye for an eye* or *lex talionis*" (*Surat Al-Baquarah—The Noble Qur'an*). This principle is enforced today by a number of states that apply sharia law, such as Saudi Arabia and Iran (Sial, 2006). However, this principle is not applied in most Western countries.

It is noteworthy that there are change and development in the child maltreatment area wherein legislation introduced in some countries under the criminal code nevertheless embodies the principles of the UN Convention on the Rights of the Child. Under this legislation, the "best interests of the child" are given paramount consideration. Countries such as the Philippines and India (Government of India Act 32, 2012) are beginning to demonstrate this trend by approving legislation with an emphasis on providing "Special Protection of Children against Child Abuse and Exploitation" (Philippine Rep. Act No. 9231, 2003). This type of legislation creates special categories, procedures, and courts to address child maltreatment issues in a criminal setting. This type of legislation changes the emphasis of traditional criminal law by introducing victim's interests and rights. This balancing of the rights of the accused against the rights of the child victim is still developing and not universally applied.

The evidentiary rules also vary between countries. The traditional rule that all hearsay statements are inadmissible has given way to exceptions, especially in the areas of recording children's statements and medical opinions offered in child physical and sexual abuse cases. The Federal Rules of Evidence under U.S. law provide a template to other jurisdictions for adoption of the exceptions to the hearsay rule (U.S. Federal Rules of Evidence, Section 803). However, the circumstances under which the child's statement is recorded and how it is used are not uniform. For example, recent legislation passed in India requires the child's statement to be recorded under very specific circumstances. It is then available for use in a special court designated to hear cases involving child sexual offenses (Government of India Act 32, 2012).

Another principle that arises in criminal courts is whether the accused has a right to confront the child witness. The right to confront one's accusers is a strong principle held in the criminal courts that are classified as adversarial. Certainly there has been advancement in the methods available to question the child. Multiple options exist, including the use of closed-circuit television, video depositions, and screening the child victim from the accused during the child's testimony, as well as questioning the child by the court or an interpreter or other individual skilled in forensic interviewing. These options are limited not only by resources but also by the individual laws of each country.

The use of the expert and scientific evidence in child abuse cases is another issue in which unanimity does not exist. Limitations on the qualifications and the use of experts as well as the extent to which an expert may render an opinion vary among jurisdictions. Scientific evidence, although helpful to the decision maker, is another issue in which admissibility in child maltreatment proceedings may be limited based on country-specific requirements for admitting expert testimony. The quantum of proof required in criminal courts has traditionally been very high and has usually been "beyond a reasonable doubt." This standard has been traditionally a Western standard in countries such as England (Whitman, 2008), Canada (*R. v. Lifchus*, 1997), New Zealand (Young, Cameron, & Tinsley, 1999), and the United States (18 U.S.C. Section 19). The presumption of innocence of the accused is not a principle that is shared unanimously. In the common law countries, the principle is applicable, and as such the burden rests with the prosecution to establish guilt. However in the recent legislation involving sexual offenses against children, the law of India provides that if a person is prosecuted for committing any offenses involving sexual assault, the court shall presume that the accused has committed the offense unless the contrary is proved (Government of India Act 32, 2012). Because uniformity is not the rule, continual review of country-specific legislation is necessary.

An additional significant difference between countries is the actual legal definition for sexual offenses against children. What is noteworthy is that the term "child sexual abuse" does not uniformly appear in criminal codes. In some jurisdictions, sexual offenses against children are categorized as rape. The definitions of such sexual crimes against a child vary based on multiple factors, including age of the child, gender, capacity to give consent, particular sexual act, degree and type of force or coercion applied, and resulting physical injury to the child. There is usually a direct correlation between these variables and the degree of punishment prescribed in the law. Whether specific facts can be established by evidence supporting these variables is often determined by the admissibility of the type of evidence received by the court. For instance, if the degree of force or coercion used in a sexual crime is a variable in a specific criminal law, the child's observation and testimony might be critical to establish the degree of force used. If the child told the investigating police officer or the evaluating medical physician about the force or coercion of the sexual assault, the officer's testimony or the physician's testimony as to the child's statements will be controlled by the exceptions to the evidence code under the hearsay rule. Depending upon the jurisdiction, the child may or may not be required to testify along with the physician or the police officer in order to establish proof of the use of force in the sexual assault. Understanding the hearsay exceptions and knowing how the victim's observations and other evidence need to be properly preserved will significantly impact the victim's role in the criminal proceeding.

The age of consent concerning sexual activity also varies among jurisdictions. Thus a child is a person under the age of 18 (Philippine Rev. Penal Code, s.4 a.) for the purpose of testifying. However, under some criminal codes, the charge of rape is applicable when "the woman is under twelve years of age" (Philippine Rev. Penal Code, s.4 a.), in which case, the element of consent does not have to be established. Whereas if the victim is 12 years of age or older, proof of force or coercion is necessary. This variation in the laws is found in the criminal code of Australia. The common-law crime of rape was abolished (Waller & Williams, 1993, p. 92) in Australia and the category of sexual offenses was substituted (Waller & Williams, 1993, p. 87). The age under which consent cannot be given for sexual offenses appears to be 16 years (Crimes Act s.4.15, 1992). Thus what some jurisdictions might consider sexual abuse might differ in other country jurisdictions.

It is critical to understand that legal definitions in criminal codes for child maltreatment will determine what facts and evidence need be established. Despite the attempts to define these terms by the World Health Organization (WHO) (Butchart, Harvey, Mian, Furniss, & Hahane, 2006) as well as other international agreements and documents, there does not appear to be one definition that is uniformly accepted and expressed in each country criminal code. Thus, familiarity with the individual country definitions of specific crimes involving children is important for the professional, since this will impact not only the type of investigation conducted and gathering of evidence, but will also ensure a good outcome for the child through the criminal system.

The outcome of criminal cases usually provides for punishment of the accused who is now categorized as the offender. This may involve incarceration or confinement in a jail or prison for either a fixed or an indefinite period of time. In addition, the law may provide for the levying of a fine and possible restitution to the victim, and also extended periods of court supervision for the offender. For sexual offenses, offenders are frequently required to register on a sex offender list, depending upon whether such a registry exists in the particular country. The length of time of confinement is typically stated in the laws. Some jurisdictions have in the past provided for capital punishment for crimes of child sexual offenses and still do today (Abolitionist and Retentionist Countries). Alternative outcomes might include placing the offender under the supervision of the agency with specific conditions for a specified period of time. This might also include orders prohibiting the offender from contacting or communicating indirectly with the child-victim. In some jurisdictions, treatment requirements might be ordered by the court for the offender.

Although criminal courts can exercise authority over the offender once adjudicated as guilty, there is usually no authority over the victim. As a result, there are no provisions to order treatment or therapy for the victim. There has been a trend in some jurisdictions to combine the authority of the criminal court with the authority of the family court. In this way, the same court would have authority to make orders over the offender as well as the victim. Some jurisdictions have created specialty courts with this type of authority (Government of India Act 32, 2012). It should be noted that this would only occur in those cases in which the victim and offender are related. The standard for ordering treatment for the victim and offender as well as possible contact would have to be reviewed in the context of the child's best interest.

Understanding the criminal courts and criminal laws from an international perspective is complex because of the variations from country to country. Understanding the particular country's laws is essential to the professional who must decide whether to access this criminal system. It is critical to identify the particular procedural requirements in a given criminal system that may impact a child abuse victim. If these two goals are accomplished, then it is easier to anticipate the potential outcomes that are available through the criminal system of a particular country.

JUVENILE/CHILDREN/FAMILY LAW SYSTEM

The second type of legal system that exists is in the category known as either the juvenile, children, or family law court system (hereafter referred to as the juvenile system). Although accessing this system may be easier, the rationale for understanding the juvenile law system is similar to understanding the criminal court system in that by identifying the particular procedural requirements and steps in the juvenile system it will be easier to understand its impact on a child abuse victim, as well to anticipate the potential outcomes that are available through the juvenile system.

Status Proceedings

The juvenile court is characterized by cases referenced, categorized, or identified as "In Care" proceedings (Children Act c.41, 1989), "Dependency" proceedings, or "Child in Need of Protection and Services" proceedings (Government of India, Juvenile Justice Care and Protection of Children Act, 2000). The title of these proceedings varies from country to country. The commonality of these cases and hearings involves issues of child maltreatment, which encompasses physical abuse, sexual abuse, neglect, or abandonment of a child.

Guilt Determination

In contrast to the criminal code, the emphasis in these proceedings is not to adjudge the guilt of the accused perpetrator. Rather, the emphasis is on whether the child fits into one of these categories or in a status as a result of being maltreated. The identity of the maltreater is not necessarily a critical element of the proof that is presented. The fact that the child is a victim of abuse is usually sufficient evidence for the court to assume jurisdiction or authority over the child. The rationale for this becomes clearer if one thinks about the types of injuries a child might suffer as a result of physical abuse. A young infant who has sustained a subdural hematoma as a result of violent shaking would be considered a victim of physical abuse. However, the identity of the abuser might not be apparent if there are multiple caregivers. With this fact scenario, criminal proceedings would require that the alleged abuser be identified and be found guilty of committing a crime in order for the court to exercise jurisdiction over the offender. With multiple caretakers, it might be difficult to identify who caused this injury to the child. If no specific individual is identified and charged, then there cannot be any intervention under the criminal system.

In contrast, under the juvenile system, it is usually sufficient to establish that the child sustained a nonaccidental injury (physical child abuse) for the court to assume jurisdiction or authority over the child with a determination that the child is "In Need of Protection and Services" (Care and Protection of Children Amendment Act No. 9, 2012). When the court finds that the facts to establish abuse occurred, the court then adjudicates the child to be in the status of "In Need of Care," "Dependent," "Neglected," or a "Child in Need of Protection and Services." Since there is no need to determine guilt of the abuser, this substantially impacts the procedures that apply in juvenile court proceedings.

Best Interest Focus

The central focus of the juvenile proceedings, unlike the criminal proceedings, is to advocate the best interests of the child. This central focus is also the predominant principle of the UN Convention on the Rights of the Child as expressed in article 3 of CRC (Convention on the Rights of the Child, 1989). The principles that fit under this focus on the best interest of the child include and would address issues of intervention, protection, treatment, providing necessary care and proper development for the child, as well as maintaining the family connections of the child where it serves the best interests and needs of the child. Although most countries have a legal system that deals solely with children who are abused or neglected, this practice is not universal. The juvenile/family law system is present in most Western countries; however, there are countries that do not have this type of legal system (Peters, 2006). In those countries, other options to protect the child need to be pursued, which may include the criminal court.

Structure

The structure of these juvenile courts can be either judicial—in which case the matter is heard and decided by a judge, a magistrate, or a panel of judges in a court system (Care and Protection of Children Amendment Act No. 9, 2012)—or the matter is decided by an administrative panel of non-legal professionals who have specialized knowledge of the issues involving child maltreatment, child development, or other issues related to children. Sometimes the panel may comprise both a judge and some nonlegal professionals. The role of the professional in either deciding or making recommendations to the decision makers in this type of legal system is much greater.

Procedural Steps and Rules

With the focus of the best interest of the child as well as the elimination of the requirement to adjudicate guilt of the accused, juvenile procedures differ from procedures in the criminal system. These proceedings are considered civil proceedings (Children Act c.41, 1989). As a result, the civil rules of procedure are typically applied in the same way as in any other civil litigation, such as contract law, personal injury, or other similar areas. The civil rules do not include the right against self-incrimination and the right to remain silent (Evidence Act R.S.C. 1985 C. C-5). This means that if a parent is believed to have caused the abuse to the child, the parent may be called to give testimony and is not allowed to assert the right to remain silent. If the parent does remain silent, the silence may be used to draw an adverse conclusion against the parent (Evidence Act R.S.C. 1985 C. C-5).

Burden of Proof and Rules of Evidence

The quantum of evidence or proof that is required to be presented also differs. Whereas in the criminal system the burden is beyond a reasonable doubt, the civil burden of proof is less. The level of preponderance of evidence or balance of probabilities (Care and Protection of Children Amendment Act No. 9, 2012) is applied, or in some jurisdictions a slightly higher burden of "clear and convincing" (Children's Code Wis. Stats. 48.299[4], 1978). The application of civil rules of evidence is similar to application in the criminal system. Thus hearsay exceptions will be allowed if provided for in law. As already noted, each country has its own civil codes for admission of evidence. Those rules would apply in these types of proceedings. The rules of evidence in juvenile court proceedings are either relaxed or suspended for preliminary proceedings that address the intervention and removal of the child. In these proceedings, the rules of evidence are not stringently applied. Some codes specifically allow for the admission of hearsay evidence as long as it has indicia of trustworthiness (Care and Protection of Children Amendment Act No. 9, 2012; Children Act c.41, 1989). The evidentiary distinction should not leave the impression that professionals gathering evidence in child abuse cases would apply less rigor in documentation, collection of evidence, and preserving evidence on the assumption that the case will only be heard in juvenile court. Rather, consistent standards need to be applied so that the evidence will withstand scrutiny whether the case is heard in the civil courts or the criminal court.

Representation of the Child

One distinction that is unique to juvenile court proceedings is the right of the child to be heard, as set forth in the CRC, article 12.2 (Convention on the Rights of the Child, BGBL, 1992). The majority of countries have some provision or mechanism to allow this to occur (Peters, 2006). In some countries the child is considered to be a legal party in these proceedings. When this occurs, the child is represented by either adversary counsel or by an attorney called a guardian ad litem (Care and Protection of Children Amendment Act No. 9, 2012). Other models provide for presentation of the child's views through a layperson (Children Act c.41, 1989; Care and Protection of Children Amendment Act No. 9, 2012). The representation of the child through a lawyer should provide for a greater degree of advocacy in a legal system and also a better opportunity for the child's voice to be heard, which is consistent with article 12 of the CRC.

Outcomes

The advantage of using a juvenile court system is its focus on the child throughout the process, including the outcomes. Whereas the criminal system emphasizes the punishment of the offender with no authority or jurisdiction over the victim of the crime, the juvenile system's outcome looks at the child from various perspectives. The treatment needs of the child, whether physical, emotional, or developmental, are only one aspect of the court's focus. Additionally, the court evaluates the safety and placement issues of the child as well as the parental deficits that must be corrected in order for the child to be safely returned to the family. If the child's safety dictates temporary placement out of the parental home, placement with relatives, foster homes, residential treatment facilities, institutions, children's homes, and other facilities become temporary options. During this placement period for the child, there is usually authority for the court to order treatment for the parent as a condition of the child's being returned to the parental home. Unlike the criminal court, the juvenile system does allow the court to exercise authority over the child as well as greater authority over the family unit through a process of court-ordered supervision and provision of services. In many jurisdictions, these services and treatments are provided through either government or non-governmental health and social welfare agencies.

This broad reach of authority allows the court to address some of the underlying causes of the child's maltreatment, such as mental health issues, drug and alcohol dependency, parenting issues, domestic violence, and others. Many systems allow for court monitoring to assess the progress of the parent as well as the child. There is an assumption that the parent is motivated to seek reunification with the child. When that reunification does not occur, then the court has the options of transferring legal custody or guardianship of the child to another relative, an agency, or some other entity. Ultimately, the court also has authority to terminate the parental rights of the parent to the child with the outcome that the child would be adopted by a third party. This option varies from country to country. Some countries do not allow for termination of parental rights and adoption (U.S. Department of State, n.d.). It is noteworthy that the focus is not intended to be, nor should it be, punitive to the child. Whatever outcome the court would order must serve the best interest of the child.

PROCEDURAL DECISION STEPS

The types of hearings existing in the juvenile system encompass the following types of issues: 1) whether immediate intervention on behalf of a child is necessary; 2) whether facts exist to establish court jurisdiction that the child is in need of care, or in need of protection and services as a result of child maltreatment; 3) what outcome or court-ordered disposition will serve the best interest of this child. The three hearings, identified by their respective issues, are referred to as 1) emergency intervention or physical custody hearing; 2) jurisdictional hearing; 3) dispositional hearing. The particular name given to each hearing will vary between jurisdictions.

However, the issues remain the same. Understanding these types of hearings is helpful for the professional to more effectively use or access the juvenile system. The previously described principles apply to these hearings and will assist in understanding what occurs.

Emergency Hearing

The emergency intervention hearing will usually result from a child abuse referral made by a professional or nonprofessional to any relevant agency or law enforcement (Children Act c.41, 1989). Once the intervention is initiated, the hearing will occur either via a child being taken into physical custody by law enforcement, a physician, or other agency representative, and brought before the court, or via an application that is presented to the court requesting that the child be removed and brought before the court. In either circumstance, the emergency nature of the proceeding will dictate that the rules of evidence supporting allegations are less formal. The rules of evidence are relaxed. Hearsay evidence that is presented should have indicia of being trustworthy. The opportunity for the caretaker of the child to be heard may or may not occur.

The child's needs for temporary measures of protection, treatment, and placement are the main considerations for the court. Typically this stage of proceeding is preliminary; investigation is not completed but is ongoing as additional facts are gathered. These hearings usually require a showing of either serious risk or actual harm to the child. At these hearings it is not unusual for the court to order evaluations and assessments of the child for the purpose of obtaining more information concerning the child's condition.

When emergency medical procedures are necessary to protect the child's life, the court usually has authority to order these procedures. These hearings often contain a mechanism for review within a particular time frame. The role of the professional is to accurately identify for the court the nature of the emergency as well as risks to the child and why court intervention is necessary for the child's best interest. Separating the child from the maltreater or restricting the maltreater's access to the child can be accomplished by removing the child from the parental home or its current placement. The court also has authority to restrict not only the parent's access to the child but also the access of other individuals, including extended family members. These temporary measures are implemented to protect and stabilize the child while additional investigation is conducted and information is garnered.

Jurisdictional Hearing

The second step in the juvenile court process is the jurisdictional hearing. This is the hearing in which the court determines whether the child is "In Need of Protection or Services" (Care and Protection of Children Amendment Act No. 9, 2012) or "In Care" (Children Act c.41, 1989) as a result of the child sustaining physical or sexual abuse, neglect, or abandonment. This hearing occurs after the evidence is gathered. Thus there is time for the parties to prepare, and this is reflected in the manner in which this hearing is conducted. The civil rules for procedure and evidence apply. The parties to these proceedings typically include the parents, the state, and the child. Parents may or may not be represented by a lawyer depending upon the individual country requirements, unlike in criminal proceedings where the right to be represented by a lawyer appears to be a universally accepted principle. Although the child is often excused from appearing, the child's voice, through either an advocate attorney or guardian ad litem, is heard. The right of the parent against self-incrimination and right to refuse to testify do not exist at this hearing as they would exist in a criminal case. The direct testimony of the child is usually not required and is frequently introduced through other individuals and mechanisms as well as broad interpretation of the hearsay exceptions. The burden of proof is lower than in criminal proceedings. The result of the court decision is not a finding of guilt but rather a determination that the child is in need of care or some similar status.

Dispositional Hearing

At the conclusion of the jurisdictional hearing, the court has the option of going directly to a dispositional hearing or continuing the proceeding to another date. The dispositional hearing may be delayed so that additional court study reports, evaluations, or other information can be obtained. The focus of the dispositional hearing is a determination of the best outcome for the child based on the child's particular needs. The options for the court should be driven by the child's individualized needs. A combination of orders addressing treatment needs; court-ordered therapy; and out-of-home placement based on safety and risk assessment issues, need for basic nutrition, supervision, care and education, as well as other needs unique to the child, are all considerations. Additionally, the court may order the parent to participate in treatment to address parenting issues and deficits. This may include court-ordered participation for the parent, including mental health treatment, drug and alcohol treatment, parenting skill improvement, and other considerations deemed necessary by the court and in the best interests of the child. Issues of parental visitation and parental contact are addressed by the court. The court has the authority to modify visitation, including suspension of parental and child contact if that is in the child's best interest. These hearings are conducted in a less formal manner than the jurisdictional hearing. The same parties from the jurisdictional hearing will participate in this hearing. The courts may also transfer legal custody or guardianship to an agency or other individuals. The courts typically enter orders for a specified period of time with some mechanism for review of the progress of the court's orders.

OTHER COURT SYSTEMS: FAMILY COURT/DOMESTIC RELATIONS/CIVIL COURTS

As previously indicated, the juvenile court's functions, as herein described, might be carried out by a court referred to as a children's court or a family court. However, in several jurisdictions, the family courts, known also as domestic relations courts or civil courts, have the authority to consider matters beyond child maltreatment issues. These systems have the authority to address family divorce and family separation issues, adjudication of paternity, domestic partner issues, and domestic abuse issues. While a discussion of these proceedings is beyond the scope of this chapter, these types of court issues may involve child maltreatment and may also provide alternative options and strategies for children who are subject to maltreatment. Thus a married parent with a child who lives with an abusive spouse might consider seeking a divorce decree along with protection orders or a domestic abuse injunction order prohibiting spousal contact along with prohibiting parental visitation as a strategy for protecting both the nonabusing spouse and the child from further child maltreatment or domestic violence. Likewise, an unmarried parent who has a child and lives with the other parent or domestic partner in an abusive relationship can seek protective orders and domestic abuse injunction orders from the court. This is a strategy that can be pursued. Typically protection orders or domestic abuse restraining orders are time limited and their enforcement may be difficult to implement depending upon law enforcement's response and willingness to enforce the orders. Violation of such orders may result in periods of incarceration.

TRADITIONAL COURTS

Other court types that exist are referred to as traditional and religious courts. These types of court are regional in nature and are driven primarily by religious and cultural traditions. Accordingly, their formality and rules are part of an oral and written tradition that codifies traditional and religious practices. Traditional leaders who act as decision makers exercise a high degree of autonomy and independence. Recent legislation introduced in South Africa reflects attempts at formalizing a traditional court in the Traditional Courts Bill (Traditional Courts Bill 76, 2011) and the Muslim Marriages Bill (Muslim Marriages Bill Act 20, 2011). This latter bill sets out a statutory framework for the legal recognition of Muslim marriages and their consequences. There are inherent strengths and weaknesses to these types of court systems.

The disadvantages are reflected in the following description of the traditional court in South Africa. In South Africa's traditional court, the tribal court is the highest court in the tribe. The chief is the only person who is authorized to pass judgment. Adult men in the tribe play a central role in assisting the chief in his judicial duties. Adult men attend court sessions and may participate in the cross-examination of the parties to lawsuits as well as of witnesses. Traditional courts settle disputes that involve two parties—for example, a victim and an offender. In criminal cases, the traditional court attempts to reconcile the victim and offender. Civil and criminal cases stemming from the same event are often heard simultaneously. An offender may be sentenced to some punishment and to the payment of compensation. The accused person must prove his or her innocence. There is no legal representation. Community courts are created by communities in order to deal with disputes locally. These courts tend to be formed in communities where the police have failed to address crime over a long period of time. Critics view these courts as vigilante courts based on cases in which alleged offenders were killed or severely injured only to be subsequently found innocent. Case studies are presented to show instances of brutality without determining the merits of the case, bias by the courts against defendants, mob influence in court decisions, bias against women, and lack of training for court officials (Bogopa, 2007).

The description of the traditional court reflects the fact that such courts do not reflect the principles of the UN Convention on the Rights of Children when dealing with issues of child maltreatment. Therefore, prior to accessing this type of legal system, serious consideration must be given to the potential impact on the child of such a system and whether it would serve the best interests of the child.

Another type of court is one that applies the sharia code, the moral code and religious law of Islam. The sharia code deals with many topics addressed by secular law, including crime, politics, and economics, as well as personal matters such as sexual intercourse, hygiene, diet, prayer, and fasting. Though interpretations of the sharia code vary between cultures, in its strictest definition it is considered the infallible law of God—as opposed to the human interpretation of the laws (Ritter, 2005, p. 349). The difficulty is that when the traditional or other courts deal with issues of child maltreatment, the focus may not necessarily reflect or implement the best interest of the child principle as expressed in article 3 of the CRC. If a country follows the sharia code and has ratified the CRC with reservations, then those principles of the CRC that conflict with the sharia code are nonbinding. This could have a negative impact on the child depending upon the type of maltreatment that the child has experienced.

INTEGRATING THE LEGAL SYSTEMS AND COURTS

Several legal systems and courts have been described in this chapter. Clearly, there are variations within each country. Despite the almost universal acceptance of the CRC, the implementation is not universally applied throughout all legal systems. The professional must therefore develop a strategy that maximizes the strength of the legal systems that exist within a given country to achieve a good outcome for the child. The discussion of the goals of each system identifies the outcomes of applying each system. Those outcomes may not necessarily serve the best interests of a child in a particular case.

Although there are several options as to how this information might be used to access the legal system that will address the child's need for protection, treatment, and stability, the more effective strategy would be to access the juvenile system simultaneously with the other court and legal systems. This might include involving the criminal system along with the juvenile law system. By simultaneously accessing both systems, the goals of each might work to protect and address the child's needs. For example, if the child is a victim of sexual abuse caused by a parent, a criminal prosecution alone might remove the parent from the house, but this might not address the needs of the child for protection or treatment. However, initiating juvenile proceedings along with the criminal proceedings gives the juvenile court authority to enter orders to protect the child and provide treatment during the pendency of criminal proceedings. Using parallel legal systems simultaneously or in tandem is a very effective strategy that addresses the child's needs during criminal proceedings, including the maltreatment.

The evidence gathered will be available in both proceedings, although the presentation and use of evidence may differ. Some of the criminal codes now provide for some of the same protections for children in criminal prosecution as exist in the civil actions, such as use of a guardian ad litem to represent the child victim in criminal proceedings (18 U.S.C. Sects. 3509, 3510). This same strategy is applicable with the other systems as well. Thus, pairing the family and civil court actions with juvenile court proceedings also provides flexibility in the use of protection or restraining orders in addition to treatment orders entered by the juvenile court. Combining court proceedings and legal systems simultaneously is one of the most effective strategies that can be implemented when dealing with cases involving child maltreatment. The key to this strategy is understanding the difference in procedures and outcomes of each system and then matching those procedures and outcomes to the needs and best interests of the child.

SUMMARY

This chapter identified various legal approaches that are available or present in many jurisdictions. The analysis included a description of the criminal, juvenile, family, civil, and traditional courts. By understanding the goals and outcomes of each system, the strategy of the professional is to access and anticipate the underlying principles and possible outcomes when a particular system is accessed. In this way, hopefully the disadvantages of one system will be reduced by simultaneously accessing another legal system with an outcome that serves the best interests of the child.

REFERENCES

18 U.S.C. § 19. (N.d.). *18 U.S C.§ 1920, Rule 11*.

18 U.S.C. §§ 3509, 3510. (N.d.). *18 U.S.C. §§ 3509, 3510*. U.S.

Amnesty International. (N.d.). *Abolitionist and Retentionist Countries.* Retrieved from http://www.amnesty.org/en/death-penalty/abolitionist-and-retentionist-countries

Bogopa, D. (2007). Critique on traditional courts, community courts and conflict management. *Acta Criminologica, 20*(1), 144–155. Retrieved from www.restorativejustice.org/articlesdb/articles/8351

Butchart, A., Harvey, A., Mian, M., Furniss, T., & Hahane, T. (2006). Preventing child maltreatment: A guide to taking action and generating evidence. Geneva:

World Health Organization (WHO) and International Society for Prevention of Child Abuse and Neglect.

Canada, R.S.C., c.46, s.14-33. (1985). *Canada Consolidation Criminal Code, R.S.C. 1985, c.46, s.14-33.*

Canada, R.S.C., c.46, s.46, 1985. (N.d.). *Canada Consolidation Criminal Code, R.S.C.1985, c.46, Part II, s.46.*

Care and Protection of Children Act 2007. (N.d.). Section 15. AusLII. Retrieved from www.austlii.edu.au/au/legis/nt/num_act/capoca200737o2007315/s15.html

Care and Protection of Children Amendment Act No. 9. (2012). *Care and Protection of Children Amendment Act, 012, no. 9 of 2012.* North Territory, Australia. Retrieved from http://www.austlii.edu.au/au/legis/nt/consol_act/capoca269/s20.html

Children Act c.41. (1989). *Children Act 1989, In Care Order, c. 41, part IV, s. 96.* Retrieved from http://www.legislation.gov.uk/ukpga/1989/41/section/47

Children's Code Wis. Stats. 48.299(4). (1978). *Children's Code, Wis. Stats. 48.299(4).* Wisconsin, U.S. Retrieved from https://docs.legis.wisconsin.gov/statutes/prefaces/toc

Clarke, S. (2007, August). *Canada: Children's rights; Law Library of Congress.* Retrieved from http://www.loc.gov/law/help/child-rights/pdfs/Children's%20Rights-Canada.pdf

Convention on the Rights of the Child. (1989, November 20). *Convention on the Rights of the Child, 1577 U.N.T.S. 3;28 I.L.M. 1456.*

Convention on the Rights of the Child, BGBL. (1992, February 17). *17577 U.N.T.S. 3 Ratified by Germany.* Germany: Budesgesetzblatt.

Crimes Act s.4.15. (1992). *Crimes Act 1900 as amended by Crimes Amendment Act 1989 and Act 1992, s. 4.15.* New South Wales (NSW).

Evidence Act R.S.C. 1985 C. C-5. (N.d.). *Evidence Act R.S.C. 1985, C. C-5 Witnesses, Incriminating Questions, Section 5.(1).* Canada. Retrieved from Laws-lois.justice.gc.ca/eng/acts/C-5/FullText.html

Government of India, Juvenile Justice Care and Protection of Children Act. (2000). *Government of India, Juvenile Justice Care and Protection of Children Act No. 56 of 2000, ch 1.2.d.* India. Retrieved from http://wcd.nic.in/childprot/jjact2000.pdf

Government of India Act 32. (2012). *Government of India Act 32 Code of Criminal Procedure, the Protection of Children from Sexual Offenses Act.* Retrieved from http://www.courts.state.hi.us/docs/financial_svcs/Solicitations/Health_Human_Svcs/J11030/J11030_section_two_specs1.pdf

Hale, S. B. (2004). *The discourse of court interpreting: Discourse practices of the law, the witness and the interpreter.* Amsterdam: John Benjamins.

In Re Gault. (1967). *387 U.S. 1, 13.* U.S. Supreme Court.

Kilkelly, U. (2001). The best of both worlds for children's rights? Interpreting the European Convention on Human Rights in the light of the UN Convention on the Rights of the Child. *Human Rights Quarterly, 23*(2), 308–326. Retrieved

from http://muse.jhu.edu/login?auth=0&type=summary&url=/journals/human
_rights_quarterly/v023/23.2kilkelly.pdf

Markel, H. (2009, December 14). Case shined first light on abuse of children. *New York Times.* Retrieved from http://www.nytimes.com/2009/12/15/health/ 15abus.html

Muslim Marriages Bill Act 20. (2011, March). *Muslim Marriages Bill Act 20.* South Africa.

Overview: Glossary; United Nations treaty collection. (N.d.). Retrieved from http://treaties.un.org/Pages/Overview.aspx?path=overview/glossary/page1 _en.xml

Papademetriou, T. (2007, September). *Greece: Children's rights; Law Library of Congress.* Retrieved from http://www.loc.gov/law/help/child-rights/pdfs/ ChildrensRights-Greece.pdf

Peters, J. K. (2006). How children are heard in child protective proceedings, in the United States and around the world in 2005: Survey findings, initial observations, and areas for further study. *Faculty Scholarship Series, Paper 2146.* Retrieved from http://digitalcommons.law.yale.edu/cgi/viewcontent .cgi?article=3181&context=fss_papers

Philippine Rep. Act No.7610. (1992, June 17). *Philippine Rep. Act No. 7610 s. 10: Special Protection of Children against Abuse, Exploitation and Discrimination Act.* Retrieved from www.chanrobles.com/republicacts/republicactno7610 .html#.UVTZyRxJPpU

Philippine Rep. Act No. 9231. (2003, December 19). *Philippine Rep. Act No. 9231: Special Protection of Children against Abuse, Exploitation and Dis-crimination Act.*

Philippine Rev. Penal Code, s.4 a. (n.d.). *Philippine Revised Penal Code, No. 004-07-Sc2000-11-21 section 4.a.*

R. v. Lifchus. (1997, September 18). *3 SCR 320 (Case no. 25404).* Winnipeg: Supreme Court Judgment.

Ritter, R. (2005). *The essential A-Z guide to the written word: New Oxford dic-tionary for writers and editors.* Oxford, UK: Oxford University Press.

Sial, O. (2006, March). *A guide to the legal system of Islamic Republic of Iran.* Retrieved from http://www.nyulawglobal.org/globalex/Iran.htm

Slomanson, W. (2011). *Fundamental perspectives on international law.* Boston, MA: Wadsworth.

Status of Treaties: Chapter IV, Section 11: United Nations Treaty Collection. (N.d.). Retrieved from http://treaties.un.org/Pages/ViewDetails.aspx?src= TREATY&mtdsg_no=IV-11&chapter=4&lang=en#16

Surat Al-Baquarah—The Noble Qur'an. (N.d.). Retrieved from http://quran.com/2

Traditional Courts Bill 76. (2011, December 13). *Traditional Courts Bill 76, pro-posed section 76, explanatory summary of bill published in government gazette no. 34850.* South Africa.

U.S. Department of State. (N.d.). *Intercountry adoption: Bureau of Consular Affairs*. Retrieved from http://adoption.state.gov/country_information/country _specific_info.php?country-select

U.S. Federal Rules of Evidence, Section 803. (N.d.). *18 U.S.C. 3482, Federal Rules of Evidence, Section 803.*

Vieth, V. I. (2006, Fall). Unto the third generation: A call to end child abuse in the United States within 120 years (revised and expanded). *Hamline Journal of Public Law & Policy, 28*(1), 85. Retrieved from http://www.ncptc.org/ vertical/Sites/%7B8634A6E1-FAD2-4381-9C0D-5DC7E93C9410%7D/ uploads/%7B9D65D957-4906-4503-BF31-04C801DE8D84%7D.PDF

Waller, L., & Williams, C. (1993). *Brett, Waller and Williams criminal law: Text and cases* (7th ed.). Sydney: Butterworths.

Whitman, J. Q. (2008, February 24). What are the origins of reasonable doubt? Retrieved from http://hnn.us/articles/47018.html

Young, W., Cameron, N., & Tinsley, Y. (1999, November). Juries in criminal trials: Part two; A summary of the research findings. *New Zealand Law Commission, preliminary paper 37.* Retrieved from http://www.lawcom.govt.nz/sites/ default/files/publications/1999/11/Publication_76_159_PP37Vol2.pdf

Zeldin, W. (2007, July). *Children's rights international law: Law Library of Congress.* Retrieved from http://www.loc.gov/law/help/child-rights/pdfs/ Children's%20Rights-International%20Laws.pdf

9

The Child's Right to Freedom from Violence: The UN Convention on the Rights of the Child and UNCRC General Comment 13

Jaap E. Doek and Kimberly Svevo-Cianci

BACKGROUND

In adopting the UN Convention on the Rights of the Child, the international community, led by children's rights advocates and professionals working with and for children, recognized that children and adolescents under 18 years of age often need special care and protection that adults do not require. Certainly, the world has made important historical advances to become the "civilized" society we know today, in terms of understanding the importance of human rights and advocating for a higher standard of living for all. Yet millions of people in today's world, including a majority of children, live in poverty, without their basic human rights to food, shelter, clothing, education, and safety. They may reach old age never aspiring to anything beyond what they have seen and known in the environment of their childhood, and with no means to do better, although the Arab Spring and other social phenomena in recent times tell us that by being more connected to the world through technology, youth as well as adults are becoming more conscious of their rights to more than subsistence. UNICEF's publication entitled *The State of the World's Children* provides statistics on the hardships that many of the world's children experience in their often very short lifetimes, such as child labor, child marriage, female genital mutilation, malnutrition, and violent discipline.

Yet even today these problems, which should not be tolerated in any country for any children, are commonplace hardships for many children in developing countries, and also for many living on the margins in almost all countries. In fact, worldwide, in most cities and often rural areas as well, good housing, education, and job opportunities are lacking or of inferior quality for many families, thereby creating barriers to higher social and economic advances for parents, and subsequently for their children. And certainly we know of urban communities plagued by high rates of crime, corruption, substance abuse, and violence, which retard the positive social development of children and youth. We can easily track how the lack of children's rights to education and the lack of basic needs required for an adequate standard of living, well-being, development, and safety set a dismal foundation for children, adolescents, and young adults to build on, thus depriving them of the right to develop the capacity to take advantage of the human rights to which they are entitled.

THE UN CONVENTION ON THE RIGHTS OF THE CHILD: A BRIEF INTRODUCTION

The history of the recognition of the rights of the child is relatively short. It started with the League of Nations' adoption of the Declaration of the Rights of the Child on September 26, 1924. After World War II there was a need to reconfirm the commitment of the international community to the rights of the child. The discussions about the text of a new document took some time, but on November 20, 1959, the UN General Assembly adopted a new Declaration of the Rights of the Child.[1]

In the meantime, the newly established United Nations undertook many efforts in service of the development and recognition of human rights. The first result of these efforts was the adoption on December 10, 1948, of the Universal Declaration of Human Rights (UDHR). It was the first international document containing all basic human rights approved and adopted by all the states that were members of the United Nations.[2] It was a nonbinding document, but meant as the basis for the development of binding international human rights treaties. Efforts to that effect resulted in the adoption of two international covenants by the UN General Assembly in 1966, the International Covenant on Economic, Social and Cultural Rights (ICESCR) and the International Covenant on Civil and Political Rights (ICCPR).[3]

After the adoption of these covenants, the international community felt that there was a need to provide more specific protection to vulnerable groups of people such as women, children, migrant workers, and persons with disabilities. Efforts to provide that protection resulted in, among other efforts, the adoption by the UN General Assembly of the Convention on the Elimination of All Forms of Discrimination against Women (1979), the Convention on the Rights of the Child (1989), the Convention on the Protection of the Rights of All Migrant Workers and Members of Their Families (1990), and the Convention on the Rights of Persons with Disabilities (2006).

The UN Convention on the Rights of the Child (UNCRC) was drafted by the Open-Ended Working Group on the Question of a Convention on the Rights of the Child in a long process (from 1979 to 1989) of discussions and negotiations.[4] The result: a very comprehensive treaty of the human rights of children. The importance of the UNCRC is, among other things, that it contains an elaboration and specification of both the civil and political rights and the economic, social, and cultural rights of children. In addition, it recognizes the right of the child to grow up in a family, the right to be cared for by her/his parents as much as possible, the primary and common responsibility of parents for the upbringing and development of their children, and the obligation of states party to the UNCRC to provide them with appropriate support and assistance in the performing of this responsibility.

A major change established by the UNCRC is that the child is not only considered as an object of care and protection, but also as a person with the right to express her/his views in all matters concerning her/himself and with a growing capacity to exercise her/his rights. The CRC has been ratified by 193 countries and therefore has achieved almost universal recognition of the child as a rights holder.[5] A list of UNCRC articles follows later in this chapter.

In 2000, the UN General Assembly adopted two optional protocols that provide an important strengthening of the right of the child to protection, the Optional Protocol on the Involvement of Children in Armed Conflict (OPAC) and the Optional Protocol on the Sale of Children, Child Prostitution and Child Pornography (OPSC). They entered into force in 2002.[6] We will discuss these more fully below.

Like all other human rights treaties, the UNCRC provides for the establishment of a committee. The 18 members of this committee are elected by the states party to the UNCRC (article 42). The core task of the committee is to examine the progress made in the implementation of the UNCRC by the states party to it. This examination is based on the information provided in the reports of these states and in reports from UN agencies (in particular UNICEF) and nongovernmental organizations. The result of this examination is a country-specific document called *The Concluding Observations*.

In this document, the committee recognizes the progress made; it expresses its concerns about still-existing shortcomings in the implementation of the CRC and outlines specific recommendations for actions that should be taken to address them.

Another important activity of the committee in order to foster the effective implementation of the UNCRC is the organization of annual Days of General Discussions. These meetings allow for in-depth discussions of certain issues relevant for the implementation of the CRC and result in recommendations for the states and others involved in this implementation.[7] Some of these discussions have had a lasting impact. For instance, the one on children and armed conflict in 1992 resulted in a UN Study (Machel, 1996),[8] the drafting of the OPAC, and the appointment of a special representative of the UN Secretary General on Children and Armed Conflict.

The discussion days in 2000 and 2001 on violence against children led to the UN Study on Violence against Children (Pinheiro, 2006) and the appointment by the UN Secretary General of a special representative on violence against children.[9]

In addition to the country-specific recommendations in the concluding observations, the CRC Committee issues "General Comments." Their objectives are to provide a fuller understanding of the states' obligations both to ensure fulfillment of children's rights, but also to provide guidance to actors involved in the implementation of the CRC, with related responsibilities. These actors, or agents, include parents, family members, caregivers, professionals, and education or service providers, as well as government officials and those monitoring and evaluating the effectiveness of CRC implementation in each nation and each community, and for every child. The General Comments deal either with a specific article of the CRC or with a particular vulnerable group of children. Since 2001, the committee has issued the following General Comments found in Table 9.1.[10]

THE UNCRC AND THE OPTIONAL PROTOCOLS: A SUMMARY OF THEIR CONTENT[11]

For a proper understanding of the role of the CRC with regard to the prevention of and the intervention in cases of child abuse and neglect, it is not enough to focus on the implementation of article 19 of the UNCRC as the most relevant provision (see the fourth paragraph). It is important to look

Table 9.1 UNCRC General Comments

	UN Convention on the Rights of the Child—General Comments (as of April 2013)
17 Advance unedited version	The right of the child to rest, leisure, play, recreational activities, cultural life and the arts
16 Advance unedited version	On state obligations regarding the impact of the business sector on children's rights
15 Advance unedited version	The right of the child to the enjoyment of the highest attainable standard of health (article 24)
14 (2013)	The right of the child to have his or her best interests as a primary consideration (article 3, para.1)
13 (2011)	The right of the child to freedom from all forms of violence
12 (2011)	The right of the child to be heard
11 (2009)	Indigenous children and their rights under the Convention on the Rights of the Child
10 (2009)	Children's rights in juvenile justice
9 (2007)	The rights of children with disabilities
8 (2006)	The right of the child to protection from corporal punishment and other cruel or degrading forms of punishment
7/Rev.1 (2006)	Implementing child rights in early childhood
6 (2005)	Treatment of unaccompanied and separated children outside their country of origin
5 (2005)	General measures of implementation of the Convention on the Rights of the Child
4 (2003)	Adolescent health
3 (2003)	HIV/AIDS and the rights of the child
2 (2003)	The role of independent human rights institutions
1 (2002)	The aims of education

at this article in connection with other articles of the CRC regarding, for instance, the right of the child to express her/his views, the right to the highest attainable standard of health, the right to a standard of living adequate for the development of the child, and the right to education. The CRC should be implemented in a holistic manner. Therefore, a brief summary of the content of the CRC and the Optional Protocols follows.

The Convention on the Rights of the Child

Part I of the UNCRC contains the rights of the child and the obligations of the states party to the CRC to undertake all necessary and/or appropriate actions for their full implementation. The rights are not presented in a specific order and this can be considered as a reflection of their indivisibility. But in order to help the states with their reporting on the implementation of the CRC, the committee has clustered articles under certain themes, as follows.

General Measures of Implementation

Article 4 of the UNCRC requires states to take all appropriate legislative, administrative, and other measures for the implementation of the rights recognized in the CRC. According to the CRC Committee, this means, among other things, that the national laws have to be brought into compliance with the CRC; that a body should be established for the effective coordination of all actions for the implementation of the CRC undertaken by governmental bodies and civil society organizations (NGOs and others); that a system should be established for the collection of all data relevant for this implementation, and a national independent body should be set up for the promotion and monitoring of the implementation of children's rights (ombudsperson or commissioner); and that information about the CRC should be systematically disseminated to children, parents, and professionals working with or for children.

Definition of the Child

For the purpose of this convention, article 1 defines a child as any human being below the age of 18, unless under the applicable law the age of majority is attained earlier. Under this article, the committee also discusses various minimum ages for, e.g., marriage, child labor, and sexual consent.

General Principles

The CRC Committee considers articles 2 (nondiscrimination), 3 (the best interest of the child as a primary consideration in all actions concerning children), 6 (the right to life, survival, and development), and 12 (the right to express one's views) as the general principles of the CRC. The fact that these are "general principles" means that these articles must be fully observed in the implementation and exercise of the other rights of the convention. Given the importance of these articles, some remarks relevant to the matter of child abuse and neglect are in order.

1. The obligation of states to respect and ensure the rights in the CRC to each child within their jurisdiction without discrimination of any kind is not just a negative one (as in, do not discriminate), but is also a positive one. This means, among other things, that the government must pay special attention to vulnerable groups of children, for instance children belonging to racial, ethnic, religious, or linguistic minorities; children with disabilities; and girls, in developing and implementing programs meant to prevent abuse and neglect in order to ensure that these children have access to and benefit from these programs. To that effect extra support measures may be necessary.
2. There is no universal and concrete definition of the best interest of the child applicable in all actions and decisions concerning children. Regardless of the circumstances, however, it must be a primary consideration, meaning that it must be the first factor in the midst of all other relevant interests, e.g., of parents. In considering all the interests at stake, the best interest of the child should ultimately be the prevailing factor. For instance, in taking measures for the protection of the child against abuse and neglect, the interests of parents may play a role, but the interest of the child to be effectively protected must be decisive.
3. Article 12 requires that children be provided with a meaningful opportunity to express their views and that these views be given due weight in accordance with the age and maturity of the child. This applies not only in legal proceedings for the purpose of protecting the child against (further) child abuse and neglect, but also in the development and implementation of prevention policies. The child should participate to the maximum extent possible in the process of decision making and policy development.[12]

Civil Rights and Freedoms[13]

Civil rights and freedoms include inter alia the right to a name, the right to acquire a nationality, and the right to preserve one's identity (articles 7 and 8);[14] the right to freedom of expression (article 13); the right to freedom of thought, consciousness, and religion (article 14); the right to freedom of association and peaceful assembly (article 15); the right to privacy (article 16); the right to information (articles 13 and 17); and the right to be protected against torture and other cruel, inhuman, and degrading treatment or punishment (article 37 [a]).

Two brief remarks: When it comes to the exercise of the right to freedom of thought, consciousness, and religion, states shall respect the rights and duties of parents to provide direction to the child in a manner consistent with the child's evolving capacities. Article 14 does not contain the explicit provision, which can be found in article 18 of ICCPR, that this freedom includes the freedom to choose one's religion.

The right to protection in article 37 (a) requires, according to the CRC Committee among others, a prohibition by law of all forms of corporal punishment.[15]

Family Environment and Alternative Care

The UNCRC contains various articles recognizing the primary and common responsibilities of parents (and other caretakers) for the upbringing and development of the child and the obligation of states to provide children with the necessary assistance and support (articles 5, 18, and 27).

Separation of the child from her/his parents is only allowed if that is necessary in the best interest of the child, and the separated child has the right to maintain personal relations and direct contact with both parents (article 9). In line with this provision, states shall take measures to combat illicit transfer and the nonreturn of children (article 11). The child who is in the care of her/his parents or others has the right to be protected from all forms of violence, abuse, and neglect, and states must take all appropriate legislative, social, and other measures to ensure that protection (article 19); for an elaboration of this right, see the fourth paragraph.

When a child is deprived of her/his family environment for whatever reason, states must provide the child with alternative care. This could include foster care, kafalah or Islamic law, adoption, or if necessary, placement in a suitable institution for the care of children (article 20). This provision clearly indicates that priority should be given to alternative care in a family setting; putting a child in a residential setting is a measure of last resort. Domestic and intercountry adoption must be in the best interest of the child and meet the standards set out in article 21, which also states that intercountry adoption should be a measure of last resort. Every placement in alternative care must be periodically reviewed, a review not only of the treatment of the child but also of all other circumstances relevant to her or his placement (article 25).[16]

Basic Health and Welfare

Every child has the right to the highest attainable standard of health. In order to progressively achieve this goal, states must take various measures listed in article 24. These measures include, among others, measures to reduce infant and child mortality, to develop primary health care, to combat disease and malnutrition, to ensure appropriate prenatal and postnatal health care for mothers, and to abolish traditional practices prejudicial to the health of children. Special attention is given to the rights of children with disabilities in article 23.[17]

Every child has the right to benefit from social security, including social insurance, and states shall take the necessary measures to realize the full realization of this right (article 26).

Every child has the right to a standard of living adequate for her or his physical, mental, spiritual, moral, and social development. Parents have the primary responsibility to secure this adequate standard of living, and states have to assist them in performing this responsibility and shall in case of need provide the parents with material support programs, particularly with regard to nutrition, clothing, and housing (article 27).

Education, Leisure and Cultural Activities

Every child has the right to education, and states are obliged to take measures with a view to progressively making that right a reality in the daily life of children, such as making primary education compulsory and free for all children; making different forms of secondary education, including general and vocational education, available and accessible for all children; and encouraging regular attendance at schools and reducing drop-out rates (article 28).

Unique in the world of human rights on education is article 29, which lists the aims of education, such as development of the child's personality, talents, and mental and physical abilities to their fullest potential; the development of respect for human rights, as well as respect for the child's parents and the child's cultural identity, language, and values; and the preparation for a responsible life in society and respect for the natural environment.[18]

Every child has the right to rest and leisure, to engage in play and recreational activities, and to participate freely in cultural life and the arts. States shall promote these rights and provide appropriate and equal opportunities for their exercise.[19]

Special Protection Measures

Millions of children live in very difficult circumstances and become the victims of economic and sexual exploitation, sale and trafficking, and armed conflict, among other eventualities. They need special protection, and various articles of the UNCRC provide them with the right to adequate protection (articles 22 and 32–38) and the right to physical and psychological recovery and social reintegration (article 39). Two optional protocols to the CRC deal in more detail with protection from sexual exploitation and from involvement in armed conflict (see the following section for more detail). The protection of children in conflict with penal law is dealt with in articles 40 and 37.

THE OPTIONAL PROTOCOLS TO THE IMPLEMENTATION OF THE UNCRC IN THE UNITED STATES[20]

On May 25, 2000, the UN General Assembly adopted two optional protocols to the CRC, one entitled "The Involvement of Children in Armed Conflict (OPAC)" and the other entitled "The Sale of Children, Child Prostitution and Child Pornography (OPSC)."[21]

These are important additions to the CRC for the protection of children against all forms of violence and exploitation. Therefore a summary of their content and some limited remarks on their implementation in the United States follow.[22]

OPAC

The main reason for this optional protocol was that many states were not happy with the low age in article 38 of the UNCRC for involvement and recruitment of children in armed conflict (prohibited for children below the age of 15). OPAC sets new and higher standards:

1. Involvement of persons below the age of 18 in armed conflict is prohibited (article 1).

2. No compulsory recruitment of such persons in the armed forces of the state party (article 2); the same applies to armed groups (article 4).
3. The minimum age for voluntary recruitment is 16, and specific conditions must be met (article 3); voluntary recruitment of persons under the age of 18 is not possible for armed groups (article 4).

OPSC

This optional protocol can be considered as an elaboration of articles 34 and 35 of the UNCRC. It contains important provisions for combating the sale of children and the exploitation of children in prostitution and pornography. It can be summarized as follows:

1. Article 2 contains definitions of the sale of children, child prostitution, and child pornography.
2. Article 3 requires states to make the activities mentioned in that article a crime under their national law and also to establish liability of legal persons if they commit one of these crimes.
3. Article 4 obliges states, among others, to establish extraterritorial jurisdiction over the crimes mentioned in article 3. It means that a person with the nationality of or a habitual residence in Country A can be prosecuted in that country for crimes as defined in article 3 outside that country; the nationality of the victim is irrelevant. If the victim is a national of State A, authorities of that state can prosecute the alleged perpetrator whether the crime was committed in or outside Country A and regardless of the nationality of the perpetrator.
4. Article 5 rules that the crimes mentioned in article 3 are extraditable offenses and should be included in extradition treaties, or the article should be used as a legal basis for extradition.

This optional protocol contains many more articles, for instance on the protection of child victims and witnesses of such crimes (article 8), on the need for awareness-raising campaigns to prevent sexual exploitation of children, and the right of victims of this exploitation to appropriate assistance for their full physical and psychological recovery and social reintegration (article 9).

Implementation of the Optional Protocols in the United States

As a state party to the optional protocols, the government of the United States has to report on its implementation of the UNCRC first within two years after the protocols entered into force for that nation and thereafter every five years (OPAC article 8 and OPSC article 13).[23] The United States has so far submitted two reports to the CRC Committee, the first one in 2005 and the second in 2010, and is therefore one of the few countries that have reported on time.[24] The first report was examined in May 2008 and the second in January 2013 in meetings with delegations of the U.S. government. After these meetings, the CRC Committee issued concluding observations regarding each of the optional protocols. These observations contain the recognition of progress made in implementation as well as concerns, along with specific recommendations. It goes beyond the scope of this chapter to present and discuss these recommendations in detail. But it is relevant to the matter of child abuse and neglect to pay some attention to the most recent recommendations regarding the implementation of the OPSC made by the committee in January 2013.[25]

In general, it should be noted that the CRC Committee welcomes in both sets of concluding observations (both paras. 4) the assurances expressed by the delegation (of the United States) during the dialogue that "the administration supports the treaty's [i.e., the CRC's] goals and intends to review how it can finally move towards ratification of the Convention on the Rights of the Child."

In the concluding observations regarding the implementation of OPSC, the CRC Committee welcomes and/or appreciates various measures taken by the United States government to address the sale of children, including trafficking, child prostitution, and child pornography, such as the development of a comprehensive strategic action plan to strengthen the services for victims of trafficking, the activities of various departments to raise awareness in particular on human trafficking, and the training of officials who may come in contact with trafficking victims.

However, the CRC Committee recommends that the U.S. government pay more attention to the sale of children and define, regulate, monitor, and criminalize the sale of children at the federal level and at the level of all states, and in particular the sale of children for the purpose of illegal adoption (para. 30 [b]).

Furthermore, the CRC Committee urges the U.S. government to effectively prevent publication and dissemination of pornographic material concerning children through surveillance mechanisms to automatically block offending Internet service providers and other media and to establish an authority for Internet safety, ISP licensing, and checks for harmful content for children (para. 28 [a] and [b]).

Regarding the protection of children victims of prostitution, the committee recommends the passage of safe harbor laws in all states that have not yet done so to ensure that prostituted children are protected and not arrested or detained, and the provision of training and funding for the promotion and application of such laws (para. 34 [c]).

The committee is deeply concerned about the severe lack of services for the recovery and reintegration of child victims of sexual and economic exploitation and other crimes covered by the optional protocol. It strongly urges the U.S. government to increase allocation and spending of resources to establish directly or through service providers the specialized services for children who are victims of crimes under the optional protocol, which should include shelters for immediate relief and longer-term services, especially family reunification, if appropriate, or placement in family settings, and health and education, in order for these children to recover physically, psychologically, and emotionally and to reintegrate into society. In addition, adequate remedy and reparation should be sought legally and through other means.

Regarding the implementation of OPSC article 8, on the protection of child victims involved in criminal proceedings as witnesses, the committee urges the U.S. government to encourage all states to undertake procedural reform to allow prosecution of perpetrators without victims'/ witnesses' testimony in court hearings and to use videotaped testimony-interviews as evidence in court in order to avoid revictimization of the child (para. 49 [e]).

ESTABLISHING A CHILD'S RIGHTS APPROACH TO CHILD PROTECTION

Depending on where we were born and live our lives, we see the world in very different ways. The reality of the world and the potential for a child or adult of the Brazilian favelas, or a Los Angeles slum, or a Thai brothel, or an African country's garbage dump, might be very different from the realities perceived by many of those reading this chapter. To what extent, however, does each of us believe that every child, regardless of her or his origins or national, cultural, or personal characteristics, has the right to every opportunity necessary for maximum development—equal to any other child in the world? To borrow from Thomas Jefferson (1801): What are the implications in terms of our individual responsibilities if we believe that nothing is more unequal than the equal treatment of children with different levels of privilege, resources, and support? And, what is each of our unique roles in effecting the UN Convention on the Rights of the Child for every child?

The Vision

The UN Convention on the Rights of the Child was conceived to address the issue of the human rights of children—to ensure their rights from birth, providing essential opportunities for their fullest personal development as children and adolescents, and enabling them to aspire to equal opportunities of any adult, perhaps becoming the first generation in their families to do so. The UNCRC therefore strives to strengthen families and communities to create an environment in which equality for all becomes probable. The CRC therefore set in motion and supported the many further efforts that have since been made, building upon its near global adoption to protect the rights of millions of children who were previously invisible to child protection systems (Eisenstein, 2009; Svevo-Cianci, Herczog, et al., 2012).

An important shift in perceptions on the issue of violence against children, which started with the UN Convention about the inevitability of this challenging social issue, was advanced still further with the 2005–2006 UN Study on Violence against Children, and the ensuing 2006 World Report on Violence against Children, in which the independent expert Paulo Pinheiro declared, "No violence against children is justifiable; all violence against children is preventable" (Pinheiro, 2006).

While the Convention on the Rights of the Child introduced and established the standard for a children's rights approach to all interactions with and for children, and regarding all issues which impact children's lives, CRC General Comment 13 (GC13) established a clearer interpretation of the CRC's definition of what a children's rights approach to protection is and requires. In fact, one fundamental assumption upon which GC13 is based is that "[a] child rights–based approach to child caregiving and protection requires a paradigm shift towards respecting and promoting the human dignity and physical and psychological integrity of children as rights-bearing individuals rather than perceiving them primarily as 'victims'" (GC13, 2011).

Further, according to GC13, governments, professionals, and all adults must establish and champion "respect for the dignity, life, survival, well-being, health, development, participation and non-discrimination of the child as a rights-bearing person" in their efforts to protect and fulfill the rights of the CRC. There is a clear shift from perceiving and treating children as objects to assist, to seeing them as "rights holders entitled to non-negotiable rights to protection." Further, GC13 emphasizes the need for duty bearers to develop the capacity to "meet their obligations to respect, protect and fulfill the rights of children," including caregivers, parents, and community members to direct and guide children "in the exercise of their rights . . . in line with children's evolving capacities" (GC13, Section V, para. 52). Finally, GC13 establishes the holistic and assets-based nature of a children's rights–based approach for maximum effectiveness and sustainability. In fact, it "places emphasis on supporting the strengths and resources of the child him/herself and all social systems of which the child is a part: family, school, community, institutions, religious and cultural systems" (GC13, Section V, para. 52).

As Finkelhor pointed out, today's understanding of the challenging need for a more holistic, and therefore complex, child protection movement has evolved from important advances made in the past one hundred years. It has

benefitted particularly from progress in women's emancipation, the development of professional discipline concentration on children and families, growing support for the view that children should be socialized through love rather than physical beatings and humiliation, and recognition that parents are not always right and should not have unrestricted authority over children. Child protection interventions have emphasized establishment of laws and regulations, including support for child welfare/protection services involved in identification and investigation of victims and perpetrators, punishment of perpetrators, separation of children from perpetrators; and, to lesser degrees, therapeutic services to those involved. (Hart et al., 2011, p. 7)

In fact, prevention must be the highest priority, as there are not sufficient resources in any nation to address the short- and long-term needs of child victims of maltreatment and their families.

Further, article 19 of UNCRC provides an advanced and comprehensive conceptualization of child protection. For example, as Hart points out, even

[t]he title of the General Comment, "The right of the child to freedom from all forms of violence," is testimony of the need for a complete change in the manner that violence against children is understood. It is the right of the child to live in an environment that is peaceful, loving, and free of all forms of violence. In the context of the full Convention, it provides the basis for a transformation in child protection toward a child rights approach. (Hart et al., 2011 pp. 10–11)

In fact, GC13 carries weight in guiding child protection throughout children's experience of prevention, as well as during child protection intervention and during long-term-care follow-up and related decision making. GC13 establishes that "[c]hildren's rights to be heard and to have their views given due weight must be respected systematically in all decision-making processes, and their empowerment and participation should be central to child caregiving and protection strategies and programmes" (GC13, 2011).

GC13 also strengthened the evolving interpretation of the UNCRC through a working group and consultations to clarify several issues that were controversial in their implementation. For instance, the development of GC13 led to changes in the world's perceptions of children without parents or guardians, establishing that such children retain their rights through the obligations of the state to provide care for them. It further disallowed the exemption of children's rights from children who had been emancipated through early marriage or self-declared emancipation, based on the understanding that children in these situations are often at high risk, and in fact must still have their rights to protection, well-being, and development upheld (Svevo-Cianci, Herczog, et al., 2011).

CRC ARTICLE 19: PROTECTION OF ALL CHILDREN FROM ALL FORMS OF VIOLENCE/GENERAL COMMENT 13

Article 19 is the key article addressing the child's right to protection from violence. It sets the stage for all actors to have a responsible role, with accountability for their specific actions, in child protection ranging from preventive social programs to intervention, and even through the child's rehabilitation and reintegration back into a family or care setting. However, it is the other articles that flush out details of the necessary and appropriate rights to care in full context of children's circumstances, and it is the CRC General Comments that, as their development over the years becomes increasingly sophisticated in supporting effective implementation of the CRC, continue to establish more specific direction and standards for the requirements mandated by the CRC in article 19, below:

1. States Parties shall take all appropriate legislative, administrative, social and educational measures to protect the child from all forms of physical or mental violence, injury or abuse, neglect or negligent treatment, maltreatment or exploitation, including sexual abuse, while in the care of parent(s), legal guardian(s) or any other person who has the care of the child.

2. Such protective measures should, as appropriate, include effective procedures for the establishment of social programmes to provide necessary support for the child and for those who have the care of the child, as well as for other forms of prevention and for identification, reporting, referral, investigation, treatment and follow-up of instances of child maltreatment described heretofore, and, as appropriate, for judicial involvement.

While all CRC articles should be applied within a holistic understanding of the whole of the convention and the child's rights to well-being, development, and protection, there are certain CRC articles that require specific attention when citizens, professionals, or governments consider child protection at levels of primary, secondary, and tertiary prevention and related protective interventions. These articles are listed below, and apply to the child's protection from violence throughout an integrated, intersectoral approach ranging from the child's protection within the family to external protections that may be necessary from the health, education, social welfare, law enforcement, and justice sectors.

In fact, it can be considered that it is only when parents/families fail to protect their children, which can often be due to a failure of community, society, and/or government to support the parents/families, that incidences of violence occur that require intervention. Therefore, the government, social, and public health investments that are most cost effective and that should be the highest priority to safeguard children, should lie in developing the capacity of the parents and families, and supporting them (through job training/placement, mental health services, counseling, access to housing, and financial assistance in times of need) to ensure their children are protected in the first place.

In 2011, the CRC Committee adopted General Comment 13 on Article 19: the right of the child to freedom from all forms of violence.[26] In this document, the committee provides states that are party to the CRC and all agencies, nongovernmental organizations, and individuals involved in the prevention of and protection from violence against children with guidance and recommendations on the implementation of article 19.

The central vision of the committee is that "[n]o violence against children is justifiable and all violence against children is preventable." The objectives of this general comment are, among others,

- to outline the legislative, judicial, administrative, social and educational measures that States Parties must take.

Table 9.2   UNCRC Articles Relating to Protection from Violence

CRC Article Number	Article
3)	Best interests of the child
5)	Parental guidance and the child's evolving capacities
6)	Child's right to life and maximum survival and development
7)	Birth registration, name, nationality, and right to know and be cared for by parents
18)	Parents' joint responsibilities assisted by the state
19)	Child's right to protection from all forms of violence
24)	Child's right to health and health services (protection from traditional practices)
25)	Child's right to periodic review of treatment
27)	Child's right to adequate standard of living
34)	Sexual exploitation of children
37)	Torture, degrading treatment, and deprivation of liberty
39)	Rehabilitation of child victims
40)	Administration of juvenile justice

- to overcome isolated, fragmented and reactive initiatives to address child caregiving and protection which have limited impact on the prevention and elimination of all forms of violence against children.
- to promote a holistic approach to implementing article 19 based on the Convention's overall perspective on securing the rights of the child to survival, dignity, well-being, health, development, participation and non-discrimination—the fulfillment of which rights is threatened by violence.

The General Comments contain a nonexhaustive overview of all forms of physical and sexual violence, including inter alia harmful traditional practices like female genital mutilation, forced and early marriage, and violent and degrading initiation rites.

Detailed information is provided on the legislative, administrative, social support, and educational measures that states party to the UNCRC should take at the national and subnational level in order to prevent violence against children and to adequately respond to all types of incidences of child abuse and neglect.

Specific recommendations are made regarding the identification, reporting, referral, and investigation of cases of violence against children. For instance, the committee recommends: "In every country reporting of instances, suspicion or risk of violence should, at a minimum, be required by professionals working directly with children" (para. 45).

Finally, recommendations are given (in paras. 61 through 65) for the development and implementation of national plans of action, which should include the establishment of a national coordinating framework to ensure their effective implementation.

General Comment 13 is a key guiding document for governments, professionals, and other key actors above. However, it is also essential for these actors to be informed by other General Comments that will influence their work to optimize efforts to protect the well-being and development of children in specific circumstances—for instance, very young children (GC7), indigenous children (GC11), children with disabilities (GC9), those in the juvenile justice system (2007), those with HIV/AIDS (2003), or in other situations. The cross-referencing of the CRC and these general comments will result in the strongest protection of rights due to the clearest understanding of how the UNCRC and General Comments must be interpreted.

CHALLENGES TO THE IMPLEMENTATION OF THE CRC

We will first briefly identify the major obstacles to realizing the rights of the child, then provide some information on the different ways and means for implementing children's rights.

Major Obstacles to Implementing the Rights of the Child

From the reports of the states party to the CRC Committee, it can be concluded that progress has been achieved, particularly in the areas of legislation and policy development. But at the same time, a variety of difficulties have been identified that impede the implementation of the UNCRC. Too many children do not yet benefit from their rights as recognized in the CRC.

The major obstacles are poverty and violence. According to recent figures, about one billion children live in dire poverty, meaning they have less than U.S. $1.50 a day for food, housing, clothes, health care, and education. Directly linked to this poverty is the fact that more than 100 million children have to work full time, and many are starting to work at a very young age. Infant mortality rates decreased over the last decade, but more than 7 million children still die before reaching the age of one year due to preventable diseases. It remains a major challenge for states party to the CRC to remove this obstacle. There is no magic bullet; it requires well-coordinated and targeted actions to promote, and if necessary initiate, the creation of jobs; to promote accessible and affordable health care and education for all; and to develop social insurance programs (family and child allowances)—in short, to invest as a matter of priority in the implementation of the rights of the child enshrined in the UNCRC. In 2000, the international community committed itself to a reduction by half of the proportion of people living on less than a dollar per day by 2015 (Millennium Development Goal).

Violence against children is the other major obstacle to the enjoyment by children of their rights. The UN study and an overwhelming body of research show that abuse, neglect, and all other forms of violence against children have a devastating impact on their development. It is a serious obstacle to the enjoyment of their rights as recognized in the CRC.

Many states party to the CRC undertake a variety of measures to prevent child abuse, neglect, and other forms of violence against children and to provide effective protection. These efforts are supported by international campaigns and by UN agencies like UNICEF and the Special Representative of the UN Secretary General on Violence against Children and international NGOs.

Another obstacle to the realization of the rights of the child is the lack of information about the content of the UNCRC and its meaning for the lives of children, not only among professionals working with and for children but also among parents and the children themselves. The CRC Committee consistently recommends that states promote and support the inclusion of teaching on children's rights in the regular curricula of professional schools as well as in primary and secondary education.

Ways and Means to Promote and Ensure the Implementation of the UNCRC

The first and most important requirement for the implementation of the rights of the child is for 193 states to meet the obligations they voluntarily undertook by ratifying the CRC. It is obvious that it is not easy to do that. Much depends on available resources, but equally important is the political will to give adequate priority to the implementation of the rights of children.[27]

The UNCRC counts on international support in particular for developing countries, as stated in article 4, with a specific reference to the framework of international cooperation as a tool for support in implementing the CRC. Article 24 (the right to the highest attainable standard of health) and article 28 (the right to education) also call for the promotion of international cooperation in progressively achieving the full realization of these rights; in that cooperation, particular account shall be taken of the needs of developing countries.

In light of these provisions, the CRC Committee has consistently recommended, in particular to the OECD countries, to fully comply with the international commitment made many decades ago to allocate 0.7 percent of the Gross Domestic Product (GDP) to international development aid. It can be considered one of the ways to address poverty, which is one of the obstacles to realizing the rights of children.

The implementation of the UNCRC is not an easy task. It requires a full understanding of the many provisions of the CRC and the obligations their implementation entail. But the states party to the CRC are provided by the CRC Committee with rather specific recommendations for actions necessary for full compliance with provisions of the CRC (for an example, see the recommendations briefly mentioned above regarding the implementation of the optional protocols by the U.S. government).

In addition, the CRC Committee provides guidance and recommendations through its General Comments for the interpretation and implementation of the CRC, either regarding specific articles (e.g., General Comment 13 mentioned above) or specific groups of (vulnerable) children, such as children with disabilities, children belonging to indigenous peoples, children infected or affected by HIV/AIDS, and very young children. However, the guidance and recommendations only have the desired impact at the national level if not only governments but also civil society organizations, in particular NGOs and professional associations, and UN agencies such as UNICEF, use them in their efforts to promote the implementation of the CRC.

Experiences in many countries show that these organizations and agencies continue to play a very important role in the realization of the rights of the child. National and international awareness raising and advocacy can, when necessary, put pressure on governments to meet their obligations under the CRC. In that regard the special representatives of the UN Secretary General on children and armed conflict and on violence against children are important advocates for the promotion of national and international actions for the prevention and adequate interventions for the protection of child victims of armed conflict and violence.

To illustrate the previous observations, a concrete example from the efforts to prevent and address adequately child abuse and neglect would be the prohibition of corporal punishment in all settings.

Corporal punishment in the upbringing of children is widely practiced in many countries and often justified by reference to biblical texts summarized in the dictum, "Spare the rod and spoil the child."[28] But research shows that corporal punishment has many short- and long-term negative consequences for the healthy development of the child.[29]

The CRC Committee has taken a children's rights approach to corporal punishment, elaborated in General Comment No. 8 on the right of the child to protection from corporal punishment and other cruel and degrading forms of punishment.[30] With reference to international human rights treaties and article 37 of the UNCRC, the committee is of the opinion that these forms of punishment are a violation of the fundamental right to respect for one's human dignity and physical integrity and to equal protection under the law (paras. 16 through 29). States party to the UNCRC must take all appropriate legislative, administrative, social, and educational measures to eliminate such punishments. Other international and regional human rights treaty bodies and regional courts, like the European and Inter-American Courts of Human Rights, share this view.

The CRC Committee systematically recommends that states prohibit corporal and other forms of cruel and degrading punishment by law. Many countries have undertaken various actions to this effect, often preceded by awareness-raising campaigns (by the government and/or NGOs) and educational campaigns with information on alternative ways of disciplining children. The prohibition by law does not necessarily mean to introduce a separate provision in the criminal code criminalizing these forms of punishment. Information shows that countries prohibiting corporal punishment have done so by introducing in the civil code or the family law a provision prohibiting the use of all forms of violence, including corporal punishment, in the upbringing of children. This means that parents or other caretakers cannot use the traditional defense that it is their right to use corporal punishment if they are charged with assault of their child. The fear that the prohibition would result in many cases of prosecution of parents for using corporal punishment is unfounded. The countries with such prohibitions do not report any increase of prosecution of parents. The key function of the prohibition is that it sets a clear standard for the quality of the upbringing of children and in case of (serious) violation of this standard, parents can be engaged in a discussion on how to improve their child-rearing practices, and guidance and support, in the context of a child protection measure imposed by the court if necessary, can be provided.[31] What all this shows is that implementation of the UNCRC requires not only legislative measures but also extensive awareness and educational campaigns to promote understanding and support within the civil society for the protection of children.

Finally, and despite the many efforts to implement the rights of children, violations of these rights do happen and must be addressed. In 1948, the Universal Declaration of Human Rights (article 8) recognized the right of every person to an effective remedy by national tribunals in case of violations of her/his rights. Article 2 of ICCPR elaborates this right, requiring states to establish judicial remedies to which everyone should have access.

These provisions show that violations of children's rights should be dealt with first by national competent authorities. Given the fact that children are usually considered as not having the capacity to be party in legal proceedings, a petition regarding the violation of a child's rights must be filed by her/his legal representatives (usually the parents). So far there are not many examples from the 193 states party to the UNCRC of cases in which children (or their representatives) have filed a petition in a court asking for a remedy for the violation of their rights.

But in some countries, petitions on behalf of children regularly make the claim that a provision of the CRC has been violated.[32] One difficult matter is the direct enforceability of social and economic rights. The core question behind this difficulty is the justiciability of social, economic, and cultural rights. It goes beyond the scope of this chapter to discuss at length the many aspects of this matter. Suffice it to say that the answer to this question seems to depend on the legal provisions of a particular country, for instance whether economic, social, and cultural rights are included in the constitution, as they are in South Africa. That may add to their enforceability. But circumstances may also play a role. According to the South African Constitutional Court, the right to housing may not include the enforceable right to a shelter for all destitute children, but only for orphans and abandoned children.[33]

In general, it seems fair to state that the courts are often (very) reluctant to see economic, social, and cultural rights as directly enforceable. Besides this particular problem, it is the reality in many countries that children have only (very) limited possibilities (or none at all) to seek a legal remedy for the violation of their rights.

This explains the development of international channels allowing children to file complaints about the violations of their rights with international courts or human rights treaty bodies. Children in countries that are members of the Council of Europe (a total of 47 countries) can file a petition with the European Court of Human Rights, and children in the Americas can do the same with the Inter-American Commission of Human Rights, which can, under certain conditions, submit the case to the Inter-American Court of Human Rights. A general condition is that all national remedies must have been exhausted. Judgments of these courts are binding. States subject to these courts must comply with their decisions, at least in principle.

All human rights treaties do have, either as part of the provisions of the treaty or in the form of an optional protocol, rules for the submission of complaints about a violation of rights enshrined in that treaty to the committee in charge of monitoring the implementation of the treaty concerned; this is known as the communication procedure. Each treaty body has developed rules for dealing with complaints. The process is conducted in writing and behind closed doors, meaning that there are no public hearings involving the complainant or the representatives of the accused state.

The UNCRC was, for a long time, an exception to this practice. But at the end of 2011, the UN General Assembly adopted a new protocol to the CRC, on the "Rights of the Child on a Communication Procedure." In order to enter into force, the protocol has to be ratified by 10 states that are party to the CRC. At the time of this writing, that is not yet the case. One should keep in mind that children can only submit a complaint to the committee about violations of their rights if they live in a country that has ratified the protocol. The CRC Committee has adopted rules of procedure for handling the complaints submitted under the protocol.[34] A very important and unique provision is rule 19, which makes it possible for the committee to conduct oral hearings involving the complainant and/or the alleged victim(s) and representatives of the concerned state party. The hearings will take place in closed meetings of the committee. The alleged victim(s) will not be heard in the presence of the representatives of the state concerned. Although this possibility is not yet effective, it may become an important tool by which children can seek remedies for violations of their rights.

In conclusion, the implementation of the UNCRC is an ongoing challenge for states party to it, and it requires systematic and long-term strategy and action plans. At the same time, the civil society organizations (CSOs) should (and do) play an important role in the realizations of children's rights. States should seek the cooperation of these organizations and take fully into account the recommendations made in both the Concluding Observations and the General Comments of the CRC Committee. Children should be involved as much as possible in the efforts of states and CSOs for the full implementation of the UNCRC. Good progress has been made in many countries, but there are still many gaps in the implementation of children's rights, and often outright violations.

However, children are not fully dependent on the goodwill of politicians or CSOs for the realization of their rights. They can (when appropriate via their legal representatives) file a complaint about violations of their rights with national courts (or similar competent bodies like a children's ombudsperson) or if necessary with a regional court of human rights or with the CRC Committee. In other words, they can claim their rights in legal proceedings and demand appropriate action to compensate for a violation of their rights and to prevent further violations.

CONCLUSION

The UN Convention on the Rights of the Child is tremendously important to the future of humanity, with professionals and advocates from nations around the world contributing to its improvement by further clarifying, updating, and strengthening it each year to ensure the ultimate protection of rights for all children. This convention has motivated child-rights advocates, protection professionals, community leaders, and youth in every country to conceive of a higher level of well-being and development for all children than has ever been conceived of before in all areas of civil, political, economic, social, and cultural rights.

Join the effort to advocate for children's rights.

To learn about the U.S. position on the UNCRC and to find supporting information on its potential ratification, refer to *The U.N. Convention on the Rights of the Child: An Analysis of Treaty Provisions and Implications on U.S. Ratification*, by Jonathan Todres, Mark E. Wojcik, and Chris R. Revaz.

POSTSCRIPT

During the writing of this chapter, on December 14, 2012, two heinous crimes were committed, at that time merely the most recent examples of brutal violence perpetrated against children. In Newtown, Connecticut, 20 children, with an average age of six, were executed in their school by automatic weapons. In central China, 22 primary school children were wounded in a knife attack in their school (as reported by CNN, Beijing, China, December 14, 2012). With the support of the UN Convention on the Rights of the Child, we aspire to the safety for all children in the future.

NOTES

1. Adoption of Resolution 1386 (XIV) of November 20, 1959. For more information on the history and development of the concept of the rights of the child, see, e.g., Veerman (1992).
2. The UN General Assembly Resolution 217A (III) of December 10, 1948. Since then, the tenth of December is celebrated as the international day of human rights every year around the world.
3. They were both adopted by the General Assembly Resolution 2200A (XXI) of December 16, 1966. The ICESCR entered into force on January 3, 1976, and is currently ratified by 161 states; the ICCPR entered into force on March 23, 1976, and is ratified by 167 states. The UDHR, the ICESCR, and the ICCPR are together also known as the International Bill of Human Rights.
4. This working group was established by the UN Commission on Human Rights (replaced in 2006 by the UN Council on Human Rights). For a full report of the drafting process by the working group, see Detrick (1992) and Ek (2007).
5. There is no other human rights treaty with so many ratifications. The only countries that have not yet ratified the CRC are the United States, Somalia, and the recently established independent state of South Sudan.
6. Both protocols were adopted by the UN General Assembly Resolution A/RES/54/263 of May 25, 2000. The OPAC entered into force on February 12, 2002, and the OPSC on January 18, 2002.
7. For more information, see www.ohchr.org/crc/english/ discussions/.
8. See also Machel (2001), the follow-up to this study.
9. For the activities of these special representatives, see www.lwv.org/content/uns-special-representative-prevention-violence-against-children.
10. For the texts of these general comments, consult www2.ohchr.org/English/bodies/crc/comments.html.
11. For more information, see, e.g., Vucovic-Sahovic et al. (2012).
12. For more information on the implementation of article 12, see *General Comment No. 12 of the CRC Committee on the right to be heard.*
13. The representatives of the United States in the open-ended working group have played a crucial role in getting these rights included in the CRC. See, e.g., LeBlanc (1995), part 2, paragraph 6, on empowerment rights, pp. 157–184.
14. The right to preserve your identity (article 8) is unique to the CRC. No other human rights treaty contains this right. The article was proposed by the representative of Argentina in the open-ended working group with reference to the disappearance of children during the Videla regime. See Detrick (1992), pp. 291–295.
15. For more information on this protection, see CRC Committee, *General Comment No. 8* (2007).
16. For more information on alternative care see the *International Guidelines for the Alternative Care of Children,* a document welcomed by the UN General

Assembly that encourages states to take them into account in developing legislation and policies and bring them to the attention of all relevant actors in the field of children's rights. *Resolution of the General Assembly, UN Document A/RES/64/142,* February 24, 2010. The guidelines are attached to that resolution.

17. For the interpretation and practical consequences of the implementation of this article, see *General Comment No. 9 of the CRC Committee on the rights of children with disabilities,* UN Document CRC/C/GC/9, February 27, 2007.

18. For the interpretation of this article and its meaning for the quality of education, see *General Comment No. 1 of the CRC Committee on the aims of education,* UN Document CRC/GC/2001/1, April 17, 2001.

19. For more information on the interpretation of article 31, see *General Comment No. 14 of the CRC Committee on the right to play,* UN Document GC/C/GC/17, March 18, 2013.

20. There is a third optional protocol on communication proceedings that allows for filing complaints with the CRC committee on violations of children rights. It was adopted by the UN General Assembly in December 2011 but has not entered into force yet.

21. Both adopted by the same resolution, *UN Document A/RES/54/263.* The OPSC entered into force on January 18, 2002 (on January 1, 2013, it was ratified by 162 states; on February 12, 2002, the OPAC was ratified by 150 states).

22. Although the United States is not a party to the CRC, it did ratify the two optional protocols. This unique situation (not ratifying the main body but only its annexes) was made possible at the insistence of the United States during the drafting of the protocols and resulted in the provision that the protocols can be ratified not only by states party to the CRC but also by states that only signed it, like the United States (see article 9 of the OPAC and article 13 of the OPSC).

23. The obligation to submit reports every five years after the first report applies only to states that did ratify the optional protocols but not the CRC. States that did ratify the CRC include, after their first report, information on their implementation of the protocols in their periodic reports on the implementation of the CRC.

24. For the reports on OPAC, see *UN Document CRC/C/OPAC/USA/1* and *UN Document CRC/C/OPAC/USA/2* and on the OPSC, *UN Document CRC/C/OPSC/USA/1* and *UN Document CRC/C/OPSC/USA/2.*

25. For the concluding observations regarding the implementation of OPAC, see *UN Document CRC/C/OPAC/USA/CO/2,* January 28, 2013, and for the concluding observations regarding the implementation of OPSC, see *UN Document CRC/C/OPSC/USA/CO/2,* January 25, 2013 (both are advance unedited versions).

26. *UN Document CRC/C/GC/13,* February 17, 2011.

27. In this regard, interesting information is provided on the political commitment to allocate budgets for children in 54 African countries in *The African report on child well-being 2011 on budgeting for children.* Addis Ababa: The African Child Policy Forum.
28. For detailed information, see Greven (1992).
29. See, e.g., Straus & Donelly (1994).
30. *UN Document CRC/C/GC/8,* March 2, 2006.
31. For more country-specific information on legislative and other measures taken in countries around the world to prevent and prohibit corporal punishment, see www.endcorporalpunishment.org.
32. See for instance the compilation of decisions of district courts, courts of appeal, and the high court in which one or more articles of the CRC were dealt with from 1995 until September 2011, Ruitenberg (2003) and de Graaf (2012).
33. For this case and others decided by the South African Constitutional Court see, e.g., Sloth-Nielsen (2008).
34. *UN Document* January 28, 2013.

REFERENCES

De Graaf, J. H., Limbeek, M. M. C., Bahadur, N. N., & van der Meij, N. (2012). De toepassing van het Internationaal Verdrag inzake de Rechten van het Kind in de Nederlandse rechtspraak. Nijmegen, Netherlands: Ars Aequi Libri.

Detrick, S. (1992). *The United Nations Convention on the Rights of the Child: A guide to the "Travaux Preparatoires."* Dordrecht, Netherlands: Martinus Nijhoff Publishers.

Ek, S. (2007). *Legislative history of the Convention on the Rights of the Child,* Volumes I and II. New York, NY: United Nations.

General Comment No. 13 of the UN CRC Committee on the Rights of the Child. Article 19: The right of the child to freedom from all forms of violence. 2011.

Greven, P. (1992). *Spare the child: The religious roots of punishment and the psychological impact of physical abuse.* New York, NY: Vintage.

Hart, S. N., Lee, Y., & Wernham, M. (2011). A new age for child protection: General Comment 13; Why it is important, how it was constructed, and what it intends. (2011). *Child Abuse & Neglect, 35,* 970–978.

Jefferson, T. (1801). Reply to address. *The Jeffersonian Perspective.* Retrieved from http://eyler.freeservers.com/JeffPers/jefpco11.htm

LeBlanc, L. L. (1995). *The Convention on the Rights of the Child: The United Nations lawmaking on human rights.* Lincoln: University of Nebraska Press.

Machel, G. (1996). *The UN study on the impact of armed conflict on children.* UN Document A/51/306. New York, NY: United Nations.

Machel, G. (2001). *The impact of war on children: A review of progress since the 1996 United Nations report on the impact of war on children.* London, UK: Hurst & Company.

Pinheiro, P. S. (2006). *World report on violence against children.* New York, NY: United Nations. Available from www.studyviolence.org, www.unicef.org, and www.ohchr.org

Ruitenberg, G. C. A. M. (2003). *Het Internationaal Kinderrechtenverdrag in de Nederlandse rechtspraak.* Amsterdam: Uitgeverij SWP.

Sloth-Nielsen, J. (2008). Domestication of children's rights in national legal systems in African context: Progress and prospects. In J. Sloth-Nielsen (Ed.), *Children's rights in Africa: A legal perspective* (pp. 53–72). Hampshire, UK: Ashgate.

Straus, M., with Donelly, D. A. (1994). *Beating the devil out of them: Corporal punishment in American families.* New York, NY: Lexington Books.

Svevo-Cianci, K. A., Herczog, M., Krappmann, L., & Cook, P. (2011). The new UNCRC General Comment 13: "The right of the child to freedom from all forms of violence": Changing how the world conceptualizes child protection. *Child Abuse & Neglect, 35,* 979–989.

UNCRC. (2007, March 2). General Comment No. 8. Retrieved from http://www2 .ohchr.org/English/bodies/crc/comments.html

UNCRC. (2009, July 1). General Comment No. 12. Retrieved from http://www2 .ohchr.org/English/bodies/crc/comments.html

UNCRC. (2011, April 18). General Comment No. 13. Retrieved from http://www2 .ohchr.org/English/bodies/crc/comments.html

UNCRC. (2013, January 28). Rules of procedure under the Optional Protocol to the Convention on the Rights of the Child on a communications procedure. Retrieved from http://srsg.violenceagainstchildren.org/document/crc-c-62-3_826

Veerman, P. E. (1992). *The rights of the child and the changing image of childhood.* Dordrecht, Netherlands: Kluwer Academic Publishers.

Vucovic-Sahovic, N., Doek, J. E., & Zermatten, J. (2012). *The rights of the child in international law: Rights of the child in a nutshell and in context; All about children's rights.* Bern: Stampfl Publishers.

Index

About the Editor
and Contributors

EDITOR

JON R. CONTE, PhD, is a professor at the School of Social Work at the University of Washington, where he teaches courses on various aspects of clinical social work. He is the editor of the *Journal of Interpersonal Violence* and *Trauma, Violence, & Abuse: A Review Journal.* The founding president of the American Professional Society on the Abuse of Children, Dr. Conte is a teacher and scholar interested in professional education, research on the effects of child abuse on human development, and psychotherapy with traumatized individuals. He received the 2009 Ron C. Laney Award for Distinguished Service from APSAC. Dr. Conte maintains a private practice in Mercer Island, Washington, specializing in forensic mental health issues related to child abuse and trauma.

CONTRIBUTORS

REBECCA M. BOLEN, PhD, is an associate professor at the University of Tennessee College of Social Work. Her research focus is child sexual abuse and female victimization, with a more specific interest in nonoffending parents of sexually abused children. Most recently she has completed a qualitative study that evaluated nonoffending parents' perspectives of supportive behaviors, and barriers to that support, after the disclosure of sexual abuse by their children. She has also recently completed a study funded through the Administration of Children and Families to assess the sexually abused children in the National Survey of Child and Adolescent Well-being (NSCAW). Dr. Bolen has published two books, *The Epidemic of Rape and Child Sexual Abuse in the United States* (Sage), a collaboration with Dr. Diana Russell, and a single-authored book, *Child Sexual*

Abuse: Its Scope and Our Failure (Kluwer Academic/Plenum Publishers). She has made numerous presentations and has published many papers in professional journals. She was awarded her PhD by the University of Texas–Arlington (School of Social Work), where she was a co-winner of the American Professional Society on the Abuse of Children's Best Dissertation Award. Prior to this, she received her master's of science in social work from the University of Tennessee. She was on the faculty at Boston University School of Social Work before coming to the University of Tennessee.

TAMARA DEE, MSW, is a PhD candidate in the School of Psychology's Senior Proven Research Team at Australian Catholic University in Melbourne. She received her MSW from the University of Washington, where she worked with 3DL Partnership to develop collaborative relationships with community-based organizations. She has had the privilege of holding leadership roles in community-based organizations in the United States, where she developed, managed, and evaluated violence prevention programs. Tamara's PhD research examines the use of restorative practices in Victorian schools. She also works as research associate and evaluation consultant to youth organizations in Australia. Tamara's research interests include trauma; restorative justice; youth engagement; social, emotional, and intellectual learning; violence and substance abuse prevention and early intervention; collective resiliency; community-based health and wellness initiatives; and participatory evaluation.

WYATT D'EMILIA is an undergraduate majoring in psychology and history at Carnegie Mellon University and currently works as an extern for Dr. David Kolko at UPMC. A member of the Psi Chi and Phi Alpha Theta Honor Societies for psychology and history respectively, he has researched cognitive development of children under Dr. Anna Fisher at CMU and social development of adolescents under Dr. Dan Hart at Rutgers University–Camden. Under Dr. Fisher, he conducted studies measuring the development of semantic knowledge in preschool-age children, presenting his results at CMU's annual Meeting of the Minds Undergraduate Research Symposium in May 2013. With Dr. Hart, he measured how depressed tendencies and impulsivity correlate with and predict changes in body mass index over a one-year period, presenting his results at the Society for Research in Child Development's 2013 meeting in Seattle, Washington. He has also worked as a counselor for Urban Promise, a summer camp for neighborhood children in Camden, NJ. After graduating in 2014, Wyatt plans to earn an advanced degree in clinical psychology.

JAAP E. DOEK is emeritus professor of family and juvenile law at the VU University of Amsterdam. He has been a juvenile court judge and a deputy justice of the Court of Appeal of Amsterdam, a member of the UNCRC Committee (1999–2007), and the chairperson of that committee (2001–2007). He is the chairperson of Aflatoun, an international NGO promoting social and financial education in 90 countries, and a member of the international board of trustees of the African Child Policy Forum.

ARIANE FLORENT is a provisional psychologist completing her master's in clinical psychology at Australian Catholic University. She has experience as a research associate within the Senior Proven Research Team at ACU. She completed her BA in psychology and sociology at the University of Sydney and her postgraduate diploma in psychology at Macquarie University. Ariane is heavily involved in an NGO youth residential care program, where she has been a carer, an intake officer, and a volunteer. She is passionate about the philosophy of psychology and contributing empirical knowledge to the improvement of community child and adolescent mental health services, trauma informed practices, and social justice.

KELLIE B. GERGELY, LCSW, is a doctoral student at the University of Tennessee in the College of Social Work. She obtained her master's in social work from Florida State University and a bachelor's of science degree in psychology from the University of Florida. She started working with abused and neglected children and their families in 2000. Prior to entering the doctoral program, she worked in child protective investigations and as a forensic interviewer. She holds licenses in clinical social work in Florida and Tennessee. Her primary area of interest is the intergenerational transmission of child sexual abuse between mothers and their children. She is also expanding her knowledge on the neurobiological consequences of child abuse and neglect on the developing brain.

SHERYL A. HEMPHILL, PhD, BBSc (Hons), is team leader of the Psychology Senior Proven Researcher Team and professor in the School of Psychology, Australian Catholic University. Professor Hemphill's research focuses on the development and prevention of externalizing behavior problems, youth violence, bullying, antisocial behavior, and related behaviors, as well as the impact of social responses such as school suspension on young people's behavior. As a senior proven researcher at Australian Catholic University, she leads a team of early career researchers and students whose research focuses on adolescents and young adults around topics including substance use, mental health, and technology use, and including vulnerable young people such as those disengaging from school, homeless, or with disabilities. The team conducts and analyzes data from longitudinal studies, with a particular focus on cross-cultural comparisons of young people's experiences, all with the aim of improving the life chances of all young people.

TODD I. HERRENKOHL, PhD, MSW, is co-director of the 3DL Partnership and professor in the School of Social Work at the University of Washington. His funded research focuses on the development and prevention of youth violence, consequences of family violence for children, and resilience in vulnerable youth and families. Dr. Herrenkohl's publications span a number of interrelated areas in violence research, prevention and wellness, and positive youth development. As co-director of the newly established 3DL Partnership, an interdisciplinary, university-based center joining the fields of social work and education, Dr. Herrenkohl and his colleagues are seeking to raise the profile and practice of three-dimensional learning—social, emotional, and intellectual—helping educators and youth organizations prepare young people for success in school, work, and life. Those affiliated with the 3DL Partnership conduct community-driven research to better understand the influence of three-dimensional learning on young people's capacity for near- and long-term success in life and provide professional development and mentoring to help students, educators, and youth service providers integrate three-dimensional learning in their work with young people. In all activities of the partnership, an emphasis is placed on sharing research findings and evaluation tools to improve practice and to influence policy at the local and national levels.

AMY D. HERSCHELL, PhD, Western Psychiatric Institute and Clinic, University of Pittsburgh School of Medicine. Dr. Herschell is an assistant professor of psychiatry and psychology at the University of Pittsburgh School of Medicine. She is also the director of outcomes research and evaluation for the Youth and Family Training Institute and the Pennsylvania System of Care Partnership. Dr. Herschell's core research interests lie in studying the implementation of evidence-based treatment (EBT) for children in community settings. She is particularly interested in understanding the variables that support or inhibit practitioner implementation of EBT. Dr. Herschell has conducted multiple studies on this topic including the completion of a five-year National Institute of Mental Health (NIMH)–funded career development award on implementation of EBTs for children who experienced physical abuse. She currently is completing a statewide trial to understand the effectiveness of common methods for training community-based clinicians to use EBTs. Dr. Herschell has served in leadership roles on state and national committees related to parent-child interaction therapy (as chair of the continuing education committee for PCIT International), child maltreatment (as treasurer for the American Psychological Association's Section on Child Maltreatment), and implementation (as leader of the Dissemination and Implementation Science Special Interest Group, Association for Behavioral and Cognitive Therapies). She has published extensively on topics related to the implementation of EBTs, child physical abuse, and disruptive behavior disorders.

KATHLEEN KENDALL-TACKETT, PhD, IBCLC, FAPA, is a health psychologist and an international board–certified lactation consultant. She is the owner and editor-in-chief of Praeclarus Press, a small press specializing in women's health. Dr. Kendall-Tackett is a research associate at the Crimes against Children Research Center at the University of New Hampshire and clinical associate professor of pediatrics at Texas Tech University School of Medicine in Amarillo, Texas. She is a fellow of the American Psychological Association in the divisions of health and trauma psychology, editor-in-chief of the U.S. Lactation Consultant Association's journal, *Clinical Lactation,* and is president-elect of the American Psychological Association's division of trauma psychology. Dr. Kendall-Tackett is author of more than 320 journal articles, book chapters, and other publications, and author or editor of 22 books in the fields of trauma, women's health, depression, and breastfeeding, including *Treating the Lifetime Health Effects of Childhood Victimization,* 2nd ed. (Civic Research Institute, 2013), *Depression in New Mothers,* 2nd ed. (Routledge, 2010), *The Psychoneuroimmunology of Chronic Disease* (American Psychological Association, 2010), and *Breastfeeding Made Simple,* 2nd ed. (coauthored with Nancy Mohrbacher, 2010). Dr. Kendall-Tackett received bachelor's and master's degrees in psychology from California State University–Chico, and a PhD from Brandeis University in social and developmental psychology. She has won several awards, including the Outstanding Research Study Award from the American Professional Society on the Abuse of Children. She was named Distinguished Alumna, College of Behavioral and Social Sciences, California State University–Chico. In 2011, she received the John Kennell & Marshall Klaus Award for Excellence in Research from DONA International (with co-recipient Thomas Hale), and the Community Faculty Award from the Department of Pediatrics, Texas Tech University School of Medicine. Her Web sites are UppityScienceChick .com, BreastfeedingMadeSimple.com, KathleenKendall-Tackett.com, and PraeclarusPress.com.

DAVID J. KOLKO, PhD, ABPP, is a professor of psychiatry, psychology, pediatrics, and clinical and translational science at the University of Pittsburgh School of Medicine. He is director of the Special Services Unit at Western Psychiatric Institute and Clinic, a program devoted to the development and dissemination of evidence-based practices for children/adolescents served in diverse community settings or systems including juvenile justice, child welfare, pediatric primary care, and mental health. He is board-certified in child and adolescent psychology by the American Board of Professional Psychology and is a fellow of the American Psychological Association. Dr. Kolko served two terms on the board of directors of the American Professional Society on the Abuse of Children, was co-chair of its research committee, and received its Research Career Achievement Award for 2001. Much of his current work is directed towards the dissemination and evaluation of "Alternatives for Families: A Cognitive Behavioral Therapy" (AF-CBT) (www .afcbt.org), an evidence-based treatment that has been adapted for family conflict and coercion, emotional and physical abuse, and child behavior problems. His book co-written with Dr. Cindy Swenson, *Assessing and Treating Physically Abused Children and Their Families: A Cognitive-behavioral Approach* (Sage, 2002), describes the underpinnings and methods of AF-CBT. His interests involve the study and treatment of disruptive behavior disorders and children's antisocial behavior, including childhood firesetting, adolescent sexual offending behavior, and child maltreatment/trauma. A sample of Dr. Kolko's clinical-research activities and articles may be found online at http://www.pitt.edu/~kolko.

ANNA LOITERSTEIN is a graduate of Carnegie Mellon University with a bachelor's of science in psychology. She will attend a doctoral program in child clinical psychology at Yeshiva University.

HENRY J. PLUM, BA, JD, is a lawyer and nationally recognized speaker and educator in the field of child abuse and neglect. As a former assistant district attorney, he has extensive experience as a prosecutor in the areas of child abuse and neglect and child-related litigation in both the civil and criminal courts. He is currently in private practice in Milwaukee, Wisconsin, and serves as a court-appointed special prosecutor and legal consultant in child-related litigation for both governmental and nongovernmental (NGO) agencies. In addition to litigation, he conducts numerous conferences, seminars, and trainings for judges, lawyers, law enforcement, medical, social work, and other professionals on child-related legal issues for state, national, and international agencies. He serves as the legal advisor/parliamentarian to the International Society for the Prevention of Child Abuse and Neglect (ISPCAN) and is the former president and current board member of the National Association of Counsel for Children (NACC). He has co-authored child-related legislation by serving on legislative committees to the Joint Legislative Council for the State of Wisconsin Legislature as well as serving as chair of the legislative committee for children and law section of the Wisconsin state bar. He has authored several books and other publications on numerous topics involving child maltreatment issues and is a graduate of Marquette University Law School.

SHANTI RAMAN, MBBS, FRACP, MAE, is the medical director, child protection, for Sydney and South Western Sydney Local Health Districts, and a senior lecturer at the University of New South Wales and the University of Sydney. Dr. Shanti Raman is a pediatrician with subspecialty training in epidemiology and public health. Her special interests include the health of migrants and refugees; poverty; international maternal, newborn, and child health; child rights; and child abuse and neglect. As the pediatrician in charge of child protection services in Sydney and South Western Sydney, she is responsible for the development and coordination of a child protection medical service across the area, providing professional development in clinical aspects of child protection and providing academic leadership in community child health. She has established a number of specialized clinics for vulnerable children, including refugee children, indigenous children, children of parents with substance abuse and/or mental illness, and children in foster care. She is a passionate advocate for children on the margins and has been involved with policy development and advocacy at state, national, and international levels, promoting a rights-based perspective to child health and population health. Dr. Raman has maintained a strong interest in international health. She has provided consultancy services in international maternal, newborn, and child health; worked on population-based research projects in India; and been involved in teaching public health. In her role at the Human Resources for Health Knowledge Hub at the School of Public Health and Community Medicine, she was the lead on a range of maternal, newborn, and child health research projects in the Asia Pacific region between 2010 and 2012. She is currently earning a PhD in international maternal and child health at the University of New South Wales.

ABBY J. REED, BA, is currently earning her degree in osteopathic medicine from the West Virginia School of Osteopathic Medicine in Lewisburg, West Virginia. Before attending medical school, she worked as a research associate with Dr. Amy Herschell at the University of Pittsburgh on Project Connect and Parent-Child Interaction Therapy. Her two years spent with Dr. Herschell furthered her interest in public health and pediatrics.

RAJEEV SETH, MD, DNBE, FIAP, DABP, FAAP (U.S.), is a pediatrician trained in Delhi, India, and San Francisco, California. He had his subspecialty training in neonatal developmental biology. For the past 14 years, Dr. Seth has worked with passion to reach out to abused and neglected children for their comprehensive needs including education, health, and rehabilitation. At national and international forums, he advocates for the protection of rights of children and influences child welfare policy development. He is the current chair of Indian Child Abuse, Neglect and Child Labour (ICANCL), president of Indian Academy of Pediatrics (IAP) Delhi, and executive councilor, International Society for the Prevention of Child Abuse and Neglect (ISPCAN). Dr. Seth was the organizing chair of the 9th ISPCAN Asia-Pacific Conference on Child Abuse and Neglect (APCCAN 2011), India, and is a fellow of the American Academy of Pediatrics and the Indian Academy of Pediatrics. At present, Dr. Seth practices in India, where he continues to work as a volunteer, providing medical care and social and rehabilitation services to orphaned and other vulnerable children. He manages four clinics for urban street children. He is also founder trustee of BUDS, a nonprofit organization involved in the education and health care of underprivileged rural children. Dr. Seth is the editor of CANCL NEWS, besides having several scientific peer review publications to his credit. He has received several honors and academic awards, including the recent Distinguished Service Award, ISPCAN (2012), felicitation for outstanding service IAP Delhi (2011), McAllister Foundation Award, and Sorel Catherine Freyman Prize, among many others.

KIMBERLY SVEVO-CIANCI, PhD, cofounded Changing Children's Worlds Foundation (CCWF) in January 2012 to strengthen holistic community-based violence prevention by working with parents, community leaders, professionals, and children/youth. CCWF's framework is Community/Caregiver/Child Capacity Development toward Violence Prevention (CCDevVP), leveraging prevention and intervention best practice to inform programs and policy to support safe, healthy families and communities, enabling optimum child/youth development and well-being. Kimberly also founded the International Child Development Program–USA branch, bringing this empathy-based parent-child interaction program from Norway to the United States through partnerships with mental health agencies, universities, school districts, and churches based in New Orleans and Chicago.

Since 2008, Kimberly has linked her UN Convention on the Rights of the Child work to local, national, and global child protection and violence prevention. Her role on the UNCRC General Comment 13: Child's Right to Freedom from Violence Steering Committee for the Committee on the Rights of the Child addressed leveraging national mandates to strengthen local violence prevention and child protection outcomes.

Kimberly was executive director of the International Society for Prevention of Child Abuse and Neglect (1995–2008), an interdisciplinary professional organization of nearly 2,000 members in over 180 countries. She has collaborated with UNICEF, the World Health Organization, Save the Children, World Vision, and other children's rights and protection organizations, professionals, and government officials. Recently, she was co-guest editor, with UNCRC Committee Chairperson Yanghee Lee, on the November 2009, January 2010, and December 2011 special anniversary issues of *Child Abuse and Neglect: The International Journal.*

As president of Child Rights and Protection Consultancy International, Kimberly Svevo-Cianci links her UN Convention on the Rights of the Child research to local and national level child protection and violence prevention initiatives in North and South America, Europe, and around the world (ICDP). Her work leverages prevention and intervention best practice toward professional, caregiver, community/youth capacity development, and engagement to inform policy and practice in creating safe, healthy families and communities, and enabling optimum child/youth development.

EDWARD G. WEEKS is a doctoral candidate in criminal justice and criminology at the University of Massachusetts Lowell, School of Criminology and Justice Studies, where he also teaches research methods. He received his bachelor's of science and master of arts in criminal justice at the University of Massachusetts Lowell. The focus of his work was domestic violence prevention and forensic criminology and he received professional certificates in both areas. Currently, as a PhD candidate, his work is focused on the cycle of violence, child maltreatment, and criminal justice system outcomes.

LINDA M. WILLIAMS, PhD, is professor in the School of Criminology and Justice Studies at the University of Massachusetts Lowell. Dr. Williams received her PhD in sociology from the University of Pennsylvania, where she studied at the Center for Research in Criminology and Criminal Law. For the past 40 years she has directed research on sexual exploitation of children, sex offenders, violence against women, and the consequences of child abuse, including several longitudinal studies and recent qualitative work. Author of several books and dozens of scholarly publications, she has lectured in the United States and internationally on many topics, including sexual violence, trauma and memory, human trafficking, and researcher-practitioner collaborations. Dr. Williams is a past president of the American Professional Society on the Abuse of Children, and served on the National Research Councils' Panel on Violence against Women and as co-director of the National Violence against Women Prevention Research Center. She has been principal investigator on 16 U.S. federally funded research projects and was recently funded by the National Institute of Justice to conduct a study entitled *Decision-Making in Sexual Assault Cases: Multi-site Replication Research on Sexual Violence Case Attrition in the U.S.*